The Germanic People in America

The Germanic People

in America

by Victor Wolfgang von Hagen

University of Oklahoma Press : Norman

Books by Victor Wolfgang von Hagen
published by the University of Oklahoma Press

Maya Explorer: John Lloyd Stephens and the Lost Cities of Central America and Yucatán (1947)
Ecuador and the Galápagos Islands (1949)
The Incas of Pedro de Cieza de León (editor) (1959)
Incidents of Travel in Yucatán, by John Lloyd Stephens (editor) (1962)
Incidents of Travel in Egypt, Arabia Petraea, and the Holy Land, by John Lloyd Stephens (editor) (1970)
The Germanic People in America (1976)

Library of Congress Cataloging in Publication Data

Von Hagen, Victor Wolfgang, 1908–
    The Germanic people in America.

    Translation based on the author's Der Ruf der Neuen Welt, published in 1970.
    Bibliography: p.
    1. Germans in America. 2. America—History.
I. Title. II. Series.
E29.G3V58   973'.04'3   75–15970
ISBN 0–8061–1317–0

This book is based on *Der Ruf der Neuen Welt: Deutsche bauen America*, by Victor W. von Hagen (Munich and Zurich, Droemer Knaur, 1970).

Preface

From the beginning of the record, men began to march. Whole tribes have moved, en masse, from one environment to another—the Israelites out of Egypt, the Etruscans out of Hither Asia—but the migration of the Germanic peoples into the Americas has no parallel in history. "Beside it," wrote an English historian, "the Völkerwanderung of the Germanic tribes in the early Christian era sinks . . . to insignificance."

"Rome was in her six hundred and fortieth year," Tacitus reminds us, "when the alarm of German arms was first heard. . . ." Rome never realized who these people were until 113 B.C. when they moved out of their forested lands. Later, after Julius Caesar stirred up the Rhine dragons, Augustus tried to push Roman frontiers beyond that stream of history, and in doing so he lost three entire legions in the Teutoburgerwald. It was a disaster of such proportions that it changed Roman history. This then led Cornelius Tacitus, the Roman historian (then forty-three years of age), to write his famous book on Germania:

The Germans themselves, I am inclined to think, are native to the soil. . . . In their ancient songs (their only form of recorded history) the Germans celebrate the earth Goddess. . . . As to their physical type (if one may generalize at all about so vast a population) it is everywhere the same, blue eyes, reddish hair and huge frames . . . their climate and soil taught them to bear cold and hunger.

The essential culture of Germanic tribes, that is, their way of life, was set down by Tacitus in ethnogeographical terms: love of forest and land, strong sense of freedom, and sanctity of home life. "On the other hand . . . their characteristic weaknesses are . . . quarrelsomeness, drunkenness and their silly passion for war."

v

Even before the great Atlantic migration to the Americas, in the nineteenth century, the German migrants, mostly peasants, confirmed the observations of Tacitus written two millennia before: "The Germans live scattered and apart; a spring, a hill or a forest entices them." The early immigrant's preference for forested lands is understandable, since Germania was one of the most richly forested lands of Europe. "Like all good Germans," wrote an American historian, "they sought out the rich soils abounding in good water and woods." This was equally true whether they settled in Pennsylvania, Texas, California, Brazil, Argentina, or Chile. Thus from the very beginning the Germans were pioneers. An observation by a noted English historian (which seems to have become dictum of American history) that the "German role in discovering and exploring the new continent was more theoretical and speculative than active and physical"—and echoed by another, far shallower opinion, that the German emigrants in the Americas "were only bemused supernumeraries"—is contrary to the known facts. From the very first German to appear in Vineland, in 1000 A.D. to that of another of Germanic ancestry, who made the moon journey in 1968, the German record as makers and finders is impressively documented.

The migration of a people is inextricably bound up with the migration of ideas. Thought is light and easily transportable, cheap at the source, dear at the market, and inexpensive to carry. With the waves of migration came new ideas, new skills and disciplines, and a technological heritage that included both philosophies and religions— for the idea of God to migrant peoples is an incitement above all else. The impact of this Germanic culture on North America, as Henry Pochmann wrote of it, is so massive in itself that this book is able to encompass only a fragment of the contributions of the Germanic peoples to the history of the Americas.

The Germanic People in America is based on *Der Ruf der Neuen Welt: Deutsche bauen Amerika*, written by me and published by Droemer Knaur of Munich in 1970. The present volume is not a word-for-word translation but an English version of the German publication.

Victor Wolfgang von Hagen

Acknowledgments

A book like this, which concerns itself with an entire continent and a time period of five centuries, cannot be the work of one individual. Persons and institutions in North and South America have helped me with it. Don Hans Lenz from Peña Pobre in Mexico put copies of documents and books about the first Germans in Mexico at my disposal; Dr. Marianne B. de Bopp helped me further with new material about Emperor Maximilian; and Mr. Herbert R. Roesler from Bogotá provided information about Nikolaus Federmann in Bogotá. In North America The New York Public Library co-operated with illustrations and suggestions; Mr. Charles Hummel from the Winterthur Museum in Delaware and Mr. Gregory Gibson of the Pennsylvania Council of Arts provided me with illustrations; Mr. Howard C. Rice of the Princeton Library furnished me the correspondence between Thomas Jefferson and Freiherr von Eisenbach; Mrs. Charles Lundgren assisted me with material concerning the economic situation of the Pennsylvania Germans in Lancaster, Pennsylvania; and the Germantown Historical Society pointed out additional material concerning the printer Christoph Sauer. The Museum of Fine Arts in Boston and the National Gallery of Art in Washington, D.C., assisted me with their staffs' knowledge as well as with prints of German artists during the Civil War.

Mr. Allen Ottley of the California State Library in Sacramento was a valuable assistant to me with papers about the German squire, Baron Sutter; the Brown University Library joined in with prints and pictures in regard to the participation of Germans in the War of Independence (1775); and the John Carter Brown Library of the same university put books about the first German immigrants at my disposal. Professor William G. Goetzmann, Director of the American Civilizations Program at the University of Texas permitted me to quote from his book *Explorations & Empire* (New York, 1967) and in addition furnished me with rare prints of the first German artists from the time of the pioneers in the West.

Special thanks belong to Mr. W. F. Davidson, who approved the reproduction of the original drawings produced for Prince Wied zu Neuwied about his exploratory trips to Brazil; and to the Jocelyn Art Gallery in North Dakota, which permitted the use of the heretofore unpublished material of the artist Karl Bodmer about the exploratory trips of Prince Wied zu Neuwied in North America in the year 1830.

The New York Leo Baeck Institutes approved publications concerning the history of the German Jews in North America. This made a complete acknowledgement of the contribution of German Jews to the history of America possible.

In Canada, thanks to the friendly recommendation of Mr. Bernard Weilbrenner, Director of the Public Archives in Ottawa, I was furnished with a comprehensive bibliography about the first German settlements in Canada as well as with a great number of photocopies by the head librarian, Miss Juliette Bourque. The university library of the Alberta Library in Edmonton assisted me, together with the staff of the Douglas Library of Queen's University in Kingston, Ontario.

Their colleagues at the British Museum in London selected the necessary, rare documents for me and the picture department produced the corresponding copies. Maggs Bros., secondhand book dealers in Berkley Square, led me to the owner of a bibliographical rarity concerning Charles V, and Mr. J. O. Oates, librarian of the University Library in Cambridge had slides made of it.

The help from Germany was comprehensive: Dr. Adolf Meyer-Abich, Director of the German Latin-America Foundation in Hamburg put a place to work in the library at my disposal—where I tracked down large stacks of important books—and Mrs. Luisa Lessmann, a staff worker of this foundation, was helpful to me far beyond her regular working hours. Mrs. Carola von Ehrenbrook (nee von Hagen), former publisher of the *Genealogical Handbook of the Nobility*, opened up her comprehensive documents with bibliographical material to me. General Johann Count von Kielmansegg relinquished the history of his family to me in which the marriage of his ancestors, Countess Sophie Charlotte and Duke Richard Howe, who directed the naval war against the American colonies, is depicted in detail. William Frh. von Nordenflycht, whose ancestor played such an important role in Peru, was so kind as to give me new, heretofore unpublished information, while his sister, Amalia de Nordenflycht, in Santiago, lent me miniatures of the metal baron of Peru. In Castle Eisenbach the Marshal of the province, Friedrich Riedesel Freiherr zu Eisenbach, showed and gave me copies of maps, pictures, and other documents concerning his ancestor, Baroness von Riedesel, whose famous book *The Business Trip* depicts the participation of her husband (and her own) in the American Revolutionary War. Herbert Freiherr von Welser furnished me material from the Welser family foundation, Carl Prince Fugger had the ducal Fugger Foundation put essential material for my chapter concerning the Fuggers and Welsers at my disposal. The Federal Military Archive in Freiburg and the Main State Archive in Stuttgart were a meaningful help, as well as Dr. Leonie von Wilckens from the Germanic Museum in Nuremberg, who saw to it that old illustrations and papers about Nuremberg were made available to me. Mr. J. Kitzinger, used book dealer, furnished many important books, and Dr. Etta Becker-Donner, Director of the Museum for Folklore in Vienna, was, as always, helpful. Thanks finally to Mr. Fritz Bolle, chief reader at the Droemer Publishing House, who helped to make a book out of this comprehensive material, and to my secretary, Miss Christine Ploetner, who worked untiringly for two years to copy it.

Victor Wolfgang von Hagen

Contents

Maps

The Germanic People in America

Lands Never Known or Found

A two-wheeled dray wagon, piled high with quires of recently couched paper, made its way from the papermill on the Pegnitz River through the city walls into Nuremberg. Then one of the richest imperial cities of the Germanies, Nuremberg was set in the midst of pine forests of the Franconian Alps and connected by well-laid roads to the world without.

The paper drayer, whose cart bore the device of the papermaker—a bull's head with an extended cross and serpent rampant—passed his wagon under the massive Läufertor, followed the river toward the principal market, and clattered into a city already in a festive mood. They were decorating the city with pine branches and buntings for the visit of the new Emperor. The walls still displayed the printed broadsides of this year, 1493, announcing the election of Maximilian.

The emperor, Maximilian von Hapsburg, was even then considered the "last knight." As a young prince he had fought in the Tilting Lists in Flanders fields, and even when king he never wearied of court pageantry. Maximilian encouraged the arts and showed a profound interest in new mining techniques and commerce. This practical side of his character overshadowed an obvious dilettantism. Having secured by marriage the "Burgundian heritage," he saw his royal influence further extended when his son, Philip the Fair, married Joanna the Mad, heiress to the crown of Castille, by which act, as a contemporary Latin couplet had it, Maximilian gained more territory through love than war: "Bella gerant alii, tu, felix Austria, nube/Nam quae Mars aliis, dat tibi regna Venus" ("Let others war, thou happy Austria, wed/What some owe Mars from Venus takes instead").

The emperorship to which Maximilian was elected was restricted almost wholly to the Germanies, a potpourri of cities and fiefs, margraviates such as Brandenburg, archduchies such as Austria, a

Nuremberg in the 16th century—the great trading center for economic and cultural goods.

galaxy of baronies and domains, of which there were more than three hundred, and free imperial cities such as Nuremberg. These formed the Germanies.

The renascence of Europe's affluence was reflected in Nuremberg. Even the paper drayer could see this as he made his way through the crowded streets toward the sign of the hooked staves and chevroned stars (a printing colophon) to deliver his load to Anton Koberger's printshop. The industry of the city, and consequently its prosperity, was everywhere apparent. There was the Haus Hirschvogel, the edifice of the patrician bankers who had interests in faraway Lisbon. The Welsers, rivals of the Fuggers of Augsburg, had their beginnings in Nuremberg, and their counting house–residence dominated the main street. Here too were the patrician Köhlers, who would one day send one of their sons to seek out the Golden Man. The Nurembergers were cosmopolitan and world traveled in their search for new business horizons. One of them, Hans Mayer, had gone on a trading mission to the Indies. Sailing out of Lisbon, he left his impressions in

Emperor Maximilian I, patron of the arts and sciences, from a woodcut by Dürer.

his *Tagebuch*. Balthasar Sprenger, voyaging under a Portuguese flag, sailed to the spice lands and gave an account of his stirring adventures. So far flung were the activities of these Nuremberg merchants that Hans Burgkmair, the artist, made an elongated woodcut illustrating these fabulous lands where Nurembergers traveled and traded.

If Nuremberg was famed for its mapmakers, globes, and calendars, along with its linen mills and metalworking, it was equally famed for its ateliers. In that section where the Woodcutters Guild was located, there was an abundance of artists, woodcut illustrators, and goldsmiths.

Anton Koberger was then one of the most renowned printers in the Germanies. He employed over one hundred craftsmen and kept his twenty-four presses in constant operation to supply an immense trade which reached to Paris, Milan, Florence, and Bologna. Koberger's publishing reflected the times. Money was plenteous and there was an intense interest in the outside world. Born here in 1440, Anton Koberger turned to the craft of printing by movable type soon after it made its first appearance at Mainz. When his apprenticeship was over, in 1473, he issued his first book.

The *Nuremberg Chronicle*, a massive world history, was the most ambitious project ever printed in the Germanies. It was "to be the crown of medieval craftsmanship in book-building," being nothing less than a total world history, an immensely complex narrative—biblical, classical, and traditional—of the world from its beginning up to the present time, that is, the month and year of July, 1493.

The author of the *Chronicle*, Hartmann Schedel, a well-known Medicus-Humanist, had undertaken with several other learned men ("Hochgelehrte Manner" as it states in the colophon) to write a world chronicle, a "register . . . of the chronicles and histories with illustrations and portraits of persons and places, of all the important events from the beginning of the world up to our own times." It was to have no less than eighteen hundred and nine wood engravings of historical events, such as the birth of the earth, views of all the important cities, portraits of famous personages, and a map of the then-known world. Having brought the *Chronicle's* history up to the final moment, it was then, on July 7, 1493, finally set into print.

The illustrators of this stupendous work, both well known beyond the confines of Nuremberg, had as an apprentice one Albrecht Dürer, who was to become one of the giants of the arts and who straddled the end of the Gothic and the beginning of the Renaissance.

Albrecht Dürer the Elder had returned from Hungary in the early part of the century and there, in Nuremberg, on May 21, 1471, was born Albrecht Dürer the Younger. His godfather was Anton Koberger the printer.

Albrecht Dürer's self-portrait at the age of thirteen (1484) was so unbelievably facile for one so young that it assured him his future, and he was articled out, at the age of fifteen, to the artist Michael Wohlgemuth. One of his first tasks was to aid in the engraving of the woodcuts for the *Nuremberg Chronicle*. It was the first time, and certainly the last, that Dürer would be anonymous; none of the eighteen hundred woodcuts bear the familiar 𝕬̄.

As the last pages of the great *Chronicle* were printed and handed over to the binder, Anton Koberger felt reasonably confident that he and his "high learned men" had produced a book that contained every important event from the beginning of history up to that time. And yet, as a final precaution, Anton Koberger had the binder include at the end of the book three blank pages so that the purchaser might add any additional world-stirring events occurring after the book had been issued. These three blank pages were to be portentous. For it was at this moment of history that his friend, Hans Amerbach, the printer-publisher of Basle, sent him a booklet of four printed pages.

It was called a *Büchlein*. A German printer at Rome, Stephen Planck, had printed it and presumably sent it on to Amerbach, and he in turn, knowing of the grand project of the *Nuremberg Chronicle*, had sent it on to Anton Koberger. The "Little Book" contained the "Letters of Columbus . . . *Epistola Christoferi Colom* . . . concerning the islands of India beyond the Ganges, recently discovered."

This Christopher Columbus—none knew the name—had left Spain on August 3, 1492, and, sailing westward, had reached several unknown islands. Convinced that the islands he had found on the new route were an outpost of India, Columbus wrote that he had found "insulis in de supra Gengem nuper inventis."

The unknown sea into which Columbus had sailed was, in historical perspective, not entirely unknown. The *mare tenebrosum*, this "repellant sea," had been crossed and recrossed since the tenth century by Portuguese fishermen who had opened up the *bacalāo* cod-fishing ground off the Newfoundland banks. Even before this the Irish had made landings in North America, and the word "Presil-Brazil" had become current in maritime vocabulary. Moreover, Bristol seamen sailing out of that port had made landfalls on North American shores.

The Vikings, as is well known, had made frequent sailings from their settlements in Greenland to the new continent, and these voyages eventually assumed the form of history. As related in the Greenlanders' Sagas, Leif Ericson landed in what is considered now to have been the shoreland above New England. On one of his scouting parties was a German named Tykir,[1] whom the Viking leader called "my foster father." Tykir came back one day bringing grapes and grapevines and was in such a state of excitement that he spoke in German. He had found the Labrasca grape. He knew, he said, what

[1] *The German Culture in America, 1600–1900.* Madison: University of Wisconsin Press, 1961.

One of the great illustrators of the 16th century was Hans Burgkmair the Elder. His woodcuts clarify the wonders of the world for his contemporaries. This curious self-portrait of 1529 shows him together with his wife.

grapes were, for he was born in the Rhineland where such grapes were no rarity and he pronounced it a "vineland."

Many Germans, including a notable number of Nurembergers, had long been part of the early exploration of the ocean seas. They had been mostly employed by Portugal, the first modern state to undertake overseas discoveries as a national enterprise. Lisbon had a large colony of German printers, cartographers, and sailors. Martin Behaim was such a one. He had entered Portuguese service as early as 1479 and had accompanied the expedition of Diego Gomes into the "western ocean-sea" as a participant in the discoveries and colonization, sailing southward along the African coastline. The first globe made by Martin Behaim in 1492 was unknown to Columbus, but it is possible that both Behaim and Columbus drew their information from the same fount.

All learned men then knowledgeable in these matters accepted the fact that the earth was round or spheroid. The scholars at Sagres in Portugal shared the common heritage of cosmography—the spherical earth and the universal ocean surrounding all the earth lands—so that Columbus knew that by sailing directly west he would reach land, presumably Asia.

It was during his return that he wrote the famous letter that was to affect Anton Koberger's *Chronicle*. When the small fleet of Columbus was making its landfall off the Azores on February 14, 1493, the ships were caught in a scathing tempest and widely scattered. Fearful that the account of his discoveries might be lost, Columbus wrote a history of this momentous voyage on parchment, then wrapped it in a large piece of waxed cloth, placed it in a large wooden cask, and committed it to the sea. It was never found.

On the following day, when the storm lessened, he wrote another letter-report to a Spanish officer, which was also lost, and yet another to the King and Queen, lost as well. Finally arriving safely on March 15 at Palos, Spain (whither he had begun seven months before), he addressed another letter-report to Gabriel Sánchez, the Crown Treasurer of Castille. It was this letter that was printed.

The printed edition of Columbus's letter was small, yet eagerly read, passing from hand to hand, so that almost all were devoured by usage. It was one of these leaflets that Anton Koberger received some time after July, 1493. All of the four distinct editions of the letters (whether printed in Barcelona, Rome, Seville, or Strasbourg) had been issued by German printers, and all of the letters told "a charming and beautiful tale of numerous islands found by the King of Spain."

It is certain that Anton Koberger wished to include this new discovery in his *Chronicle*. The Latin edition was distributed and beyond recall; however, he still was printing the German version, which did not appear until December, 1497. Therefore, a new paragraph, in holograph, was included in the German edition implying that Martin Behaim had reached these lands before Columbus. This made the *Nuremberg Chronicle* the first book ever to mention the discovery of America.

Within a year "the landes which were never knowen" was part of the German experience. Sebastian Brant, the poet, brought its discovery into focus in his *Narrenschiff*. This "Ship of Fools," illustrated

The reports of Amerigo Vespucci, an Italian sailor in Portuguese service, provided the German Martin Waldseemüller the bases for his large world maps. They caused him to give the name "America"

to the newly discovered continent on a map originating in 1507. The illustration shows a portrait of Vespucci engraved by Waldseemüller in copper.

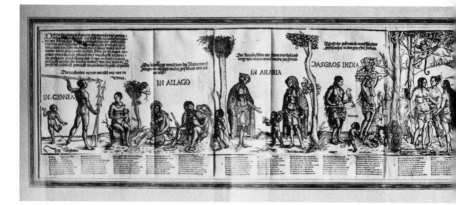

Draftsman and cartographer Theodor de Bry thus depicted an event which would change the world—the voyage of discovery which led Christopher Columbus to the coast of America.

by Albrecht Dürer, satirized man's follies and foibles. The author wrote in a memorable verse: "For newes of late hath large londe and ground/Ben founde by maryners and crafty governors/The londes whiche never knowen nor found. . . ."[2]

German printers in Strasbourg, Augsburg, Cologne, and elsewhere continued to publish and republish the 1493 letter of Columbus: "A charmingly beautiful booklet on some enchanting islands recently found by the King of Spain." These were followed in the first years of the new century by a narrative of one Amerigo Vespucci which told of "other new islands so recently found by order of the King of Portugal."

By 1505 the newly discovered islands had metamorphosed into a continent, and one printer unhesitatingly entitled his booklet *Mundus Novus.* A printer of Nuremberg issued his version of the lands "now wonderfully found," and in the same year a printer in Mainz was happy to tell his readers that his edition of *The newe founde Region* was "pulled out of the original Latin."

[2]When the *Narrenschift,* translated as *The Shyp of Folys,* was published in England in 1509, it became the first book to mention the "new founde lands" in English.

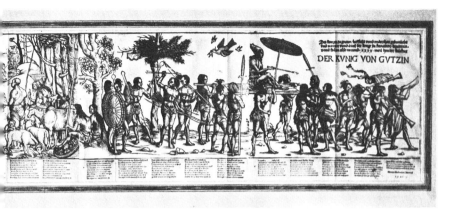

The newly found continent could have retained its original name of Terra Sanctis Crucis—"The Land of the Holy Cross"—or have become "Atlantia" or even "Hesperidia," or perhaps "Iberica" after the Spaniards who financed the voyages. Or it could have been called "Colombia" after its discoverer, had Columbus not so vehemently denied he had found a new world at all. Instead, it was named "America"—named not by the voyager himself, who timidly thought that it could be a "Mundus Novus," neither by the Medicis (who were his masters), nor even by the kings of Portugal. Following a concourse of preestablished harmonies and quite in keeping with this comedy of geographical errors, it was named "America," baptized thus by a German cartographer in the little town of St. Dié in Lothringen (Lorraine).

He called himself "Hylacomylus," Hellenizing his name in the conceit of the times, yet he was really Martin Waldseemüller, who, born at Radolzell, had studied at the University of Freiburg. Under the patronage of Renatus (René) II, Duke of Lorraine, there had been set a group of cartographers who had interested themselves in the discoveries of the New World.

Sometime in the autumn of 1504, Martin Waldseemüller began the work on his huge world map, which for the time was amazingly accurate. He had, of course, access to many of the new geographical discoveries, such as that of Pedro Álvares Cabral, a Portuguese captain whose ships, sailing by way of the Cape of Good Hope to India, had been blown off course and, caught up in ocean currents, had landed on the coast of "Brazil." So Waldseemüller had information "of the 'parrot-lands' newly discovered." Then there was Juan de la Cosa, the famed Spanish cosmographer, who had drawn a map in 1500 representing America as a continuous land body from the Arctic to well below the equator. And finally, Waldseemüller knew of the maps of Sebastian Cabot, who had delineated North America by 1497.

While writing the *Introduction to Cosmographia*, the text that was to accompany his great map and globe, Waldseemüller became aware of Vespucci's small booklet, *Mundus Novus*, since his colleague, Martin Ringmann, had collected most of them and printed the voyages himself in 1506.

Amerigo Vespucci had been in Seville for many years. Born in Florence (1476), educated by a learned friar who was his uncle, Vespucci, in 1490, arrived in Seville, where he became a factor for the Medicis. He was responsible, among other tasks, for victualing the ships of Columbus's third voyage in 1496. In 1501, Vespucci secretly quitted Spain and entered the Portuguese service. It was during these five years that he voyaged to the lands which bear his name.

"During each of these voyages," he wrote in a recently found letter, "I have made notes of the more marvellous things, the whole of which I have put in one volume, and put it down in a geographical style . . . titled 'The Four Journies.'"

On the top of his immense map Martin Waldseemüller, in 1507, drew the portraits of Ptolomey (the most authoritative geographer of the ancient world) and opposite him a portrait of Vespucci. He then put the word "America" in bold letters on that portion which is now *South* America. "I named it," he wrote, "after Americus, its discoverer, a man of sagacious mind, Amerigo, that is the land of Americus, or America."

The "New Founde Land" was henceforth proclaimed as America and took on immediate currency. Yet it soon became obvious to those of a critical turn of mind that the lands Columbus had found were identical with those described by Vespucci and now named for him. Waldseemüller later realized his mistake when publishing his *Carta*

Sechste Theill/

Kurtze / Warhafftige

Relation vnd beschreibung der Wunderbarsten vier Schiffarten/ so iemals verricht worden Alsnemlich:

Ferdinandi Magellani Portugalesers/mit Sebastiano de Cano.
Francisci Draconis Engeländers.
Thomæ Candisch Engeländers.
Oliuarij von Noort, Niderländers.

So alle vier vmb den gantzen Erdtkreiß gesegelt/auß vnterschiedenen authoribus vnd sprachen zusamen getragen / vnd mit nötigen Landt Charten/seinen Figurn vnd nützlichen erklerungen gezieret/ vnd verfertigt. Durch/

LEVINUM HULSIUM

Prima ego veliuolis ambiui Cursibus Orbem
Magellane nouo te duce ducta freto
Ambiui, meritoq pocor VICTORIA: sunt mi
Vela, alæ, precium gloria, pugna, mare.

FERDINA MAGELLAN
1520

SEBAST. DE CANO
1521

Paragones Magellanici Fretum
Terra de fogo
1577

FRANCISCVS DRACO

OLIVIER A NOORT VLTRAIECT
1601

VICTORIA

Conueniunt rebus nomina sepe suis.

Albrecht Glockenton descended from an artist family in Nuremberg. As "illuminator" he executed church commissions, but also produced woodcuts like this one, which made the strange and adventurous reports of the voyagers understandable for all contemporaries.

The travels of the great discoverers gave rise to an abundance of books and pamphlets in which an eagerly attentive public discovered how limited their field of vision had been previously. Sailing around the world, proof that the earth is round—this unbelievable fact excited all of Europe.

Marina, a new chart of the Oceans; he decided to call it "the land of parrots." It remained, however, America.

One can still grasp the excitement of public interest in the new discoveries. The German printing presses worked overtime attempting to supply the demand for information on the New World, and the whole of Europe seemed to be fevered by the idea of a Utopia, a dream of earthly paradise. They wanted something other than the huddle and squalor of their present society. Everyone was haunted by the idea that somewhere "out there" were new lands of infinite promise. The letters of Columbus told of gold and pearls in the islands, treasures that would one day dwarf those of Solomon. Shrill-voiced rumors made their way into hamlets and villages and gathering places within high-walled cities. Everywhere it seemed there were broadsides which spoke of "The Joyfull Newes Out of the Newfound Worlde." Voyagers hinted at a terrestrial paradise of women who walked about naked, of barbaric princes who trod streets paved with gold, fertile lands filled with delectable fruits that had no need of cultivation, new spices and herbs, and oysters the size of soup plates.

IOHANNES SCHONERVS.
Caroſtadienſis.
Celeberrimus Profeſſor Publ.
Mathematum in auditorio Ægid. Norico.
symbol.
Nat. A. 1477. d. 16. Jan. Mathefis Soli index Denat. A. 1547. d. 16. Jan. æt. 70.

Johannes Schöner, Nu-remberg astronomer and geographer, used the name "America" on the earliest globe produced by him.

The people of Europe seemed to be waiting breathlessly for the flood-gates of plenty to pour over them.

But the dream of plenty ended even before it began. A hint of things to come had already appeared in one of Columbus's letters to the King, wherein he had suggested that only Spaniards should be allowed entry to the new paradise. It was not until the new announcements were plastered over the time-stained broadsides speaking of the "Joy-full Newes" that people became aware of what had occurred.

It seems there had been a conference in Spain during the summer of 1494. After having jumped through all the paper disks of ecclesi-astical reasoning, Pope Alexander VI (Rodrigo Borgia) met with the kings of Castille and Portugal at the city of Tordesillas. The result: a north-south line was drawn running from the poles 370 leagues west of Cape Verde, Africa. All newly discovered lands east of the line—that is, much of Brazil, all of Africa, and the "Spiceries"—were to belong exclusively to Portugal. All the rest of the American lands found and still unfound were to belong exclusively to Spain. In his *Bula dela concession* Pope Alexander had given Spain and Portugal *de jure* possession of all the "Newfound lands." All other nations in the world were to be excluded.

Those in Europe who had placed such high hopes in the New

World's dream of plenty were understandably aghast at this turn of events. The King of France demanded to see the "clause in Adam's testament which entitled the Kings of Castille and Portugal to divide the world between them." His protests availed him nothing. The Americas were to be reserved exclusively for the Portuguese and the Spaniards.

The Feathered Serpent

II

The year 1519 was notable among other things for two events: Hernando Cortes, in the act of conquering Mexico, entered Tenochtitlán; and, in Innsbruck, Maximilian von Hapsburg, king and emperor, died.

The Holy Roman Empire, which began in A.D. 800, was political, since the Emperor theoretically ruled over all the Germanies and Italy, and religious, insofar as it drew its spiritual power from the Pope. The Empire was an accepted device; it held together most of its discordant members while providing the Emperor with a resounding title that gave him precedence above all the kings and princes of Europe.

The Empire Maximilian received was not the same establishment he yielded up when he died. During his lifetime printing from movable type was invented (1452), and with it the New Learning appeared; the invention of gunpowder (1450) changed the art of warfare, both in attack and siege; the American continent was discovered (1492), and within two years one of its dubious gifts, syphilis, was introduced into Europe.

In 1496, Maximilian's son, Philip, married Joanna the Mad, the third child of Queen Isabella. She had been fragile and flighty from birth, and was already deemed eccentric when residing in the Netherlands, which had fallen to Philip as part of his feudal suzerain. There she had given birth to numerous progeny, of which two were sons, when her madness finally pushed her over the barriers of sanity.

When she returned to Spain in 1503, her mother, Queen Isabella, knowing she could never rule, had a clause placed in her testament that Joanna would be the "Queen-proprietress of Castille," while her husband, Philip, would be only the consort to the queen. Charles, Joanna's son, would be the heir to the throne. Thus at the age of seventeen, Charles, known as "the First," the oldest child of the mad Queen, became King of Spain.

Yet not at once quite king. Charles, who had been born in Ghent and reared in Flanders, spoke no Spanish. Moreover, his French was impure and the German he spoke was the gutteral dialect of the Lowlands. At first the Spaniards found little about him to inspire devotion. He had the shovel jaw of the Hapsburgs with a protruding lower lip, he lacked the gaiety one associates with youth, and his habits were gluttonous. Few then, either in Flanders or Spain, would have foretold that this Charles would one day emerge as a "good European" and be beloved by all in the Spains.

There were then many Spains, and many royal courts. Before each of them—Castille, Aragon, and all the others—Charles had to take an oath to observe the customs and *to withhold offices from all non-Spaniards*; thereupon he was given a grant of money. Thus dutifully did the young king go from court to court, taking these oaths, receiving homage and grants of *escudos* or *maravedis*, until he arrived at the last, the Catalonian court.

It was here, in Valencia, while his ministers were haggling over the terms of his kingship, that on January 11, 1519, the news arrived that his grandfather, Maximilian, had died. The title of Holy Roman Emperor was vacant.

Charles decided to press his claims for the Emperorship. His personal funds were scant, however, and he had taken an oath to all of the courts of Spain that he would not request more funds except for extreme necessity. So from whence would come the money? From the source where most princely loans had their origin of course: the Fuggers. Since the Fuggers had been bankers to Maximilian, they felt it their financial, as well as knightly, duty to extend the same support to his grandson. Charles I of Spain could obtain money from the Fuggers by which the favor of the Electors could be influenced—that is bribed.

The patrician bankers of Augsburg, the Fuggers, were a new class of men, enlightened capitalists. Since most knew, as the Spanish had already observed, "Muy poderoso caballero es don Dinero," the Fuggers had obtained power and patents of nobility through banking.

Naturally, it had not always been thus. The first Fugger, Johannes, had been born in 1348 and in time became a master weaver. He settled in Memmingen, a city-state in Swabia, and began weaving on a large scale. In time the Fugger mills were weaving linen and wool and importing cotton directly from India. From weaving the Fuggers expanded into factoring and then banking. As Renaissance science brought in new technologies, mining became profitable, so the Fuggers moved into that field as well. Jacob Fugger, "The Rich," who was born in the same year (1459) as Maximilian, became in effect his private banker, and this brought about their first ennoblement.

The Fuggers soon were operating on a worldwide basis with offices and factories in Antwerp, Venice, Seville, and Valencia, as well as in many parts of Germany and Austria. They were creative capitalists who also risked their capital in research. Jacob Fugger was to aid in financing a voyage "round the Horn" to the Moluccas, the famed Spice Islands. They employed architects and the finest artists of the period—Hans Holbein, Dürer, Hans Maler, Bellini. Equally profound was their interest in literature; their library was well selected and as catholic in taste as was their religion.

Their interests were also vertical. Though they walked with the well placed, they were also aware of the "undeservedly impoverished," and in 1521 they began the Fuggerei, the oldest social-welfare settlement in Europe. In the heart of Augsburg they built a self-contained corporation of dwellings, each small house amazingly compact. The occupant paid then, as now, one Rhine guilder a month for rental. Such philanthropies caused them little financial hardship, however, for by 1530 they could reckon their metallic wealth at fifteen tons of gold.

Therefore when Charles was disposed to borrow three hundred thousand ducats to bribe the electors of the Holy Roman Empire, the purse of the Fuggers was at his command. In like manner, the Welsers, although not with such largesse, gave a contribution of 141,000 ducats. This loan was to open up the closed portcullis of the Americas.

The election of the Emperor was memorable. Never had such sums been spent to "persuade" the electors, the reason being that Henry VIII of England coveted the crown, as did Francis I of France. So determined were the patricians of Augsburg that Charles I of Spain should be elected that they decreed that anyone who loaned money to the King of France for the purpose of being made Emperor would be

III

During the reign of Emperor Charles V, Mexico and Peru were conquered and the Spanish colonial empire was founded. This portrait of the youthful Charles V of 1519 was erroneously attributed to Dürer because of the monogram.

liable to be hung, drawn, and quartered. As surety for the loans, the Fuggers asked Charles, when he became Charles V of the Holy Roman Empire, to pledge almost to its entirety the crown property of Castille. As for the Welsers, they obtained grants and privileges that would lead eventually to the golden path of El Dorado.

As soon as Charles had confirmation of his election, he had his courtiers proclaim it throughout the Spains, announcing the King's new dignity. Then he made immediate preparations to leave for Aachen in Germany, where he was crowned. From Aachen the spectacular train of nobles and patricians went on to Brussels, and there, on July 12, 1520, America dramatically intruded itself into the proceedings.

At Brussels the triumphal procession had been brought to a halt by the most extraordinary proceedings. Among these were the golden treasures brought by the conquistadors, who had traveled from the coast of Mexico to bring Charles tidings of a new extension of his overseas empire. The ambassadors of one Hernando Cortes, who was then in the act of making a conquest of Mexico, brought with them natives of the land dressed so outlandishly that the people who saw them swore that they had seen nothing like it before.

The two ambassadors supplied the Emperor with the needed information. Cortes, after an eventful voyage out of Cuba, had landed his expedition, on Holy Thursday, April 21, 1519, on the shores of Mexico, which they called Verz Cruz. Cortes had studied law at Salamanca, left it at sixteen, and had early attained intellectual maturity so that his keen understanding came well clad to ripen in the Indies. Cortes had first arrived in Cuba in 1511 and had taken part in many probing expeditions. In 1518, with an equal amount of audacity and farsightedness, he thwarted the governor, outfitted ships with stores and men, and set sail toward Mexico.

On the shores of Yucatán, where the water is as limpid as sapphire and the beaches are bleached golden by the sun, Cortes took a final muster of his expedition: five hundred and eight men. Of this complement, five were German: Johann of Hotzenplotz (age sixteen), whom they called Juan Aleman; Johann Berger, who settled in Puebla-Zacatula; another Johann, whom they called "Juan Armero" since he was by profession an armorer, and who later took part in the Cortes expedition to Baja, California; a German knight, George Ritter von

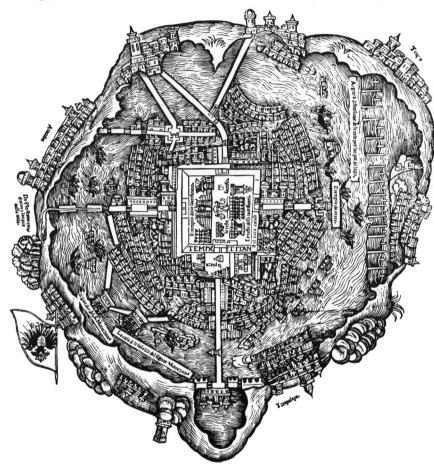

Hernán Cortés drew the first map of Mexico-Tenochtitlán as an illustration to his letters, two of which were published in the year 1524 in Nuremberg.

Nürnberg, who served later in the conquest of Guatemala; and, finally, one registered in the lists only as Juan the Landsknecht, expert with the long foliated partisan, a kind of halberd or pike.

When Cortes and his small army landed on the coast of Veracruz, he made contact with the Aztecs and several feather-cloaked ambassadors from Montezuma. They were soon overwhelmed with gifts of "novelty and value." Bernal Díaz, present when this happened, described the metallic hoard:

The first was a disk in the shape of the sun, as big as a cartwheel and made of a very fine gold. It was a marvellous thing, engraved with many sorts of figures and, as those who afterwards weighed it reported, was worth more than ten thousand pesos.
There was another larger disk of brightly shining silver in the shape of the moon. . . . Next came twenty golden ducks, of fine workmanship and very realistic, some ornaments in the shape of their native dogs, many others in the shapes of tigers, lions, and monkeys, ten necklaces of very fine workmanship. . . . Next they brought crests of gold, plumes of rich green feathers [Quetzals], silver crests, some fans of the same material . . . decorated with feathers of many colours, and so many other things.

It was now two of these gentlemen from Mexico who had brought things of "novelty and value" and set them before the youthful Charles. And, as pleasant fortune would have it, Albrecht Dürer was there to see it, having followed in the Emperor's procession from Aachen. "Historians," complained the author of *Don Quixote*, "usually relate matters so consciously that we scarcely have a smack of them, leaving the most essential part of the story drowned in the bottom of the ink horn. . . ." Not so Albrecht Dürer. He was the first qualified European to gauge the quality of American art.

I saw such things [he recorded in his diary] which were brought to the King from the New Golden Land [Mexico]; a sun entirely of gold, a whole fathom broad; likewise a moon entirely of silver, just as big; likewise sundry curiosities from their weapons, arms and missiles . . . all of which is fairer to see than marvels. . . . These things were all so precious that they were valued at 100,000 gulden. But I have never seen in all my days what so rejoiced my heart as these things. For I saw among them amazing artistic objects and I marvelled over the subtle ingenuity of the men in these distant lands. Indeed I cannot say enough about the things which were there before me.

A superb addenda to the Aztec gold were the feathered weavings. One was a ceremonial Aztec shield consisting of a feathered mosaic: two rounded disks of woven wickerwork covered with *amatl* paper to which was fixed a background of roseate flamingo feathers and against which was a springing animal, a coyote, made of turquoise-

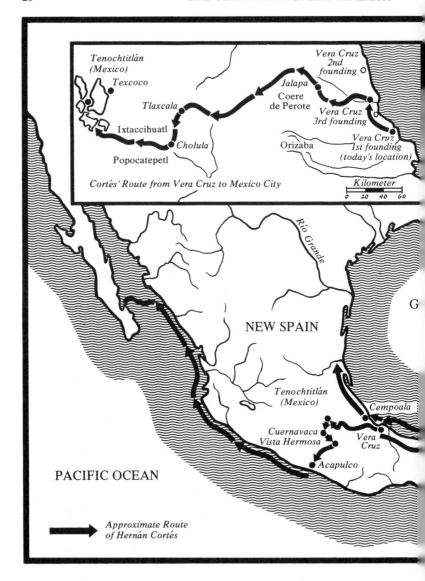

Tenochtitlán (Mexico)
Texcoco
Tlaxcala
Ixtaccihuatl
Cholula
Popocatepetl
Jalapa
Coere de Perote
Orizaba
Vera Cruz 2nd founding
Vera Cruz 3rd founding
Vera Cruz 1st founding (today's location)

Cortés' Route from Vera Cruz to Mexico City

Kilometer
0 20 40 60

Río Grande

NEW SPAIN

Tenochtitlán (Mexico)

Cuernavaca
Vista Hermosa

Cempoala

Vera Cruz

Acapulco

PACIFIC OCEAN

Approximate Route of Hernán Cortés

The route of Hernán Cortés in Mexico.

colored *cotinga* feathers, the tufts and teeth of the coyote being outlined with strips of fine gold leaf. The other was an immense feathered headdress, the symbol of Quetzalcoatl, the feathered serpent, which Montezuma had sent to Cortes because of his belief that Cortes was the returning White God, Quetzalcoatl. It consisted of over one hundred and twenty long green tail plumes, not just green, but a luminous jade green of metallic brilliancy. The plumes came from the quetzal bird (*Pharomacrus mocinno*) which lived in the high cloud forests of southern Mexico and down to northern Panama.[1] The feathers were of immense value to the Aztecs and very rare, since each male bird yields only four such meter-long tail plumes yearly. The golden objects Charles V himself retained: the feather ornaments he turned over to his brother Ferdinand, who deposited them in his collections at the Schloss Ambrass near Innsbruck. That they were there is confirmed by an inventory taken in 1596.

Meanwhile, Cortes undertook the conquest of Tenochtitlán, which was accomplished only by the total destruction of that watery city. All such feather ornaments were destroyed. Those stored in Schloss Ambrass were the only examples to survive—those pieces which so "rejoiced" Albrecht Dürer's heart.[2]

The impact of these golden Mexican ornaments on those who had the good fortune to see them before they were melted down in the crucibles of Charles's mints was most infectious. At that time gold, as money, had not circulated in Europe, so the fact that barbarous peoples in the Americas, of whom they had never heard, had gold so plenteous that they could even use golden fishhooks made the Aztecs fabulous in European eyes.

For the avid public, the German printers—then the principal artisans of the "new art" throughout Europe—were quick to sense a market. An anonymous publication of three unnumbered pages, stating that it had been taken out of the *Spanische sprach*, first told of Mexico. "Not far from the same island they have conquered is a city called Tenustitan [Tenochtitlán], wherein sixty thousand hearths [that is, houses] have been counted." Another booklet in 1522 was called *New News from Yucatán*. Cortes had written these letter-

---

[1]The author was the first to study the quetzal *in situ*, photograph and capture it alive.

[2]Now on display at the Museum für Völkerkunde, Vienna.

reports during the intervals of battle. They were as vibrantly alive as if they had been written in blood, for he wrote of the conquest while the flesh of history was still warm. At last Europe, after hearing for thirty years about the new-discovered lands and having seen nothing (aside from syphilis), now at long last had actual confirmation of the promised riches.

The Cortes letter had first been printed in Seville by Jacob Cromberger, a German. He was already renowned in 1519 as a printer-publisher for his publication of *Summa de geographia*, the first geographical book on the Americas.

While Cortes's letters gave Europe its first real glimpse of the ancient American cultures, his conquistadors were consuming much of it. The conquest was still in progress when, in 1524, the most sumptuous printing of Cortes's letters, the first Latin edition of the third letter, was printed in Nuremberg. Its title page exhibited a woodcut profile of Charles V, to whom the letters were addressed, and had as an illustration the first map ever drawn of Tenochtitlán, sketched by Cortes himself and said to have been engraved for the book by Albrecht Dürer, who was in Nuremberg when the book was being printed. It was a map from which all subsequent maps of the ancient Aztec capital were drawn.

The conquest went on for two years until, on Saint Hippolytus' Day, August 13, 1521, in the stench of a thousand fires, the Spanish Conquest was complete and the Aztec civilization passed into limbo.

America had suddenly become very much alive to the Germans.

The Streets of Magellan III

At the same time that Hernando Cortes was locked in battle with the Aztecs (November, 1519), Ulrich von Hutten, the most exalted poet of the Germanies, was locked in battle with his personal enemy—syphilis. He was also in the process of publishing the first book on the history, symptoms, and cure of this *morbus gallicus.*

While it is true that the conquest of Mexico had brought Europe its first golden hoard (which momentarily appeased the principal creditors of Charles V, the Fuggers and the Welsers), the first contact with the Americas had also brought another gift of dubious social value. It was syphilis, and it instantly took on the dimensions of a plague.

Syphilis appeared in Naples in December, 1494, twenty-one months after Columbus' return from America. A physician in Naples first observed the disease among sailors who had served on Columbus' ships. Since French troops controlled Naples at that time and were first infected, it was instantly called *morbus gallicus.* In an official account the private secretary of Emperor Maximilian described it: "Many of those poor fellows were covered from head to foot with vile running sores and looked so repulsive that their own comrades would not go near them. Others had certain parts of their bodies . . . covered with hard scales like the gnarled lumps found on a tree trunk. In their pain, the poor devils would tear off these scabs with their fingernails, revealing the purulent flesh underneath."

Many panaceas were advanced for its cure until Ulrich von Hutten popularized, in November, 1519, a cure by drinking an infusion made out of the bark guaiacum, an American tree.

Hutten sprang from one of the oldest and noblest families in the Germanies. Born in Schloss Stackelberg, he fled from an abbey near

Fulda in the summer of 1505 and went to Cologne to study the new humanism. With a restlessness that matched his capabilities, he wandered from city to city. After a sojourn in Vienna, he wandered into Italy, and while there, in December, 1515, cajoling some nameless bumpkin, he met the "sinister shepherd."[1]

"Ulrichus de Hutten equites Germaniae" was the way this disorderly knight of the Empire styled himself when he published the virtues of guaiacum wood as a specific for the cure of syphilis, so authoring the small book on the disease "wryten at Moguntia [Mainz] with myn own hande." Hutten, who thought so much of this booklet that he published his portrait with it, correctly laid down the history of the disease. It appeared first in Spain in 1493. He then told how "this pestiferus evyll crept amongst the people. . . . This disease not longe after its Begynnyng entered into Germania where it hath wandered more largely than in any other place." He wrote frankly of his own infection, relating how he had tried all the other cures. Then he came upon guaiacum wood. "The use of this wood was brought to us out of an island namyd Spagñola[2] and this ylonde [island] is in the west nigh to the contrey of Amerik set in that place where the length of Amerike, stretchynge into the northe doth ende: and was founde of late dayes amonge the newe landes, which were unknowen in the olde tyme."

Although the Welsers specialized in consumer goods such as spices (ginger, pepper, nutmeg, cinnamon, cloves, dyewoods, indigo, and the like), they also dealt in medicinal plants. Guaiacum, called by them "indisches Holz," was a tree with a very hard, brownish-green wood which grew in the West Indies. The natives thought it to be an elixir for all diseases. The Welsers secured the bark in quantities through their Spanish contacts and in time it became a source of considerable trade. They even sponsored publications attesting to its efficacy. One, appearing in 1524, gave an "approved prescription of a wood that is called *guaiacum* that grows on the islands of Spagñola . . . which heals all wounds caused by the French disease."

[1]The word syphilis was taken from a poem, *Syphilis sive Morbus Gallicus*, published in 1530 by Girolamo Fracastoro of Verona, a physician, astronomer, and poet. The hero of Fracastoro's poem was the shepherd hero Syphylus, Niobe's elder son. Hence, "the sinister shepherd."

[2]Hispanola, now Santo Domingo.

The year 1519 was one of the most notable in the history of the Americas. It was a year which witnessed the death of Maximilian, the election of Charles I of Spain as Holy Roman Emperor, the conquest of Mexico, and the publication of Ulrich von Hutten's application of practical humanism, that is, the curing of syphilis. The year 1519 also marked the push of the Germans into the Pacific through their connection with Ferdinand Magellan.

Fernando de Magalhães, as he was correctly called in his native Portugal, was to redraw the picture of the world by making its first circumnavigation, done at the cost of his own life. At the same time, to give the commercial spirit its rightful due, the voyage permitted Heinrich Ehinger, a Welser employee, to purchase all of the spices for the German market brought back by the voyage.

Let it be known that it was the tradesman and the businessman who were the driving forces of these new discoveries; it was their mercantile spirit that financed these explorations and extended the boundaries of the world. "Behind the hero," Stefan Zweig has written, "stood the trader. . . . And the quest for spices began it." A dash of pepper, a minute addition of nutmeg, a little ginger or cinnamon gave taste buds a "bounce" in an era when diets were monotonous and food, especially meats, were poorly preserved.

Pepper, before 1500, was counted by the peppercorn and was worth its weight in silver. Many city-states even kept their accounts in the value of pepper rather than gold. A sack of pepper was worth more than a human life. The palaces of the Doges in Venice, as well as those of the Fuggers and Welsers (the Palazzo dei Tedeschi by the Rialto Bridge is an example), were built from profits out of its export.

Jacob Fugger was aware of Magellan's projected voyage to the Spice Islands, for he was, in essence, the Emperor's financial adviser. Charles of Spain was then eighteen years old and only recently made King, yet he had been won over by Ferdinand Magellan's belief that "I shall find the pass—the strait—that leads to the Spiceries and only I alone know where to find it." Recognition of Magellan's qualities

Traveler Martin Behaim had the oldest globe manufactured which is in existence today. Recognition that earth is a ball and the discovery of new worlds made possible by it slowly penetrated the consciousness of the people in the 16th century.

was one of the most enduring acts of Charles's reign. On March 22, 1518, he signed his name—"Yo el Rey"—to the contract, a binding agreement with Magellan. The Fuggers, hearing of the planned voyage, wrote from Augsburg in August, 1519, instructing Christobal de Haro, who often acted as their representative in Spain, to invest ten thousand ducats in the enterprise. There was also attached to the instructions an inquiry: who in God's virtue, was Ferdinand Magellan?

The German merchants, cartographers, and printers who crowded the ports of Lisbon knew him well enough. True, the precise date of his birth was unknown, but it was thought to be 1480. At the age of twenty-four he took part in the expedition to the Spice Islands, and in Africa was wounded in the knee and lamed the rest of his life. He returned without awards. Magellan was thanked by no one and greeted by no one after seven years of service. It happened that while looking into the Portuguese archives he discovered that the Moluccas were within the Spanish boundaries of land alloted by the Treaty of Tordesillas. In resentment over Portuguese indifference to his services, Magellan renounced his citizenship and went to Spain, where, after the usual tossing on the seas of indifference, he turned to Christobal de Haro. Haro put him in touch with one in high office, who in turn wrote the King that Magellan was "one who might do a great service to His Majesty."

In August of 1519, while Cortes was moving inland toward Mexico with a small army, Magellan was moving the five small ships of his fleet down from Seville to the sea. Among his junior officers was a supernumerary named Antonio Pigafetta. A sprig from a noble Italian family of Vicenza, Pigafetta, then nineteen years old, heard of this mysterious expedition and, wanting "*di andare e vedere parte del mondo e le sue meraviglie*," he applied to the King, who in turn recommended him to Magellan. Pigafetta became Magellan's closest companion, his admirer and biographer. He was to be one of the eighteen survivors of the great voyage and author of a book of such merit that parts of it would be cribbed by Shakespeare for *The Tempest.*

The Magellan fleet made its first Brazilian landfall at what is now Pernambuco. They kept to the coast, testing the larger estuaries, and around the fortieth parallel began a frenetic search for the mysterious passage—the strait to the southern seas of which Magellan possessed a secret map made by Martin Behaim of Nuremberg, the cosmographer long in the employ of the King of Portugal and the same who had made the first world globe in 1492.

The secret German map was guiding the Magellan fleet none too well. There were, as usual in such voyages, mutterings and mutinies. Yet they kept to a southward course, and once below the fiftieth parallel they were in the first narrows of the strait. The pass was not, as the Fugger's factor Hans Prunsberger described it, a "Magalhãesstrasse," implying an open canal. It was a treacherous channel, filled with islands, and clotted with icebergs and massive, floating tree trunks.

On these fierce, windswept shores they met huge native giants with feet so large that Magellan called them *patagōa* ("big feet"), from which the term "Patagonia" is derived. All this and more was set down in the journal that Antonio Pigafetta was keeping. The ships moved through the second narrows and Pigafetta set down further notes on these desolations. The scrubby woodlands, eternally ablaze, were kept so because the natives did not know how to make fire, and thus a fire started accidentally was kept burning. Because of this Magellan called it Tierra del Fuego—"land of fire." Pigafetta further noted the storm-tossed waves and the utter desolation of the shore lands with the fissured hills torn by constant earth tremors and shores whipped by winds.

On the morning of November 28, 1520, the narrows opened widely and the sea became calm—pacific. This was the long-sought Southern Sea[3] which no man in recorded memory had crossed. Now Magellan was about to begin one of the deathless deeds of man. And yet, strangely enough, the crossing would be first told by a German who was not even present. Still, through his informants, he grasped the emptiness of this nameless ocean, "a sea so vast that the human mind can scarcely grasp its immensity."

Magellan did not live to gain his rewards of discovery. On April 27, 1521, after crossing the sea, he was killed by natives on the island of Mactan in the Philippines. Command was assumed by Juan Sebastián

---

[3]It had also been seen in 1513 in Panama by Núñez de Balboa, who took formal possession of it for Spain. Actually, the first European to sail on the Pacific Ocean was Martin de Benito on September 23, 1503.

del Cano, and only one ship, the *Victoria*, with eighteen survivors, including Pigafetta, and with an amazing cargo of spices entered the same Spanish port in 1522 that it had left three years before. Charles V had just returned from the Germanies in a royal rage. At the Diet in Worms he had had to witness a resolute Martin Luther challenge the spiritual unity of the church. The Emperor's mind was still acrid from this experience, so he was pleased to learn that his first royal sponsorship, the voyage of Ferdinand Magellan to the Spice Islands, had succeeded. As he was impatient to hear the details, three of the crew were ordered to bring him every document of the journey. He also saw and read Antonio Pigafetta's diary.

Juan Sebastián del Cano, who did all that he could to hinder Magellan yet lived to bring the *Victoria* home with the spices (which the Welsers purchased), was awarded a life pension of five hundred ducats, a patent of nobility, and a grant of arms: a globe for a crest with the motto, "Primus circumdedisti me." It was at this point that Maximilianus (a German despite the Latin name) enters history.

Matthaeus Land, Archbishop of Salzburg, having sired a son, despatched him to Spain to mature under the guidance of Pietro Martire d'Anghiera, known in English as Peter Martyr. This Italian-born humanist, who held a position of high trust close to the Emperor, was a scholar of great erudition as well an assiduous letter writer on the new events coming out of the Americas. Pietro Martire assigned the Archbishop's son, who bore the name Maximilianus Transylvanus, to examine all the survivors of the Magellan expedition and their documents, and from these compose for his Archbishop-father a report in formal Latin. Out of this assignment came the first notice of the momentous Magellan voyage.

Maximilianus called his report a "letter" and dated it October 22, 1522, but it so pleased the Archbishop that he entitled it "De Moluccis insulis . . ." (the long title did not even mention Magellan) and sent it on to a printer in Cologne, where it was published in January, 1523.

"A letter . . ." it opens, "very delightful to read concerning the Molucca islands and also many other wonders." Maximilianus kept to the facts. He wrote about the uncertainties of finding a strait, for "it was uncertain whether ingenious Nature, all whose works are wisely conceived, had so arranged the sea and land that it might be impossible to arrive by this course at the Eastern Seas." He told of the giants of Patagonia: "These Indians were very tall, ten spans high [7' 6"], clad in skins of wild beasts, darker complexioned than would have been expected in that part of the world. . . . To excite our admiration they took arrows a cubit and a half long and put them down their own throats to the bottom of their stomachs without seeming any the worse for it." He wrote how, after sailing for twenty days through "perpetual winter," the fleet finally sailed into the Pacific.

The "Letter" of Maximilianus was immensely popular and went from press to press. Its success caused Antonio Pigafetta, whose journal had been read by Charles V, to write his own narrative of his participation on the Magellan voyage: "I hope that the renown of so high-spirited a captain will never be forgotten. Among the many other virtues which adorned him, one was especially remarkable, that he always remained exceptionally steadfast even amid the greatest misfortunes. . . . The truth of this is proved by the way of which he brought to light things which no one before him had ventured to see or to discover."

The picture of the earth's size was now changing from month to month, year to year. German cartographers in Augsburg, Nuremberg, and Strasbourg were hard put to keep pace with the demand for new maps. Hardly had the cartographers revised their maps with the latest reports when new reports arrived. That which was first listed as an island, such as Yucatán, became part of a peninsula; other islands became whole continents. Cartographers never before, or since, had known such frenzied advances in so short a time. The interstices of the new lands were slowly being filled and German cartographers were avidly competing with Portuguese and Spanish cartographers, who had the advantage of being close to Seville, the source of overseas exploration. There was also a demand for stories, travels, and globes showing the New World. To meet this demand Johannes Schöner published the "Letter" of Maximilianus together with a terrestrial globe, the first to bear the name America.

The shape and size of the American continent was sufficiently detailed after the First World Geographical Congress, held in the spring of 1524 at Badajoz, Spain, and attended by all the famous pilots, geographers, and cosmographers, who were invited to bring their globes, maps and instruments, for the Welsers to realize that there was in America a massive slice of unclaimed land. This territory, which lay between the Isthmus of Panama and the Orinoco, was neither effectively occupied by the Spanish nor claimed by the Portuguese. Maracaibo, a large, brackish, inland lake connected with the sea, had been discovered by Spanish sailors and named by Vespucci "Little Venice," that is, Venezuela. And it was Venezuela that the Welsers, in view of their contribution of 141,000 ducats to Charles V to acquire the Emperorship, now demanded from the King.

Thus the Germans, through the commercial activities of the Welsers, had broken the strictures of the Treaty of Tordesillas, those clauses which excluded all except Spaniards and Portuguese to take part in the exploitation of the New World.

The Golden Man IV

At Burgos, Spain, on January 3, 1528, the representatives of the King and those of the Welsers met to sign the *capitulacíon*, the contract for the exploration of a vast territory then known vaguely as "Venezuela." The Venezuelan territory was not sold or given in grant; it was a contract for exploitation of the riches of this land for a period of twenty-five years to repay the Welsers the 141,000 ducats advanced for bribing the electors of the Holy Roman Empire and as an additional security for one million ducats of credit granted Charles V.

It was an indisputable fact that the Welsers had stolen a march upon the Fuggers. Anton Fugger, now head of the house, was not prepared to allow his rivals the lion's share of the Americas, for was not the King of Spain in greater debt to the Fuggers than to the Welsers? Jacob Fugger himself had reminded the King of "the obvious and well-known historical fact that Your Imperial Majesty would never have attained to the Holy Roman Crown without my aid."

It happened then that the Fuggers heard through their financial agent in Seville, Alberto Kohn (one of the first German Jews to have business dealings with the New World), of the new land called "Peru," and with it a new conquistador, Francisco Pizarro.

Pizarro arrived in Seville in the summer of 1528 and sought out and was received by the King, before whom he told of his adventures in the New World and ended with the astonishing news that he had found a kingdom of gold. The King examined the exquisite gold and silver ornaments, now familiar to him from the Aztec gold he had seen in Brussels. Won over by Pizarro's promise of an immense golden hoard, Charles, after many months of delay, signed the capitulation on July 26, 1529, giving him titles, salaries (to be paid out of

IACOBVS·FVGGER· CIVIS·AVGVSTÆ

Jacob Fugger II, called Fugger the Rich. The Fugger factories were, along with those of the Welsers, the outposts of civilization in the New World.

the conquest loot), officers, and military retainers. His partner, Diego de Almagro, was also rewarded, but less so, which would be the source of future quarrels. Pizarro's territory, New Granada, was defined, as much as one could where precise geography was unknown, as going from a place called Chincha, north to Tumbes near the equator. The territory south between Chincha and the Straits of Magellan had not then (in 1529) been assigned to anyone. It was this vast piece of real estate that the Fuggers demanded from Charles V on the same conditions that he had yielded Venezuela to the Welsers.

So, in a small Fugger countinghouse in Augsburg, the Germans had bargained for one-sixth of a continent without knowing anything of the land or the distances involved. Everything, on paper at least, was in exquisite detail. The Fuggers could nominate their own pilots and shipbuilders; they were permitted to export slaves and horses: and they were allowed *encomiendas*, the right to reduce to serfdom those Indians who fell under their jurisdiction. In short, the Fuggers had the right to exploit the largest estates in the world.

The contract was signed on June 28, 1531, making the Germans masters of more than one half of the South American continent—the Welsers (called by the Spanish "Belzarés") in the north; the Fuggers (called "Fúcares") in the south.

These proceedings were unknown to Pizarro, and he was unaware when the Fuggers had moved to take over their gargantuan land holdings in South America: two hundred leagues (1,100 kilometers) in length and of a depth that would have taken in half of Peru with Cuzco, all of Bolivia with Lake Titicaca, all of Chile, and a good part of Andean Argentina, including the control of Patagonia and the Magellan Strait. Who were their advisers? There is a record of only one, Hans Prunpecher of Augsburg, who had gone out with Sebastian Cabot's trading fleet in 1526 and knew of the lands which are now Argentina and presumably Patagonia. Aside from this, the Fuggers had no idea of the land or the people.

The Chilean-Peruvian coast is a desert, three thousand miles in length, broken every forty miles or so by valleys into which flow rivers, permanent or seasonal. Men filtered into these valleys in the earliest times and formed tribes; in time they extended these valleys by careful irrigation, artificially increasing the areas of fertility. In effect, each tribe was isolated by the desert, one from the other, causing them to develop, over great reaches of time, highly individual traits and cultures. The Incas under Topa Inca, during the years 1471–93, had conquered all tribes and land down to Chile. They had finally absorbed all these southern tribes only forty years before the Fugger contract.

The Fugger fleet was assembled in 1533 in Spain under the overall command of Simon de Alcazaba, one of the many Spanish navigators employed by the Fuggers, and so took its measured way toward the American lands, flying the pennant of Anton Fugger: a golden roebuck on a field of azure.

Meanwhile, in March, 1534, Cuzco quickly succumbed to Pizarro's army. Along with an additional harvest of Inca gold, Diego de Almagro, the original partner of Pizarro, now demanded his just share of land. The Spanish Court, fearful of a civil war between the conquistadors, granted Almagro the same territory—that part which lay between Chincha in Peru and the Straits of Magellan—that it had conceded to the Fuggers three years previously. Almagro moved quickly into the land vacuum.

Bartholomew Welser—here shown from a silver portrait medallion—founded in 1518 with his brother Anton the new Welser Trading Company, which gave preferential treatment to trade with Spain and her colonies.

The Fuggers met immediate disaster. Their fleet was wrecked on the wild shores of the Magellan Strait and a report to Seville relates how Pedro de Lerija, who worked for the Fuggers, tried to save horses and equipment. The wreck had occurred at night and darkness added to the confusion. Daylight brought the Indians down on them—"muy bellicosos y flecheros," the report reads. By the time the Fuggers could mount another expedition, the followers of Almagro had taken possession of the lands.

In the north the Welsers were in a different position. They had taken over their Venezuelan fief with organized promptitude, although they were subject to the same conditions imposed upon Spaniards who contracted for rights of conquest, which were "conquistar y poblar." These conditions were minutely laid down by the Casa de Contratación, a sort of Board of Trade in Seville. They were allowed to conquer and populate the lands, take the titles of Governor

Ferdinand, Archduke of Austria (1529–95), the husband of Philippine Welser.

and Captain-General, and construct fortifications out of the King's fifth, that is, his royalty.

Since the time of Columbus, Santo Domingo, first called Hispaniola, had been the administrative center of the Antilles and all other known lands in the New World. Since all matters were expected to go through these offices, Bartholomäus Welser, in 1528, sent his agents to Santo Domingo, and from here the Welsers sent supplies to the mainland. They raised livestock, processed sugar, built a gold-washing

The proud armada of the Welsers. Ambrosius Alfinger was the captain of the merchant fleet, which arrived in Venezuela in 1527.

plant, and worked a copper mine. From here they operated with goods, cattle, and slaves for the Spanish colonial empire.

The mining operations of the Welsers were the first of such American ventures, for in the sixteenth century mining and German were inseparable. As the Welsers operated many mines, principally in the Saxonian Erzgebirge, their agents contacted their miners in Joachimsthal. Hans Reiss and Jörg Neusser, finding the Welser plans feasible, gathered so many volunteers that the recruiting stations at Leipzig became riotous and the Bürgermeister had to call out the Watch to hold back those clamoring for work in America. The contract seemed generous; the miners would get one-sixth of the gross profits from mining operations in the New World after the expenses of the trip

Regions of influence of the Fuggers and Welsers in the year 1534.

Reports of El Dorado—the Golden Man—enticed the Spanish conquerors on perilous expeditions into the interior of the country. In this copper engraving Theodor de Bry shows a chief being sprinkled with gold dust.

and sustenance were deducted. Should anyone find the climate unsuitable, he could return to Europe in one year, but he must first agree to work as a sailor on the outbound voyage. One of the miners was allowed to bring his wife to cook and wash. Whoever that "she" was became the first German woman to arrive in the Americas.

Coro on the Venezuelan mainland was the Welser headquarters. It was then a small settlement of Spaniards, living almost as primitively as the Coriana Indians (hence the name Coro). Coro's advantage was that it lay in a bay protected by the Peninsula of Paraguaná within the larger Gulf of Venezuela. The original Spanish settlers were set aside by the Welsers and the settlement officially founded as a city—the first in Venezuela.

The interior of South America at that time was vague and shadowy. The Germans thought, as did everyone else, that the whole of Venezuela was an island because its first discoverers, on sailing into the immense Maracaibo lagoon, saw houses on stilts and thus thought of it as "Little Venice." Even Diego Ribero, the famed cartographer whose outline chart of the Americas in 1529 was a landmark in early American cartography and who at one time was employed by the Welsers to map the regions under their control, wrote on the margin of his Welser map: *"Está es la gobernación del la gran casa compania de Belzarés hasta el estrecho de tierra de Magellanes"* (These are the lands governed by the great House of Welser [Belzarés] which extend down to the land of Magellan—a geographical oversight of 4,200 miles!

Ambrosio Alfinger of Ulm, dubbed at once "Micer Ambrosio" by the Spaniards, was the Welser governor. Though he was then only twenty-nine years old, the Welsers chose him because of his proven loyalty, organizational ability, and firmness. More important, he could speak Spanish. As soon as Alfinger had officially taken over Coro and established his factors and officials—mostly Spaniards—he ordered his ship *Victoria* to sail for Lake Maracaibo.

While Micer Ambrosio was there, the Indians told them in vague terms that they trafficked with a mountain tribe for emeralds and that they were so rich in gold their king walked about coated with it. Thus the Germans learned through Ambrose Alfinger's interpreter about El Dorado, the "Golden Man." The search for this specter throughout the century would be the undoing of many lives. It would also be the undoing of the Welsers.

Alfinger returned to Coro, organized a land expedition to seek out the Golden Man, and set off with eighty men and two hundred Indian "volunteers" to find El Dorado. It was like a journey into hell. In his *Información de Servicios*, which he wrote when he returned, Micer Ambrosio gave in considerable detail the trials and tribulations of his journey. The jungle swallowed them, and month upon month passed without further notice of Micer Ambrosio. At last, presuming him to be lost, the Welsers ordered a new governor to replace him.

On April 18, 1530, the new governor announced himself Nikolaus

Federmann of Ulm. A professional soldier, pilot, tradesman, and factor, fluent in Spanish, he was sent by the "Welsers, my masters" to take over the governorship of Venezuela. Upon seeing this red-bearded, red-haired Swabian, the Spaniards gave him the name Capitán Barbarossa.

Nikolaus Federmann was to be the catalyst in the search for the Golden Man, opening up immense and unknown areas. In doing so Federmann would write the first ethnographic survey of an American Indian tribe and cover as well a huge area of geography.

In his narrative Federmann said that he sailed from Spain on October 2, 1529, with soldiers and twenty-four German miners and reached Santo Domingo in December, 1529, sailing after that to Coro on the mainland. "Here was I staying in Coro," he begins, "with too many idle soldiers on my hands. So I decided to travel myself toward the South Sea [Pacific], hoping I could achieve something useful. I prepared all that was necessary for such an expedition."

He left on September 16, 1530, together with one hundred six Spanish footsoldiers and sixteen cavalry. He went off "in the direction where the sun sinks," the direction of the Golden Man. Strangely enough, however, he did not go westward, but southeastward, without any precise knowledge of the geography. In the course of his journey Federmann took down the notes which became the first book ever to be written on the tribal ethnography of South American Indians.

By January 3, 1531, they were still continuing "their journey to the South Seas," although in reality they were close upon the Atlantic. Federmann was in such high fever that it "was so heavy upon me that I could hardly sit upon my horse." Hunger pursued and engulfed them, until in desperation they killed and ate a jaguar: "It had a strong smell, but we were so hungry that we would have eaten anything."

On March 17, 1531, they stumbled into Coro. There, while recovering from the harrowing effects of his march, Federmann wrote his *Indianische Geschichte*. The subtitle read, "The charming and agreeable Tale of my first Voyage." But if Federmann thought his trip would be "very pleasant to read," it was not so to Ambrose Alfinger, for he had meanwhile returned alive, resumed the governorship, and thereupon exiled Federmann for five years for insubordination.

The conquistadors Philipp von Hutten, Nikolaus Federmann, and Ambrosius Alfinger (from left to right) on the search for the Golden Man, drawn by Hieronymus Köhler.

Whereupon Micer Ambrosio himself again set out with a sizable army to look for the Golden Man. After a heroic march of three hundred miles through jungle and plain they entered the frigid uplands, over three thousand meters high. Their horses were eaten. Eight soldiers, including Hans Kasimir of Nuremberg, and one hundred Indians, died from the cold. After two years of search for the Golden Man they turned back. Close to Lake Maracaibo they were attacked, and Micer Ambrosio was struck in the throat with a poisoned arrow. There they buried Ambrose Alfinger of Ulm, first German governor of Venezuela and co-discoverer of the Río Magdalena.

The legend and name of El Dorado go back to a custom of the Muiscas in Colombia. Their cacique, covered with gold dust, was taken out on the Lake of Guatavita, where he made sacrifices and washed the gold dust away with water. Alexander von Humboldt drew the first view of this mysterious lake in 1801.

The Welsers were being consumed by what they had first called the "Spanish disease," that metallic fever for which gold was the only cure. They sent out a new governor, no less than Bartholomäus Welser, the heir, namesake, and eldest son of the paterfamilias of the Welsers. With him went Philipp von Hutten, cousin of the famous Ulrich.

The Welser governorship was given to Georg Hohermuth, from Speyer-am-Rhine. The expedition gathered in Seville in 1534 for their official departure. By happenstance the young Hieronimus Köhler, then only twenty-three and a scion of the patrician Köhler family of Nuremberg, was one of the expedition. He made a record of the ritual surrounding the mounting of an expedition to the Americas,

The gravestone of Philipp von Hutten in Maria Sontheim near Arnstein. In the background is a portrayal of his adventurous trip to South America in 1535–38.

drawing the portraits in a naïve style of the principal German conquistadors—Hohermuth, Federmann, Hutten, Welser—as well as the flagbearers, the soldiers, the carpenters with all their implements, and the conquistadors armed with daggers, pikes, and swords. By some small bibliographical miracle, all that Hieronimus Köhler set down was preserved. This, with the diary of Nikolaus Federmann and the letters of Philipp von Hutten, form an unique record.

Philipp von Hutten, born in 1511 to an old Franconian family, was the second son of Bernard, then the Emperor's representative in Königshofen. His brother was an official at the court of Charles V, and in his youth Philipp had been a playmate of Ferdinand II, Archduke of Tirol. Hutten was young, scarcely twenty-four, ambitious, romantic, and the adventures ahead had an irresistible attraction for him. "God is my witness," he wrote to his brother, "it is the trip that lies ahead that interests me; I am not motivated by the idea of riches, but to satisfy a strange desire."

By the second year of their expedition, they had reached and passed the Guaviare River, a large tributary of the Orinoco; by the third they came to the Río Caquetá, an immense tributary of the Amazon. By December, 1537, after a futile search for the Golden City, they began the death march back. "Only God and ourselves," Hutten wrote later to his father, "know the privations, the misery, the hunger, the thirst which we . . . suffered. . . . I am full of admiration for the human spirit that it could withstand for so great a length of time in these fearful exertions. . . . We were so reduced to starvation at one time that we boiled and ate the deer hides which the Indios used for making their war shields."

On May 27, 1538, three years to a day since they set off to find El Dorado, that which was left of the expedition straggled into the colony of Coro. Captain Gundelfinger, one of the more robust, brought in forty-nine walking skeletons. Hohermuth, with Hutten, headed a long line of eighty-five half-clothed men, covered with festering sores. "We were clothed no more," wrote Hutten, "than the naked Indians." Hohermuth had lost three hundred men, and even when he was moribund his head still swam with visions of gold and golden cities. Even while Hohermuth was dictating plans for his new expedition, death put an end to it.

In the meantime Federmann waited. Then, after 1537, as they did not return and were presumed dead, he advanced with his own expedition toward "that certain golden king." At first Federmann followed the unmistakable spoor of the Hohermuth expedition: graves, burnt villages, and bits of iron rusting in the jungle.

For one of the most fascinating moments of American explorations there was to be no historian, no scrivener, royal or private, who would be there to describe the famous meeting of Federmann, Jiménez de

Quesada, and Benalcázar. There is only the acrimonious letter of Nikolaus Federmann to a friend, describing the emotions of one who had spent ten frenetic years in search of a golden vision, only to see it dissolve into myth again just as he was about to embrace it.

From this one letter we learn that he first followed the Hohermuth group, but as Federmann had no intention of being merely a relief column, he set off to find the Golden Man himself. Within months he had found the passage into the Andean heartland. After all these years of advance and retreat, Federmann had gained the heights, and now only the *páramo*, the high plateau, had to be crossed. The intensely cold heights of those four thousand meters had killed most of the Indian carriers. The earth was so deeply frozen that they had to leave their dead unburied; twenty horses were lost on the first day.

It was now 1539. It had taken Nikolaus Federmann two years to reach El Dorado, and there before him lay the Lake of Guatavita, fashioned round like a cup so as to catch the first and last rays of the sun. Lake Guatavita was no wider than three crossbow shots at its greatest diameter. It was only one of the myriads of loftily placed lakes around these high, bare mountains. And yet Guatavita gave birth to the myth of El Dorado, the Golden Man.

In some faintly remembered past, a meteorite, its molten fire flowing golden in its descent from outer space, had fallen with violent impact onto the páramo of Zipaquirá.[1] It struck and buried itself 150 meters into the ground, making a vast crater. Then time, bringing with it a generous incidence of rain, filled the gargantuan crater and it became the Lake of Guatavita.

This incident lived long in Andean folk memory and became the personification of a golden Sun God. When the Chibcha tribes peopled the land they did homage to this god. As gold seemed to be the color symbol of his golden ascent, gold became the motif of their obeisance: "There was a certaine king," the troubador sang, "who when dismantled and smeared on his regal body with a fragrant resin. Over this was coated powdered gold from feet to highest brow so that with his skin of gold he seemed as resplendent as the beaming sun." This chieftain was wafted by balsa raft into the center of Guatavita, while around the high rim of the lake were gathered those who had made

---

[1]The site is only 65 kilometers from Santa Fe de Bogotá.

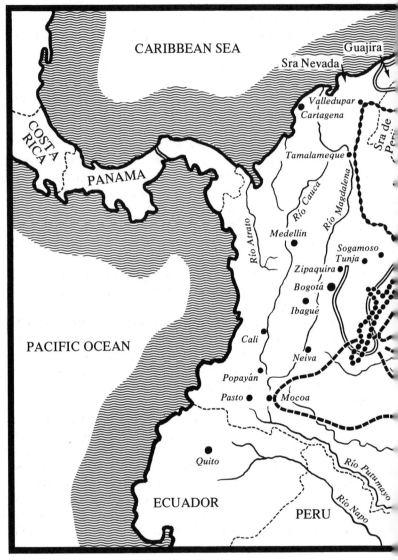

The route of the German conquistadors Alfinger, Federmann, Welser, and Hutten on the search for the Golden Man.

Coro

Barquisimeto

VENEZUELA

Río Orinoco

Río Meta

GUIANA

OMBIA

Río Guaviare

Río Orinoco

BRAZIL

Río Japurá

Río Ica

●●●●●●●● Alfinger

■■■■■■ Federmann 1st trip

▭▭▭ Federmann 2nd trip

●●●●●●●● Welser-Hutten

Kilometer

| 0 | 100 | 200 | 300 | 400 | 500 |

pilgrimage to witness the ceremony. As the Golden Man made his ablutions in that frigid tarn to wash off the gold so that it might drift down as offering to the deity, the tribesmen threw their offerings of golden *tunjos* into the lake. And so was born the story of the Golden Man.

Federmann had found the lake of El Dorado, but so had two other Spanish captains, Gonzalo Jiménez de Quesada and Sebastián de Benalcázar. Each with his small army had arrived before Federmann and each one of them believed that El Dorado lay under his territorial jurisdiction. All three captains had about the same number of combatants. It was the plain geometry of equilateral military forces. Strangely enough they did not war. Federmann was paid off with some gold and emeralds. Then all three conquistadors departed to Spain to lay their jurisdictional quarrel before the Spanish Council. In February, 1542, Federmann made his final exit.

Philipp von Hutten and Bartholomäus Welser, despite the intense suffering of their first expedition, decided to go on. In 1538, Hutten, now Captain-General of Venezuela, set out with Welser and one hundred mounted men to "look for the place called El Dorado which lies in the confines of the Amazon."

In his own world—that is, the world of the patricians in Augsburg—Bartholomäus Welser (the sixth of that name and line) was pleasant and well informed. ("A clever young man," according to Hutten.) However, Welser came to his new, raw, undisciplined world without any experience for what would lie ahead. He was rich, heir to the Welser fortune. His father had been ennobled, and his aunt, Philippine, secretly married to the Archduke Ferdinand, so it would have been unnatural of him had he not allowed these prerogatives to betray him in arguments with Spaniards of base birth. In the end, his pride would cost him his head.

In their second expedition Welser and Hutten reached the lower Río Caquetá where it enters the Amazon, site of the Omagua Indians. Forty of the mounted conquistadors looked down on the most populated village they had ever seen in all their years in the Americas. They descended to attack. The Omaguas' priests blew sacred bamboo trumpets. The war drums beat the staccato warning of attack, then the Omaguas (Hutten thought that there were over a thousand) swarmed about the horsemen. Unable to maneuver, they retreated to

the higher cleared area where they could use their horses more effectively. The Omaguas followed in such masses that even the conquistadors' lances were ineffective. All were wounded, Philipp von Hutten
seriously. They retreated and were set upon continuously until they
reached the boundary of the Vaupés River. There the Welsers called
a retreat and so began the long return march to Coro.

During their absence there had arisen throughout Venezuela a
deep wave of anti-Welser feeling, derived from the Spanish reaction
to Luther's reformation. It was clear, moreover, that the Welsers
were losing their power at court and Charles was listening more
closely to his council, who advised him to abrogate the claims of the
Welsers on Venezuela. In his long absence Hutten had been sup-
planted by a new Spanish governor. On his return he was arrested.
There was a mock trial. Hutten, Welser, and two Spanish captains
were judged guilty.

The mirage of El Dorado led Philipp von Hutten into lands never
seen before by white men. He had traversed a good part of *terra
incognita*, had taken part in great discoveries, and now the heads-
man's ax fell. Philipp von Hutten had not quite reached thirty years.

The Fuggers seemed to know of this event even before their rivals.
A letter, dated September 25, 1547, "aus dem Welser-land," gave an
account of the decapitation. By 1555 the Welser interests were
finally liquidated in Venezuela.

"I, Ulrich Schmidel of Straubing . . ." V

Ulrich Schmidel's introduction to the New World was scarcely auspicious. The ship on which he was sailing, one of fourteen that made up the armada of vessels to Argentina under the command of Pedro de Mendoza, was entering the estuary of the Río de la Plata when a furious *pampero*, a strong, cold wind, swept out and destroyed his caravel. "Our ship was fragmented into a thousand pieces," wrote Schmidel, but he and five companions saved themselves by hanging onto a ship's spar until they were thrown up on an inhospitable shore. From there, with neither arms nor food, they walked fifty leagues through an unknown country in order to reach the Spanish colony.

Schmidel was to remain in America for nineteen years (1534–53) and was the only eyewitness to write about the conquest and settlement of these lands. Without him we would have no record at all.

"I, Ulrich Schmidel of Straubing [on the Danube]," as he began his book, ". . . saw many nations and countries. . . ." He was young, in his late twenties, and had enough learning to set down his remarkable account. He was far from being illiterate, as some have described him; neither was his sense of geography "extremely defective." The distinguished Spanish geographer, Félix de Azara, who spent twenty years at the end of the eighteenth century in those austere lands, wrote well of him.

Schmidel was no ordinary man. Soldier he may have been, but he was also the business representative of the Welsers in Seville. As a full-time factor and a part-time gunner, Schmidel was one of a large company sailing with Pedro de Mendoza in the largest armada which had ever been sent to the Americas: fourteen large ships, seventy-two horses, and twenty-five hundred men. The Welsers sailed their own ship in the armada, on which there were eighty Germans.

The Fuggers, keeping pace with their rivals, already had two factor-

*The Straubinger mercenary Ulrich Schmidel participated in Spanish
service in the capture of the La Plata province in 1532–52. In his
book* True Stories of a Wonderful Voyage, *he relates in lively fashion
his adventures and observations. This illustration shows an encounter
with an anaconda and testifies to Schmidel's keen talent of observation.*

representatives in residence: Hans Prunsberger, who had taken part
in Cabot's voyage, was doing business on the Río de la Plata until he
died in 1545; and by the time Schmidel arrived, Prunsberger had been
joined by another factor named Sebastian Kurz.

Pedro de Mendoza, commander of this great armada, looked toward
the interior of the continent, for it was here that silver was believed to
have come from. The native name for the Río de la Plata was Paranaguazú, "river like the sea." Beyond the Paranaguazú, fading into
the horizon, the land was clothed with purple blossoms and was inhabited by a warlike tribe known as the Charruas.

Beyond, in a westerly direction, lay what is now Paraguay. It was to
this vast, wild jungle area that Mendoza directed his captain, Domingo
Martínez de Irala. One of this company was Ulrich Schmidel, who
went, as he wrote, "with Captain Irala . . . in the second month of the
year 1548 . . . with upwards of 7 brigantines and 200 canoes, while
another host of people, those who could not fit in the ships, walked
the shore of the river with 130 horses." They moved into what is now

Paraguay, looking for the source of silver mines. They did not know that the silver which had come down to Sebastian Cabot on his expedition was obtained from the Incas, five hundred miles westward.

They moved through a galaxy of Indian tribes—Abipónes on the west bank, Guaraní on the east, and many others—all speaking variants of the same Tupí-Guaraní language. It was when they moved away from the rivers that their troubles began: "We were exceedingly hungry and had no longer anything to eat but wild honey." Here Schmidel learned of the hammock ("made of spun cotton and fashioned like a net"); each man after that carried his net bed. He observed the animals, the customs of the Indians, their mode of warfare, the manner in which houses were constructed—and the women. "A woman could be bought for a shirt or a knife or a hatchet. . . . They attend to anything that we needed." He admired the way the women painted their bodies: "A painter in Europe would have to work hard to equal it."

Somewhere on the pampas, probably southwest of the Abipóne tribes, where the jungles halt and the vast grasslands begin, he had first sight of a llama and its relative, the wild guanaco. He called them Indian sheep, "of which they have two different kinds . . . the native [llama] and the wild ones [guanaco]. They use them for riding and cargo, as we would use horses. I myself rode on such a 'sheep' for more than 40 miles when I broke my leg."

They went westward by river and then by land following, it is believed, the Pilcomayo, one of the larger tributaries of the Paraná River. They followed this until "we arrived," Schmidel wrote, "in a land where the people are called Peionas. There we found enough to eat: geese, deer, sheep [llamas], ostrich, parrots, etc. There was also plenty of Indian Turkish corn [maize], other roots [sweet potatoes and manioc] and fruit [papaya and *chirimoyas*]. But there was little water, nor was there gold or silver." Later, after they had traveled over five hundred miles—although according to "their astronomical calculations they were 372 miles from Asunción [in Paraguay]," they reached what Ulrich Schmidel called the river of Machcasies (in Bolivia). This was the closest route to the mines of rich Potosí. But since they found no silver in Paraguay, they returned to the land of the Guaraní.

Here, in 1553, at one of the permanent stockades in Paraguay,

Schmidel found letters waiting for him. One was from his brother urging his immediate return, as well as one from the Welsers asking him to return to Antwerp, from where he had departed twenty years before.

After consulting with his captain, Schmidel was given liberty to return to Europe. With six soldiers, German and Spanish, and twenty Indians, they had to ascend the Paraná, bypass the great falls and cataracts of Iguassu—the most impressive waterfall in the Americas—and move over the Tropic of Capricorn to the Paranapanema, a large tributary of the Paraná. This was followed down to the seaport of São Vincente in Brazil. Even Schmidel complained of the thousand miles through raging rivers, terrifying waterfalls, and myriads of different tribes.

In São Vincente he found a German factor who, though constantly warring with the Indians, was operating a sugar mill for the Welsers. Soon there appeared a trading vessel belonging to Johann von Hulst of Lisbon and it was loaded to the gunwales with brown sugar loafs and Brazilwood for dyeing. On January 20, 1554, Schmidel landed at Antwerp. "And so after the lapse of twenty years, . . . I have returned to the place whence I set out; but meanwhile I have in my peregrinations of these Indian nations experienced no little danger to body and life, great hunger and misery, care and anxiety, sufficiently made known and set forth in this historical narrative."

Later, in Regensburg, he began to write *A True and Agreeable Description,* first published in 1567. It was still immensely popular in 1599, when Théodore de Bry, the Huguenot publisher and illustrator living in Frankfurt-am-Main, published it again in Latin.

Hans Staden continued the German contribution to American history precisely at the same port of São Vincente (now Santos, the port of São Paulo) whence Schmidel set sail to Europe. Little is known of Staden other than what he tells of himself—a not unusual condition of that century when base-born men remained anonymous.

Staden was a *villein*—a townsman—of Homburg in Hesse. There his parents had settled, and there he was born about 1515. He was near thirty when he first left for America, "if God willed it," to see the Indies. Accordingly, he embarked for Lisbon, where he "lodged at an inn owned by the younger Leuhr, a German. I told him that if it were at all possible, I desired to see the Indies." Staden was directed

to the offices of the Fuggers, Welsers, and others, where he secured employment as a gunner on a Portuguese trading ship. He sailed on his first voyage in a ship fitted with "every kind of war contrivance," having with him two other Germans. Then, having once gained shore at Pernambuco in Brazil, they had their first skirmish with the natives before they were able to load Brazilwood and sugar.

On the next voyage Hans Staden left Seville in Easter Week of

The mercenary Hans Staden, shown on page 62, went twice to Brazil in Spanish and Portuguese services in 1545–55. Staden describes his month-long imprisonment by the Indians in his True Story, *also called* Cannibal Book.

1549. It took them six months of sailing until they made a landfall on the island harbor of São Vincente, close to the port of Santos. There they ran into a wall of high water, the ship was destroyed, and Staden drifted to land hanging onto a ship's mast, an incident that he illustrates in his book. "We stayed there for two years in the wilderness," he wrote, "in great peril and so straitened for food that we were forced to eat lizards and field-rats . . . and sea creatures. Most of the savages who had at first supplied us with food departed . . . when they had obtained sufficient wares from us. . . . It seemed as if we must remain there and die."

They then made their way to a Portuguese trading station, where Staden was given employment along with other Germans who were among the pioneers operating the first sugar mill in Brazil. Hunting one day with friendly Indians, Staden was set upon by Tupinambás and captured. It is to this event that we owe his illustrated ethnographic monograph. Like Federmann in Venezuela and Schmidel in the south, Staden's narrative is of utmost importance in the prehistory of the Americas.

There were two subtribes of Tupís: those called Tupinambás, who were his captors, living in a northern coastal territory, and the Tupinikins, with whom they waged perpetual war. Staden was con-

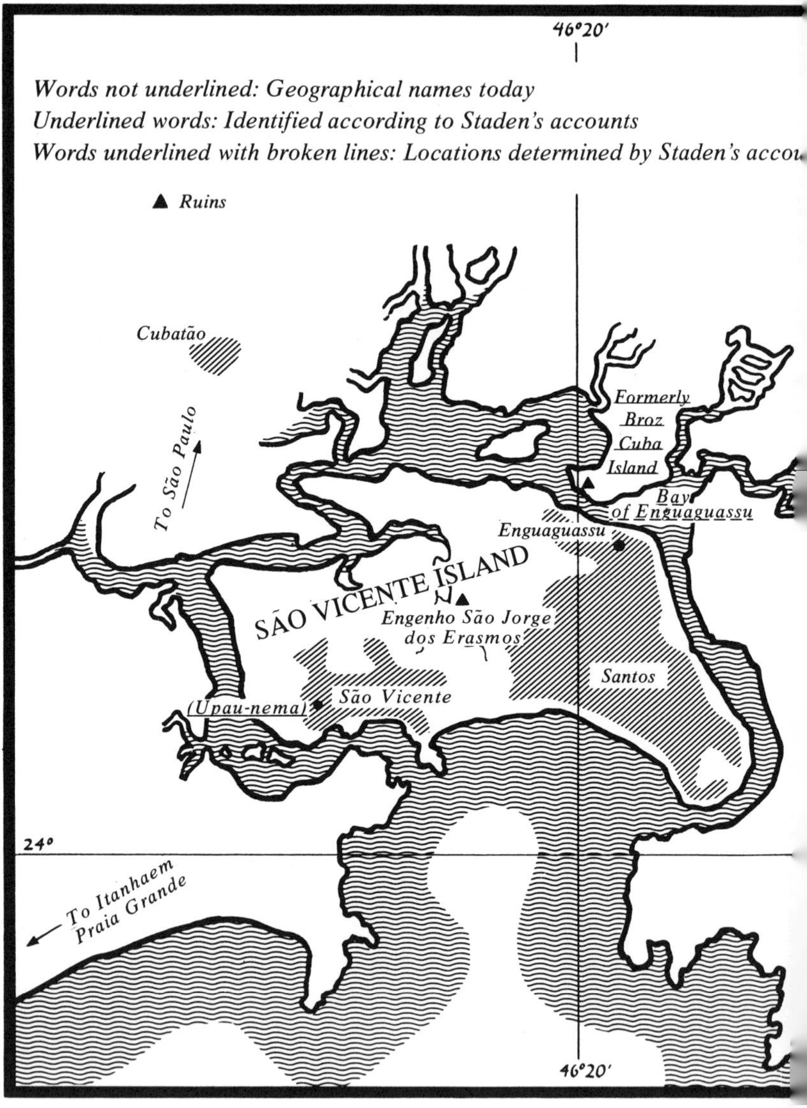

Words not underlined: Geographical names today
Underlined words: Identified according to Staden's accounts
Words underlined with broken lines: Locations determined by Staden's accou

▲ *Ruins*

Cubatão

To São Paulo

Formerly
Broz
Cuba
Island

Bay
of Enguaguassu

Enguaguassu

SÃO VICENTE ISLAND

Engenho São Jorge
dos Erasmos

Santos

(Upau-nema)   São Vicente

To Itanhaem
Praia Grande

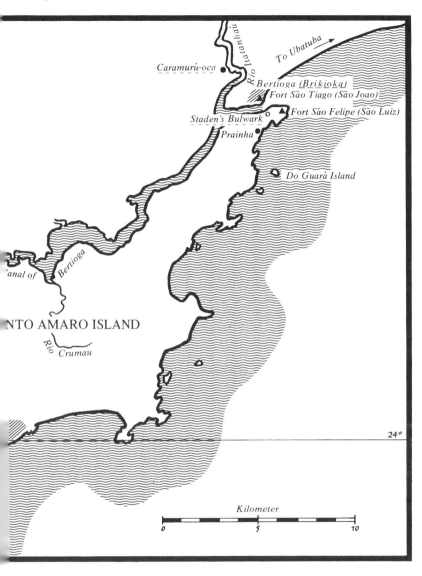

From Staden's True Story, *the coast of São Vicente (today Santos, harbor of São Paulo) to Bertioga.*

fined behind the stockaded village, the entrance to which was fes-
tooned with the skulls of those whom the Tupinambás had consumed
in ritual cannibalism.

But as the natives were used as allies by the contending Europeans,
Indians fought Indians to obtain the monopoly of white man's gee-
gaws. In the end, this allowed the white man to gain the foothold
which was the end of the Tupinambás. The Portuguese had established hereditary captaincies and colonies in Brazil to protect their
monopolies, but, by 1548, relentless war had broken out between the
Indians and the colonists, the French and Portuguese playing each
other off against the Indians.

The Tupinambás told Staden he would be fattened and then eaten;
therefore, as was their custom, they shaved off all his facial hair,
including his eyebrows. Staden's long reddish beard proved too much
for them, however, and it remained his only clothing. Hans Staden
happened to have been captured by the Tupinambás, who had attached themselves to the French; therefore he was, they said, a
"Portuguese." But he insisted, "I am not Portuguese, but a kinsman
and friend to the French and my native land is Allemania." This
saved him.

During the eight months of his captivity Staden learned the Tupí
language and carefully remembered in ethnographical detail the
material culture of these coastal people. It was well that he did. In
many instances it is our only history.

*A True and Brief Account of all that I learnt concerning the trade
and manners of the Tuppinbas* (Tupinambás), a book of forty pages,
was illustrated under his own supervision. The facts of the Tupinambás' religion, war, material culture, and the flora and fauna of the
country were all set down by Staden with sustained and penetrating
observation. It became fascinating reading for those Germans who
now saw the New World opening up through personalized adventure.

Staden told how the Tupís lived ("their communal dwellings are
fourteen feet wide, 150 feet long . . . and rounded at the top like a
cellar"); their manner of sleeping ("in hammocks with a fire underneath to keep warm"); their methods of firemaking, fishing, pottery-
making, and the preparation of food and beer. As a German, he
observed the beer with special care. Boiled manioc tubers were chewed
by the women, and when masticated with their saliva the enzymes of

Colonial cities in Brazil (with founding dates).

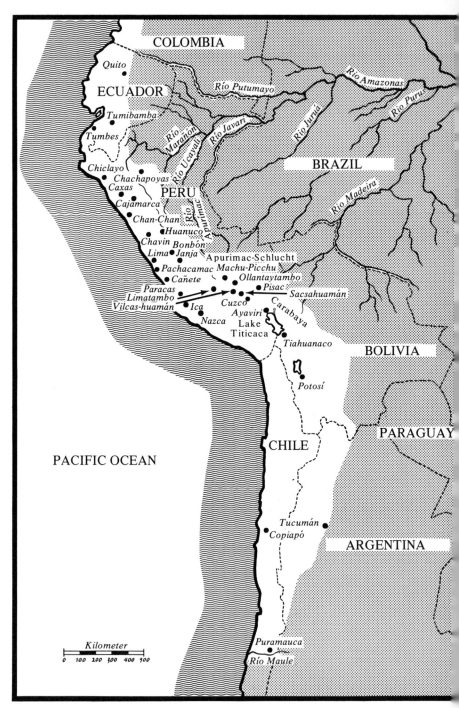

The empire of the Incas stretched over more than 5,000 kilometers along the west coast of South America.

starch were converted into sugar, causing fermentation within two days. It produced a strong, maltish-tasting liquor. He dealt with their body decorations, their marriage and possessions, their beliefs and their cannibalism. All this he properly assessed as ceremonial cannibalism, and he correctly gauged that "they do it not from hunger, but from great hate." After living for eight months under the fear of a cannibalistic death, Staden eventually bargained his way aboard a French ship. It touched at São Vincente and then sailed to France.

Once having returned alive to Germany in 1555, Hans Staden immediately settled down at the village of Wolfhagen and began to write *A true history and description of a country of savages, a naked and terrible people, eaters of men's flesh, who dwell in the New World called America, being wholly unknown in Hesse both before and after Christ's birth until two years ago, when Hans Staden of Homburg in Hesse took personal knowledge of them and now presents his story in print.* The book's obvious honesty ("I subscribe myself in all humility") maintained its suspense and held the reader while he wrote about their customs and material culture.

Hans Staden's literary fame was given further emphasis by the magnificent publication of his adventures by Théodore de Bry. This engraver-publisher of travel books did more to make America known to Europeans than all others before him. Born at Lüttich (1528) of a well-known and prosperous Huguenot family, he was trained first as a goldsmith and then as an engraver. Thrust out of his own land, he worked first in Strasbourg, then settled, in 1569, in Frankfurt-am-Main. After his death (1598), his son Jean continued the work. The result was the *Great Voyages* in German, Latin, French, and an astonishing list of other publications.

While Prunsberger, the Fugger agent, remained in Argentina, Sebastian Kurz was sent by the Fuggers to Yucatán, the peninsula below Mexico. The name Yucatán had early entered the German vocabulary, even before the name Mexico. An anonymous printer had somehow acquired a letter written in 1519 by one of Cortés's companions, made an extract of it, and printed it on March 18, 1522, as *News out of Yucatán.* The small pamphlet told the avid public of "the land that the Spaniard hath found in 1521 known as Yucatán."

It was amazing what correct information the *News out of Yucatán* contained. The people had gold, finely woven cotton garments, and also the famous feather weavings. Their temples were stone built, but roofs were thatched with straw. In the center of the city was a principal building (the writer called it "Rathaus") and a plaza where people traded. They made a drink called chocolate out of a seed shaped like an almond. The writer noted that the Mayas were really "business men," for they kept their accounts in books on paper made from the inner bark of a tree (*amatl*), and it mentioned "König Mathotzoma," who was, of course, Montezuma. All very correct as far as it went, except the writer was describing Mexico, not Yucatán.

After aiding Cortes in his conquest of the Aztecs, Francisco de Montejo had returned to Spain and enticed his wife to sell her estates and pawn her jewels to finance his own expedition. Montejo was "somewhat middle-sized, [with] a merry face and one who was fond of rejoicings and a good horseman, . . . who was liberal with his own money as well as that of others." He had applied for and been granted by the Spanish crown the rights to conquer and then colonize the whole of Yucatán.

In 1527, Francisco de Montejo arrived in Yucatán with ships, men, and cannon—as well as smallpox—and began the conquest of the Mayas. This was done first by occupying the walled cities of Xelha and Tulum, which lie on the immediate coast.

Some years later, in 1534, Sebastian Kurz arrived and began trading in the wake of the Maya conquest. His object was twofold: to secure usable products from the conquest and to sell trade goods— iron implements, guns, mirrors, combs, and all the other ill-sorted gewgaws that accompanied conquest everywhere. Kurz found that the land of Yucatán appeared to be like some gigantic up-raised thumb projecting into the Caribbean Sea. The peninsula was all limestone. There were no surface rivers; all water ran thirty meters underground and yet supported forests of dry scrub. There were also low, wetland jungles. In the lowland areas where the great temple cities—Tikal, Uaxactún, Yaxchilán, Calakmul—the lake was El Petén. There rain forests alternated with depressed areas that became seasonal swamps; high bush alternated with savannas covered with tall grass.

In the northwest of the Yucatán peninsula was Campeche, a rolling country of forests and rivers, and west of it the lushly tropical Tabasco, covered with swamps and quagmires, a network of bayous, creeks, rivers. The land was made for cacao plantations, and the Indians planted little else, depending on the exchange of cacao for cloth, salt, and corn.

Population centers were compact and self-contained. These sprang up over all these areas during the long formative period between 1000–300 B.C. Trade, language, and common culture rather than political ties held the Maya together.

War, although continuous, was waged in relatively short campaigns occurring in October when the farmer-soldier did not have to work his cornfield. Mere slaughter was not the primary aim of warfare, for like the Aztecs the Mayas wanted prisoners—the distinguished ones for sacrifices, the less worthy as slaves. After a victory the dead were decapitated and their jaws cleaned of flesh "and worn on the arm." Shields were heavy. Warriors wore quilted cotton jackets soaked in salt brine to toughen them.

Francisco de Montejo settled first at Xelha on the coast, where skirmish and sickness whittled away his forces. He then moved up the north coast, encountering one large Maya city after another. Yet at every turn the Indians attacked, chewing up his small troop. By 1535, there was not a white man left alive in the whole of Yucatán.

What happened to the Fugger factor Sebastian Kurz in all this? No one knows. There is little except the orderly records of the Fugger archives, where there is recorded in bare, unadorned prose that the first German to see the Mayan civilization before it succumbed to conquest was Sebastian Kurz.

German Pioneers in Mexico

The pyramid of the Great Square at Tenochtitlán had already been pulled down by the time that Jakob Cromberger the Younger arrived in Mexico. In place of the Aztec temple a church was being built with the stones of the demolished Aztec structure to be enlarged one day into the cathedral.

Hernando Cortes, the Captain-General, now known as the Marqués del Valle, though fallen from power, was living in luxury on his estates in Oaxaca. The day of the conquistador had passed. By 1539 it was the time of the administrator. The Viceroy, Antonio de Mendoza, was then, by the gracious consent of Charles V, the ruler of the Aztec realm, and to him Jakob Cromberger the Younger had come bearing a letter from the King. By decree and contract, the House of Cromberger was to set up in New Spain the first printing press in the Americas. It was to antedate by a full century a printing press in the English colonies of North America.

Jakob Cromberger the Elder was a printer-publisher who had come down to Spain from Cologne and, with other German printers, had settled in Seville. He married a Spanish widow and began publishing books under the imprint of "Jacobu crumberger alemanu." The most important books relating to the discovery of the Americas came from his press. He printed the "American" books of Peter Martyr, the Italian humanist living in Spain; he issued the *Suma de Geographía* of Martin Fernández de Enciso in 1519, the first complete book printed in Spanish relating to the Americas; and he printed the first letter of Cortes's discovery of Mexico, as well as the *Historia General y Natural de las Indias Occidentales* of Oviedo.

When the Archbishop of Mexico wanted a catechism in Spanish and Nahuatl (the Aztec language) to aid in the conversion of Mexican Indians, the Crombergers were asked to print it. The difficulties of

The colophon of publishers Jacob and John Cromberger.

producing such a book in Spain were such that Jakob Cromberger the Younger decided to send a printer, an Italian from Brescia known in Spain as Juan Pablos, and a printing press to Mexico.

In 1539, Jakob Cromberger the Younger arrived from Spain with printing press, printers, and type founts. He set up his presses in Casa de las Campaña and here produced the first book printed in the Americas.

The contract with the Crombergers was signed in the King's name "para imprimer libros de Doctrine Cristine de todes maneras de ciencia," assuring the House of Cromberger that for "the said ten years, no other person shall print in the said area of New Spain."

Sixteen known books were issued by the press under the imprint "en la Casa de Cromberger." The first book, known only by its title, was issued in 1539; the second, *Manual de Adultos*, of which there is one known surviving copy, was printed "en la gran cidudad de Mexico . . . casa de Juá Cromberger."

The incidence of Cromberger, a German, living in Mexico was not an isolated case; many came from the Germanies. They mostly worked as stone masons, charcoal burners, watchmakers, ironmongers,

The Crombergers established the first publishing house in Mexico in 1539 with a franchise from the King of Spain.

armorers, and gunsmiths, as well as shipwrights and sailors, usually from Hamburg or other Hansa cities. Some were bakers. "You should know," wrote Charles V in a personal note to his Viceroy, "that I have made an agreement with the German [bakers] Heinrich and Albert Goun [Kohn], in order to produce cake and saffron in New Spain. I want to inform you of this contract, and since this business will be of great use to our royal incomes, I recommend that you grant it and give it your special attention and protection so that it may succeed. I urge that you fulfill the conditions which were agreed upon with the Germans in the said contract."

German miners were the next to arrive. German mining techniques were the most advanced in Europe as systematic mining had been practiced there since 745 A.D. It was not until a great textbook appeared on every aspect of mining (embodying centuries of practical information gathered from medieval miners) that it passed into science. *De Re Metallica* was written by Georg Bauer (d. 1555), who had taken the name of Agricola. A Saxon, he had studied medicine in Italy and then settled down as a physician at Joachimsthal, where he was the first to make a systematic study of mineralogy. *De Re Metallica* was profusely illustrated with woodcuts detailing how a mine is opened, types of mining tools and ore containers, the way to do mine trucking, methods of drainage and ventilation—all of which was engrained in brains of the well-trained Saxon miners. When the famous silver mines in Guadalcanal, Spain, were reopened in 1551, the government asked "for 200 Germans skilled in mining and metallurgy"; when Christian VI opened the famous silver mines at Kongsberg in Norway he "was pleased to give his name to the first mine groove for the miners sent from Germany."

The fifty German miners brought out by the Welsers to Santo Domingo in 1528 failed to find workable ores on the mainland of Venezuela. They had been wasting their talents and lives on that island for a decade. Mexico now seemed the promised land. Martin Berger, Christoph Kaiser, and Johann Engel, three of the fifty miners who had come out to the New World, signed a petition to the Viceroy to make known that these "master miners through whose diligence and knowledge were found the gold and silver mines and other metals in the lands and islands" should be employed in Mexico. By 1557 they had moved their operations into the richly veined silver mine at

Pachuca, using the Spanish invention of amalgamation by the use of quicksilver. But it was not the exhaustion of the silver ore that ended the first German mining efforts in Mexico. It was the Inquisition that consumed them.

The Catholic reaction to the Reformation was having an immediate impact on the Germans in Brazil, Venezuela, Peru, or Mexico, wherever they chanced to be. Moreover, its effect on the Germans would be such that they were virtually cut off from the history of the Americas for more than a century. The Reformation and the reaction to it, while European in origin, had a far-reaching effect on the history of the Americas; it would be the primary cause for populating the Americas and Canada with Germans.

Charles of Spain had hardly taken up his Emperorship at Aachen when the religious schism was upon him. The Diet of the Holy Roman Empire met at Worms in 1521. Luther was excommunicated and pronounced an outlaw. Charles could only see the Reformation as an insurrection, a religious aberration, a political crime. Martin Luther was personally incomprehensible to the Emperor, who countered the evangelical opposition by threatening to put it down by force.

In 1544 the Counter Reformation began in earnest. The Jesuits founded a college in Cologne to train fighters against Protestantism in Germany. The prerogatives of ecclesiastical law were extended to the Pope, who "could issue decrees of his own, which might not be set aside by any other person. No council might enact canons without his approval. He was supreme judge of Christendom." The result was the Inquisition and the establishment of the Holy Office to examine, prosecute, and execute all heretics.

It is an unfortunate commentary on the mores of humanity that it was only in their persecution that the names and personal history of those early German pioneers in Mexico have been preserved. Without the Inquisition we would not know who they were.

One of the first charged with heresy was Gerhard Albert. He had migrated from the dukedom of Geldern, was an alchemist, and the first to import aqua fortis (nitric acid) into Mexico. In the beginning he waxed rich, then he was made poor by the Inquisition. With Gregor, his brother, he was sentenced in 1601.

Heinrich (called Montalvo) of Hamburg, the powdermaker, was

tortured by the Inquisition. Marthaves Berg, called "Monte" (Berg), from Kaldenkirchen, had become wealthy in Tlaltilco from his profession as a watchmaker. Accused of being a "Protector of heretics," he managed to escape. Johann Perez of Emden was likewise accused. Johann Boss of Lübeck, a sailor, confessed to being a heretic; he was released "since he was already poor and penitent." Wilhelm of Bremen, sometime interpreter for the Inquisition, turned out, in 1596, to be a heretic himself.

Albert Meffenger and the one the Mexicans called "Rodrigo," both from Nuremberg, had set up a small forge at Zacatecas in northern Mexico. As armorers they had manufactured the first armor and swords in Mexico. Andreas Morab, a lapidary, admitted that he was a Lutheran, but as the Inquisition found nothing else against him he was lectured and fined 506 pesos, a lordly sum for the time. Daniel of Hamburg, a master tailor, was given the relatively light sentence of two years in jail.

The number of Germans then in Mexico is astounding. Their otherwise anonymity is only revealed in their persecution. Johann Müller of Hamburg, Detlef of Dithmarschen, Johannes of Emden were jailed for life. Melchior of Bremen admitted eating meat on fast days; Franz of Hamburg, who confessed to having heretical thoughts, got life imprisonment.

The Holy Office gave the young life of Jakob Gewert of Hamburg a preternatural aging by its method of truth extraction. He had come to Mexico at the age of seventeen and had briefly served as a muleskinner at Jalapa, the first official stop out of Veracruz on the Camino Real to the capital. The Inquisition found him working at the mines of San Luis Potosí with Lucas Prestel, who came from Cologne. He was pulled away from his prosperous works, which he shared in partnership with Herbert Rudrich, whose father had been, he told the Inquisition, a boatman on the Rhine. Although both were Catholics, the Inquisition gave them the same treatment as the others, since to them "German and Luther are as one in our eyes."

Heinrich Faneck, who worked in the port of Veracruz, was forced to leave there when the English corsairs, Hawkins and Drake, were raiding the coasts. The officials feared that the *luteranos* might aid them. Faneck was marched off toward the capital with those whose names are only given as Johann, Hadrian, Joachim, Jakob, Hermann,

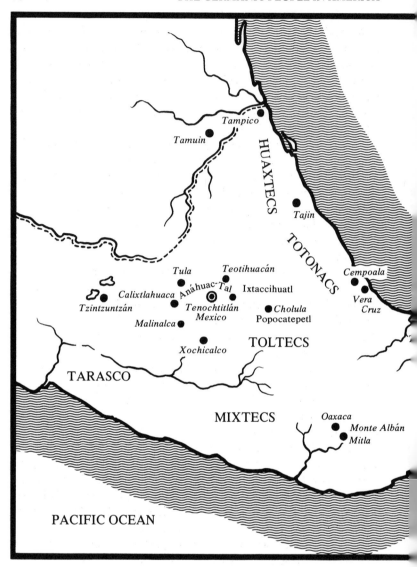

View of Mexico at the time of the Spanish conquest (the border of the Aztec influence is shown by broken lines).

ULF OF MEXICO

Chichén Itzá

Uxmal

Tulúm

Xicalango

MAYA

's

TABASCO

La Venta

Palenque

Tikal

OLMECS

TECS

Kilometer

0   50   100   150   200   250   300

Konrad, and Wilhelm. All of them were young, footloose fellows who had come to New Spain in order to try their luck.

Before long all were caught in the dragnets of the Inquisition. It certainly aided no one when Johann Thames of Hamburg shouted under questioning, "The saints are dead since a long time and the Bible does not say any word about their resurrection!" So why should one suffer Lent when priests have a good breakfast! Thames was sentenced, escaped in 1602, was found again, and given a life sentence aboard a prison galley.

Jacob van der Becken had the distinction, if such it could be called, of being the only German to be burned at the stake by the Inquisition. He had been born, the records say, in Wildeshausen in Oldenburg. At the age of twelve he had been taken to Danzig and apprenticed to a furniture maker. Having become proficient at his trade, he worked in Paris and then Seville, where he served as a furniture maker for the prestigious Duke of Medina. After that he went to Veracruz in Mexico where, in time, he fell into the hands of the Inquisition.

Heinrich, a Lübecker, revealed the most fascinating personal history of all those who were tortured and questioned. At the age of eleven he was taken to London, where he learned English. Then he went to Denmark and learned to be a weapons and powdermaker. He was captured during a sortie, jailed in England, and released to go to Venice, where he learned a second trade as a carpenter. Then, in the port of Cádiz in Spain, he was recruited as gunner for the armada of the Duke of Medina that sailed against England in 1588. Heinrich, one of those who survived the destruction of the Invincible Armada, returned and became a gunner, this time in the armada of Admiral de Avellaneda. He was captured in battle by the Turks, put into a galley, and on his exchange decided to find peace and security in Mexico. He fell back on his old craft as furniture maker and then walked right into the arms of the Inquisition.

Thus disappeared, in one way or the other, all of the German colony in Mexico until the coming of the German Catholic Jesuits a century later.

William Penn's Holy Experiment   VII

The religious upheaval that engulfed the Germanies after 1580 was the direct cause of one of the greatest migrations in history. The Protestant movement had begun with a clear mandate for change. For a brief moment it seemed that Lutheranism might dominate all the Germanies. Then it fell into disputes which brought disunity—and hatred. Internal dissents so wracked the Protestant movement that one sensitive humanist "welcomed death as a release from the raving of theologians."

Protestant sects multiplied. There were the Anabaptists, who disapproved of infant baptism, preached and practiced religious toleration, and were convinced that religious reform must have social consequences. Menno Simons, a Netherlander born four years after America was discovered, preached a new life and urged his followers toward religious simplicity. They were against war and the taking of oaths. The Mennonites played an important part in pioneer immigrations in Canada, North America, Brazil, and Paraguay. There were other pietistic sects—Dunkards, Moravians, Herrnhuters—which fragmented the original Protestant movement. All of these and many others would play an important part in the history of the Americas.

The prevalency of protest brought on a Catholic reaction. A Fugger newsletter announced: "A new edict was proclaimed [October 18, 1585,] which threatens all Huguenots in France with pain of death and the loss of their goods and chattels if they do not leave the country within fifteen days." Protestant and Catholic faced each other with increasing hostility; tolerance all but vanished. Religious sects were persecuted in France, Bohemia, Austria, the Low Countries, and the Germanies.

The witchcraft craze was an outgrowth of this religious neurosis. One reads of it in the Germanies, in England, and even beyond, in

William Penn attempted to establish an "ideal state" in his colony of Pennsylvania in which there would be neither poverty nor class differences. He brought the Indians gifts and concluded a trade agreement with them.

North America and Mexico. The intellectual and spiritual life of Europe was overwhelmed by it; business and politics were conditioned by it; everywhere whole communities were engulfed by it. The Popes forwarded the craze; it was even pressed on society by some of the best known Protestant reformers and scholars. Witches were the agents of Satan in the struggle for control of the spiritual world; for one long moment the witch replaced the Jew as the social scapegoat. They were driving out devils in Vienna. On September 3, 1583, "The Jesuits . . . in company with the Bishop drove out a devil from a poor maid. . . . First they exorcized in vain, but finally she was given a drink of holy water."

The confidence that Europe had felt in the first part of the century was gone, the religious strife was reflected in the gradual economic decay of the Germanies. Those people who had so long held primacy in North Europe in financing, cartography, and printing were now silenced. The religious wars deprived the German peoples of the leadership in the sciences, the arts, and the crafts.

The Dutch and their English rivals took over maritime trade, exploration, piracy, and economic development. A Fugger newsletter of July 2, 1600, from Antwerp confirmed it: "England and Holland have conquered the trade of the world. From Holland and Zeeland we get written tidings that four ships from the East Indies and others from the West Indies have again sailed into Plymouth in England heavily laden with spices."

The only commodity that the Germans seemed now able to export were its *condottieri*. The Protestant electors of Brunswick, Hesse, and the princes of Pomerania sent, after 1589, thousands of soldiers to fight for Henry IV of France, or to Scotland or Denmark. By 1600 there were fifty-eight thousand soldiers fighting outside the Germanies. Those unfortunates who survived the struggles were eventually brought back again, for in 1618 the Thirty Years' War began. It was an event that would make the Rhineland veritably uninhabitable and begin the mass exodus to the Americas.

The suffering that the German people endured brought on a pietism, reflected in the religion of the Shakers, Dunkards, Quakers. People sought a spiritual retreat from such fearful violence; it made them want to stand apart from the life about them. This evangelical spirit found a musical expression in the hymns, motets, and passions of Heinrich Schütz.

The Thirty Years' War struck hardest at the peasants of the Palatinate, the homeland of thousands who would migrate and populate the Americas. The Elector of the Palatinate stood at Mannheim once, sadly looking over the devastated lands. He counted in one day alone twenty-three villages in flames. "Not a vine," he said, "or an almond tree was to be seen on the sunny hills." It was virtually a desert. More than half the population had disappeared. Almost all the villages had ceased to exist; one part of the Palatinate had been plundered eight times in two years. Wolves roamed the streets; education disappeared; there was a coarsening of manners and a drying up of industry. The loss of women and children almost equaled that of men; thousands of peaceful citizens had been driven into exile and exposed to misery, exploitation, devastation, and disease.

The peasant had been taught through centuries of experience that his task in life was to labor early and late, that matters of state were beyond his knowledge, that he must accept wars and crushing taxes as he accepted drought or pestilence. Bound to the soil, he could not even marry without permission of the landlord. Still, in normal times he was not dissatisfied with his life. His wants were few, his tastes simple. He loved his home and his fields and felt himself a part of the land; he was steeped in its customs, traditions, superstitions, and art. But when landlords and princes took the food from his mouth, when foreign soldiers laid his home in ashes and slaughtered his cattle, when he was subjected to religious persecution, he finally was willing to turn his back on his homeland with all its traditions and seek a place of peace, even in a wilderness three thousand miles away.

It was then that the peasants listened to tales of America's riches. Many read glowing letters sent back by fortunate relatives who had reached the land of promise. They turned a willing ear to *Neuländers*, men hired by immigration and shipping companies to loaf about villages in gaudy clothes boasting that their fortunes were made in the colonies.

German emigrants had made their appearance in North America early in the seventeenth century. A Rhinelander born in Cleves, Peter Minnewit (known later as Peter Minuit), arrived in 1626, bought Manhattan Island for $24, and became director-general of New Netherland, the Dutch colony that would one day become New York City.

The German pioneer also appeared early in Virginia. Sir Walter Raleigh, with Queen Elizabeth I's tacit consent, had attempted to colonize Virginia in three expeditions, the last being Roanoke, the famous "Lost Colony." The type of colonization first used by Europeans was to set up a trading post, collect raw materials from the natives, and pay with trade materials. Indians were numerous enough, but their material culture was economically insignificant. What was needed was to set up a permanent colony to develop agriculture by having the colonists work the soil and export the agricultural products. German presence in these early colonial experiments is only inferential; archaeologists have found numerous casting counters, "Jettons," that had been made in Nuremberg by one Hans Schultz sometime after 1550.

King James I of England authorized in 1606 one colony to be set up in what is now Virginia, located in the tidewater area below Chesapeake Bay. The coastal land there was rich with pines and cypress, while the inland area was densely covered with forests of hardwoods teeming with deer, buffalo, bear, wild turkey, otter, and beaver. Ducks were of such multitude they darkened the skies for seven miles while in flight; fish were so numerous that sturgeon could be killed with an ax; oysters were twelve inches across the shell.

To this Virginia colony, in 1607, came Captain John Smith, founder of the first permanent English settlement in North America. He brought over three shiploads of 105 laborers and "gentlemen," of which three were Germans. Captain Smith settled in a place he called Jamestown. Three German carpenters, Unger, Folday, and Keffer (Keifer), were assigned to build a house for Powhatan, the Indian chieftain who was father of the famed Pocahontas.

A colony was not then easy to maintain. The planters were massacred in 1622. Undaunted, new settlers arrived and were soon encroaching farther into the Indians' communal hunting lands. Since successive tobacco plantings without crop rotation exhausted the land's mineral salts, further land expansion became necessary, so that with each planting the pioneers pushed even farther into the wilderness. A second Indian uprising in 1644 stayed, but did not prevent, the settlers from expanding tobacco planting, their one reliable cash crop. As the colony grew and prospered, the need to know more about the unknown land west of the Blue Ridge Mountains made it necessary to have a land survey done by some qualified person who could use compass and surveying instruments. For this task Sir William Berkeley, the Virginia governor, chose John Lederer.

When and why John Lederer came to Virginia is not known. It is possible that he was lured to America by the exciting reports which appeared in print, or perhaps by the universal wanderlust which led so many after the Thirty Years' War to seek other lands. Lederer was born in Hamburg (1644), attended the Hamburg Academic Gymnasium, where he must have studied medicine as he later became a much sought-after physician in the North American colonies.

By 1669, Dr. John Lederer, then twenty-five years old, was in Virginia, setting out to explore and find a path through the Appalachians. The Virginia settlements were then mostly coastal, hugging the tidewater areas. In less than two years Lederer made three expeditions into the Appalachians with Indians as guides and occasionally with "other Gentlemen." He was the first European to stand on the highest peak, on August 20, 1670, and to look into the Shenandoah Valley, which in short time would be the goal of many German immigrants. He found the gap, later called "Harpers Ferry" (after another German immigrant), and opened up a trail to the Catawba tribe for fur trade. Lederer also left intelligent instructions "touching trade with Indians."

Between 1710 and 1722, Governor Alexander Spotswood herded the Indians of the piedmont onto a reservation. Then, in 1714, he brought out forty German ironmongers to work the iron deposits on the upper Rappahannock River. He made a settlement especially built for them and called it, appropriately enough, Germanna. Other furnaces were set up in Fredericksburg.

In 1716, Spotswood directed an elaborate exploring party through the James River watergap into the Shenandoah Valley, which resulted in the German settlement of Orange County. Thus began the movement of Germans into Virginia when families crossed the Southwestern Mountains and followed the Monocacy River into the Potomac Valley, where they built the town of Frederick.

Adam Müller was the first Palatine to make his way (1727) into the Great Valley of Virginia. Within three years he lured more German families to his clearing. More prominent was the town of Winchester, laid out in 1731 by a band of eleven families under Justus Hite (Heydt). This became a center for the German migration that filled the Virginia back country during the next decade. By 1740 their settlements extended as far west as Patterson Creek and south to the James River, while an overflow was already spilling eastward through the mountain gaps into the piedmont. Then in 1751 a colony of German Moravians purchased 100,000 acres near the Yadkin River and the march southward began once more, ending a decade later when the North Carolina Great Valley and Piedmont were comfortably settled. Then John Peter Pury, a Swiss-German from Neuchâtel, arrived with a sizable group of silkworkers. They were assigned to a tract of land of forty thousand acres; there they planted white mulberry trees for the silkworms and grape vines for themselves. They called the place Purys-burg. In time, they sent thousands of pounds of raw silk to England.

In all this peopling of Virginia, John Lederer was the pioneer. His geographical explorations reversed the fantasies of the times. No mountain peak is named after Lederer; no roadway records his journey along the now industrialized Piedmont route that he helped open to commerce. He might say about this oversight, as he commented on another similar situation, "I have lost nothing by what I never sought to gain—popular applause."

In the Carolinas the Germans appeared in force by 1710. Many had read, if they had not been told, of "the fertile Carolina . . . raising infinite profits to the Adventurers and Planters." The immigrating Protestant Salzburgers went through the Carolinas and were given land in Georgia. Booklets had been distributed all along the Rhineland telling of "the great Profits . . . in the hott [Carolina and Georgia] than in the cold parts of the coast of America . . . inviting Rhinelanders and other men inclyned to Plantations in America." Tobacco was the principal cash crop; aside from its use for smoking, one author declared it "a Panacea, an Universal Medicine, the Wonderful vertues of Tobacco Taken in a Pipe, with its operation and use both in Physick and Chyrurgery."

The Salzburgers had long been prosecuted in their native land; as early as September, 1588, a Fugger newsletter made known the "Persecution of the Protestants in Salzburg." Before leaving they had to register all their real estate, sell their houses and other property, and give up their civic rights to trade and travel: "All are to leave our town of Salzburg of this date and none are to be encountered here again." It was not until 1734 that they could leave Europe to find peace and land in Georgia.

General James Oglethorpe, who had served in the European wars under Prince Eugene and then later sat in the British Parliament, was given a land grant (1730) by George II—hence Georgia. His purpose in obtaining the empty land was to settle English debtors, as well as "poor, humble and neglected English folk," including the Salzburg Protestants. Oglethorpe set out with a hundred and fourteen "worthies," founded the city of Savannah, and personally conducted the poor "persecuted Salzburgers" to a settlement twenty-one miles from Savannah where they would preserve their customs and language. On March 1, 1733, they erected at the place a "pillar which we called Ebenezer."

Baron von Reck visited them there and his heart warmed at what he saw: "We see Industry honoured, and Justice strictly executed, and Luxury and Idleness banished from this happy place, where Plenty and Brotherly Love seem to make their Abode, and where the good Order of a Nightly Watch restrains the Disorderly and make the Inhabitants sleep, secure in the midst of a Wilderness." A few German Jews were already there and "the Saltzburgers have (as the other Settlers in Georgia) received a gift from the trustees of Arms, Houshold Goods, and working Tools (that is Kettles, Pots, Dishes, Saws, Axes, Shovels). We found them very willing to serve us. They are so honest and faithful, and the like is hardly to be found, as appears by Examples. . . . They were born in Germany, and talk good German."

John Lederer had problems in Virginia. He was in financial difficulties and indebted to several persons, so he fled into neighboring Maryland. "He was," said Sir William Talbot, "forced . . . into Maryland." Talbot found him "a modest person, and a pretty scholar [and so] made me desire *this* account of his travels which have been faithfully rendered out of Latine from his own writing." Since Lederer was unable to write literary English, he composed his report in classical Latin, something few then in the colonies could have done. His small, important book was translated and published by Talbot as *The Discoveries of John Lederer.*

So he came under the protection of Charles Calvert, the third Lord Baltimore and governor of Maryland, who gave him carte blanche. "To all Persons to whom these presents shall come, Greeting: . . . know ye that whereas Iohn Lederer a Hamburgher born but now Resident in Calvert County in the said Province of Maryland having formerly discovered several Nations of Indians . . ." etc., etc. The province of Maryland, that rich land between the south bank of the Potomac River and the fortieth parallel, was granted to the Calvert family. They took possession of it by 1632; by the time John Lederer arrived in 1673 he found many Germans already there.

Augustin Herrman was one. Born in Prague in 1621, he had, by 1644, at the age of twenty-three, joined a merchant firm when New York was still New Amsterdam and ruled by the Dutch. In New Amsterdam, Herrman came in contact with cartographers, and about the middle of the century he himself prepared a pictorial map of New

Amsterdam.[1] Thus it was Herrman who drew one of the first views of the village destined to develop into one of the greatest cities of America. In time he ran afoul of the redoubtable peg-legged Peter Stuyvesant. As a result he was more than delighted to settle his family, servants, and slaves on five thousand "good plantable acres" in Maryland. There he built a mansion and called it Bohemian Manor.

His contribution to Maryland in trade, politics, and history was ample. Boundary lines were vague in Maryland, as elsewhere. Therefore, in 1670, Augustin Herrman completed a map of Maryland consisting of four separate sheets. At the lower left he drew two Indians and between them a tablet with the title of the maps and at the lower right a picture of himself.[2]

The best known German in the early history of Maryland was Georg Hack. Born in Cologne about 1623, he studied medicine, moved down to Holland, emigrated to New Amsterdam, and in time formed the firm of Hack and Herrman, the largest and most successful tobacco house in America.

In the early eighteenth century a new phase began. The new German immigrants now left the coastal regions and began to pioneer Maryland's interior. Settlements metamorphosed into villages with names such as Germantown, New Market (Neumarkt), Frederick (Friedrich), and Brunswick. Log cabins soon yielded to brick; Thomas Schley built the first stone house in Frederick. Jonathan Hager arrived from Westphalia and was granted two hundred acres in the middle of the forest near the Pennsylvania line, thirty miles from the nearest inhabitants. He called his grant Hager's Fancy, and in 1762 he began to lay out lots which in time became Hagerstown, now the second largest city in Maryland.

It was Pennsylvania, however, that attracted the largest number of German immigrants. In 1682, William Penn appeared in the Rhineland seeking converts to the Quaker religion, as well as Protestants to settle in Pennsylvania. His publications in German, which had pre-

[1]This sketch appeared in a book by Arnoldus Montanus, *De Nieuve en Oubekende Weereld: of Beschrijving van America* (Amsterdam, 1671).

[2]Most of the copies of Herrman's compendious map have been destroyed by time and decay. Only two copies are extant today: one in Europe, in the British Museum in London; the other in America, in the John Carter Brown Library in Providence, Rhode Island.

Many persons from Salzburg accepted William Penn's invitation to come to Pennsylvania. This engraving by

David Ulrich Bocklin shows "The Friendly Welcoming of the Salzburgers."

ceded him, "made publick the information for such that may be disposed to Transport Themselves or Servants . . . to a Country in America that has fallen to my Lot." When Penn appeared at Frankfurt in 1684 to bring news of his Holy Experiment, there were, as well, a considerable number of Germans who had heard of the Americas through friends and relatives who already had journeyed there.

The son of a famous admiral who, for his long services to the Crown, was awarded a huge tract of land in North America, the younger Penn had been brought up in luxury and sent to Oxford University. There, to his father's chagrin, he was sent down for espousing Quakerism, an extreme Protestant sect founded by George Fox in 1650. The Quakers derived their name from Fox's admonition that members should "quake" at the word of God. At that time Quakerism was equated with high treason, since they would neither serve in the military nor take oaths. The old Admiral sent his son to Paris, hoping that exposure there might correct his religious leanings. It did not. He espoused more than ever the cause of the Friends, as they called themselves, and in 1668 he was tossed into the Tower of London where he wrote *No Cross No Crown*.

In 1670, Admiral Penn died, leaving his son a sizable income as well as the large tract of land in North America which he called Pennsylvania. There, after Penn had made his treaty with the Indians in 1682, he laid out the city of Philadelphia and left, in 1684, for Holland and the Germanies to seek out people who would come as convert-settlers to his Holy Experiment.

Penn had gone to the New World with a Quaker's faith in attainable goodness. His vision was that of a government based on people's wishes, changeable according to their needs, in a land without war or class barriers, where the poorest man could live in peace and support himself in decency. As absolute proprietor of Pennsylvania's twenty-eight million acres, William Penn could have made himself a feudal lord in the New World, yet his only use of power was to divest himself of it. "Let men be good," he wrote, "and the government cannot be bad."

A resident of Heilbronn wrote to his son in New York in 1681: "Along the Rhine a number of families have banded together to accept the invitation of an Englishman named William Penn . . . to settle in that beautiful land of America. We, as also the Platenbach family, are only waiting a good opportunity when the dear Lord will take us to you. Your brother Peter is learning shoemaking and will soon be free. America is the only dream of Elizabeth. Catherine, only six years old, asks us daily, 'Will we soon be going to our brother in America?'"

On October 6, 1683, the sailing ship *Concord*, the "Mayflower" of German emigrants, put into Philadelphia. On board, led by Francis Daniel Pastorius, were thirteen families, the first organized group of German immigrants, who, Pastorius said, had the "desire . . . to lead a quiet, goodly and honest life." In time they were established by the Quakers on a forty-three thousand acre tract, which was called Germantown.

Pastorius had been educated in theology and law and was a polylinguist whose commonplace book recorded his thoughts in eight languages. His *New Primer* (1698) was the first schoolbook published in Pennsylvania; even still more important, he published the first formal protest against slavery ever to be made in North America.

Once established, the settlers brought in other emigrants, most of whom were Pietists and Quietists—a reaction to the wars which had destroyed their lives. Anabaptists, Mennonites, Moravians, Amish, Dunkers, Schwenkfelders, Herrnhuters—all made their way to North America by various ways. They did not all arrive as free men; many came as indentured servants to pay for the voyage and were bound to service for a stipulated length of time. One of them, a German, recalled: "The ship becomes a market. The buyers make their choice and bargain with the immigrants for a certain number of years and days, depending upon the price demanded by the ship captain or other 'merchant' who made the outlay for transportation."

Many of the Germans lost their names as soon as they set foot on American soil, for nothing changes names more than the abrasion of common speech.

The captains of ships landing at Philadelphia [wrote H. L. Mencken in his study of the American language] were required to furnish the authorities with lists of their passengers, and after 1727 this order was usually complied with. In addition, every immigrant was required to subscribe to an oath of allegiance, and to another abjuring the Church of Rome. . . . When the newcomers got to the Pennsylvania uplands their names were barbarously manhandled by the officials, usually Scotch-Irish, of the local courts and other officers of record. Almost every "Johannes Kuntz" of the ship lists thus became a "John Coons" in the interior, and every "Pfeffer" a "Pepper," and every "Schmidt" a "Smith."

The German immigrants also brought with them a firm idea of what they wanted. Settlers expected to exchange poverty for prosperity and oppression for freedom. But at the same time they expected, as a matter of course, to retain their language, religion, architecture, agricultural methods, folk arts, food habits and drink, music, and habits of dress.

If the newly arrived Germans were stolid, they were also solid. They brought crafts and craftsmen to the new colonies. Among the Mennonites who arrived in 1709 the lists included fifty-six bakers, one hundred twenty-four carpenters, sixty-nine shoemakers, ninety-nine tailors, twenty-nine butchers, forty-five millers, fourteen tanners, and a scattering of barbers, weavers, locksmiths, glass-blowers, wool and linen weavers, hatters, engravers, silversmiths, blacksmiths, and potters.

"Among the recently arrived German immigrants came eighteen hundred vinedressers and vintagers from regions of the Rhenish Palatine." So wrote Dr. Benjamin Rush, whose book *Manners of the German Inhabitants of Pennsylvania* was a perceptive study of a migratory people and their culture. Born in Pennsylvania about 1745, Rush studied medicine in Edinburgh and on his return became a professor of chemistry at the University of Pennsylvania. (Later he would be a member of the Continental Congress, a signer of its Declaration of Independence, and Surgeon-General of the American Army.) He knew that, while the Labrasca grape was native to the Americas, vine culture was generally undeveloped until the arrival of the Rhinelanders. The Pennsylvania soil, however, did not contain the proper amount of moisture. Insects appeared in force and the vintagers were not able to cope with them. Eventually the German vintagers found upper New York state more promising.

Jean de Crèvecoeur, whose *Letters from an American Farmer* (1782) was written under the pseudonym J. Hector St. John, considered them the most adaptable of all those pioneering in the forest-covered lands. "How much wiser, in general, the honest Germans than almost all other Europeans; they hire themselves to some of their wealthy landsmen, and in that apprenticeship learn everything that is necessary. . . . They observe their countrymen flourishing in every place; they travel through whole countries where not a word of English is spoken; and in the names and the language of the people, they retrace Germany. . . . The recollection of their former poverty and slavery never quits them as long as they live."

Benjamin Rush also praised the German immigrants as being the most successful farmers in Pennsylvania. Their farms were distinguished by the "superior size of their barns," he wrote, "the height of their enclosures [fences], the extent of their orchards, the fertility of their fields, the luxuriance of plenty and neatness in everything that belongs to them. This success must be attributed in part to their training in husbandry, in part to their thrift, in part to their capacity for hard and unremitting labor." One historian explained that the Germans' capacity for saving was developed by the fact that in their fatherland they had been compelled to utilize every inch of soil, to expend their last bit of strength in order to keep body and soul together. "Their severe training, more than their greed, compelled them for the first generations at least to follow the same methods and practice the same rigid economy as their fathers."

In the process they also brought the German barn to America. The style and function are unmistakably lower Saxon, the *Niedersächsisches Bauernhaus*, invariably and mistakenly called the Dutch barn. It had its origin on the lower Elbe and Weser river valleys, and from thence spread over much of Germany. Barn and house were one. The back part was for the cattle and other livestock, threshing floor, hayloft, and stalls. The house consisted of a sitting room, chambers, bed alcoves, one or more fireplaces, spinning wheels, and the iron stove. Many German settlers in Pennsylvania still retain these barnhouses.

And as the *bauernhaus*, so the iron stove. While it was only one of the items among the folk art brought to the Americas by Germans and German-Swiss, it was one of the most important. The stove, in the humble homes of the Rhine Valley or the Black Forest, was the center of family life. It took on the sanctity of a shrine. Benjamin Franklin, who adopted the iron *ofen* of the Old World as the "Franklin stove," wrote about its construction. He said that it is "composed of five iron plates scru'd together and fixed so that you may put the fuel into it from another room. . . . This invention certainly warms a room very speedly, thoroughly, with little fuel."

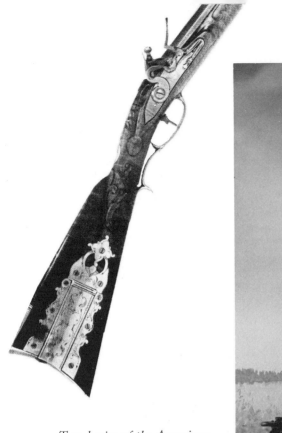

Two basics of the American frontier were the Kentucky rifle and the Conestoga wagon. The Kentucky rifle, which German gun makers had developed further, was an indispensable weapon in the wilderness. The Conestoga wagon, built on the principles of the German farm wagon, was suited to the demands of the new homeland. It made possible the long treks westward.

Pottery followed traditional folk-art designs: simple, functional, strictly utilitarian, but with a grace and style of its own. It was customary in Germany for a groom to present his bride with a set of furniture, beds, cupboards, chests, and chairs; this custom was retained for a long time in the Americas.

The Germans were the inventors—or better, the adapters—of the Old World peasant wagon into the Conestoga wagon, one of the factors that helped open the West. The Moravian sect had settled among the Conestoga tribe in southeastern Pennsylvania, and the township was so named until it later acquired the name of Lancaster. The first wagon built at Conestoga, from a German model, was purely a freight carrier; the driver rode one of the horses or stood upon the footboard outside. As soon as its practicality was seen, the Conestoga wagon replaced pack horses. Benjamin Rush described it as "a large, strong wagon (the ship of inland commerce), covered with a linen cloth. . . . In this wagon, drawn by four or five horses of a peculiar breed, [the Germans] convey to market, over the roughest roads, 2,000 and 3,000 pounds weight of the produce of their farms. In the months of September and October it is no uncommon thing, on the Lancaster and Reading roads, to meet in one day fifty or one hundred of these wagons on their way to Philadelphia." He acknowledged that it was due to the "perfection of German wheelwrights, carpenters, blacksmiths, machinists, living in and about Lancaster [Conestoga]." The wagon wheels were invariably painted bright red, the body of the wagon Prussian blue, and the cover was of gleaming white canvas. By the end of the eighteenth century thousands of wagons were trafficking with Philadelphia, a traffic so dense that the first formal road built in North America, the sixty-two-mile-long Philadelphia-Lancaster turnpike, was surfaced with crushed stone.

A companion to the wagon was the Kentucky rifle. German gunsmiths in Lancaster were the first to conceive of the "grease pad" technique of loading, by means of which a small piece of cloth or deerskin dipped in grease was wrapped about the bullet and rammed down into the muzzle. It required a smaller bullet and made loading easier. The next step, one of the great contributions of German gunsmiths to the opening up of the West, was the Kentucky rifle. A huntsman or soldier could fire it more rapidly than the heavier European rifle. Its history runs counter to the usual course of transplanted crafts, which often deteriorate after introduction. Here the reverse was true; the Kentucky rifle evolved from the heavier one used by German Jägers. The American woodmen required a lighter, more accurate rifle, with a smaller caliber and with rifling to propel the bullet farther so that it would rotate during its trajectory. There was not one inventor of the Kentucky rifle, but many. The records of Germantown and Lancaster have preserved a long list of its gunsmiths: John Lassler, John Moll, Frederick Zorger, Peter Brong, Jacob Newhardt, Daniel Kliest. In the beginning it was adopted by the United States Continental Army. John Quincy Adams, attending the first Continental Congress, saw it being used in target practice and wrote to his wife: "A peculiar kind of musket called a rifle used by riflemen from Pennsylvania, Maryland, Virginia . . . the most accurate marksmen in the world." A huntsman or soldier could fire a Kentucky rifle more rapidly than the European musket since it was not necessary to stop after a few shots to clean the fouled barrel. It became one of the deadliest weapons of its time and of vital importance in opening up the western United States.

The German immigrant in Pennsylvania was also intensely religious. Their pietism was echoed in their music, as essential to the German as bread. They became the primary manufacturers of musical instruments; the zithers of Bucks County and the organs, pianos, spinnets, and hand organs of Lancaster found their way into homes and churches all over Pennsylvania. David Tannesberg, who came from Lititz, Pennsylvania, built organs with a tone said to equal any European organ.

To the Quakers, however, music was sinful; insidious and sensuous, it bewitched the heart with temporal delight. There was much ado when Ludwig Kahn, in 1758, opened a school "at the sign of the Golden Rose" to teach the guitar and flute. It was not music alone that disturbed the Quakers, who also objected to the theater because of the passions simulated by the actors. Christianity, in their view, required simplicity and truth, and it was contrary to their beliefs to create imaginary scenes and episodes.

Aside from their insistence on music, the ruling Quakers found initially that the Germans gave rise to few political problems. They were mostly apolitical. The peasants and craftsmen from the Palatine, Alsace, Baden, or Zurich rarely participated in politics. At first the

German settlers founded the city of Bethlehem in Pennsylvania, the so-called Christmas city. It was supposed to become a center of German culture in America.

Germans found no reason to change their attitudes. They were accustomed to paying tithes and taxes, and thus considered themselves fortunate to have their own land, to worship as they pleased, and to be otherwise undisturbed.

The Herrnhuters changed this political inertia. Belonging to the Moravian Brethern, they had come to Pennsylvania to share the religious freedom of the land. Nikolaus Ludwig von Zinzendorf, born in Dresden and educated at Halle, turned to the role of religious reformer and welcomed to his estates whole groups of Moravians. There they consolidated their colony and called it Herrnhut, "the Lord's keeping." The Saxon regime took umbrage and Zinzendorf was exiled. He went to England while the first of his Brethren went off to Pennsylvania, where, in 1741, they founded the settlements of Bethlehem and Nazareth on the Susquehanna River in Pennsylvania.

The Herrnhuters lived on the very edge of the frontier and thus were exposed to Indian attack. From all sides of the frontier the Germans, as well as the Scotch-Irish, made urgent appeals to the Quaker assembly for protection. "Why not vote money for arms or, if not arms, then money and construct forts to which the frontiersmen might flee when attacked." The ruling Quakers refused to compromise, with the result that in one of the Indian uprisings the Herrnhuters were frightfully massacred.

Benjamin Franklin himself "undertook this military business." He was sent with an armed relief party and found that "the Indians had burned Gnadenhutten, a village settled by the Moravians who were massacred." He found the larger buildings defended by a stockade and the Germans armed and ready to fight. Bethlehem was also destroyed. The mutilated bodies were packed into a wagon, brought back and exhibited in the streets of Philadelphia, and finally laid out in front of the State House. Four hundred Germans crowded into the Assembly Hall and faced the officials. With peasant bluntness they demanded protection.

The Germans were now no longer apolitical. In Germany people read of the terrors of frontier life and the massacre of the Moravian colony in a book published by Georg Loskiel, whose pertinent observations on Indians and their culture have long been considered some of the best on the subject. From that time forward the Germans kept their Philadelphia printing presses busy publicizing their affairs.

In an attempt to come to some understanding between Indians and white men and to prevent further massacres, Conrad Weiser volunteered to settle deep in the Indian territory. Born in Württemberg, Weiser had come early to the Americas. He learned the dominant Indian tongue and settled in a log cabin at Tulpehocken, in Pennsylvania territory. Through friendship and knowledge of Indian custom and speech, Weiser won their confidence. He advised the German settler pioneers on how to get along with the Indians, but at the same time he also urged the Quaker government that they should abandon their conciliatory policy. While this was going on, Weiser installed an organ in his log cabin. He composed church music, read Voltaire and Armholtz and still he found time to lay out the town of Reading, Pennsylvania, and keep up a lively correspondence with Benjamin Franklin. His daughter married the famed Peter Muhlenberg, pastor and general.

Thus it was that out of these stern, simple, no-nonsense German families that many of the great American fortunes had their rise: the Wistars, Wanamakers, Drexels (originally Drechsels), Pennypackers, Rockefellers (originally Roggenfelder, "rye-cutters"), Rittenhouse (Rittenhuysen).

But if their fortunes flowered, their German speech did not. A learned German traveler found that "the language which our German people make use of is a miserable, broken, fustian, salmagundi of English and German. . . . People come over from Germany forget their mother tongue in part while seeking in vain to learn the new speech." Christopher Sauer (Sower) of Germantown, who printed the first Bible in German in America, urged them to defend their native tongue, vowing to read and think in German. He imported German books, founded a German newspaper, and set up a firm to print and publish books in German. When Franklin first came to Philadelphia in 1742 he was amazed by the bilingual quality of the city. "The street signs of our Philadelphia," he wrote in his *Autobiography*, "have inscriptions in both languages and some places only in German."

Franklin's great passion was books. He began his career as a printer's devil in 1717 by being apprenticed to his half-brother, James. Then he moved to Philadelphia to work as a printer for a German Jew named Samuel Keimer. "He wore his beard at full length because somewhere it is so stated in the Mosaic law. . . . He kept the 6th as

◄(No. I)►

Philadelphische Zeitung.

SAMBSTAG, den 6 Mey. 1732.

An alle teutsche Einwohner der Provintz Pennsylvanien.

NACHDEM ich von verschiedenen teutschen Einwohnern dieses Landes bin ersuchet worden, eine teutsche Zeitung ausgehen zu lassen, und ihnen darinnen das vornehmste und merckwürdigste neues, so hier und in Europa vorfallen möchte, zu communiciren; doch aber hierzu viele mühe, grosse correspondentz und auch Unkosten erfordert werden: Als habe mich entschlossen, denen teutschen zu lieb gegenwärtiges Specimen davon heraus zu geben, und ihnen dabey die Conditiones welche nothwendig zu der continuation derselben erfordert werden, bekent zu machen.

Erstlich, müsten zum wenigsten, um die unkosten die darauf lauffen, gut zu machen, 300 stücks können gedruckt und debitiret werden, und müste in jeder Township dazu ein mann ausgemachet werden, welcher mir wissen liesse, wie viel Zeitungen jedes mahl an ihn müsten gesandt werden, und dor sie dan weiters einen jeglichen zustellen und die bezahlung davor einfordern müste.

Vor jede Zeitung muss jährlich 10 Shillinge erleget, und davon alle quartal 2 sh. 6 d. bezahlet werden.

Dagegen verspreche ich auf meiner seite, durch gute Correspondentz die ich in Holland und England habe allezeit das merkwürdigste und neueste so in Europa und auch hier passiret, alle

woche einmahl, nemlich Sonnabends in gegenwärtiger form einer Zeitung, nebst denen schiffen so hier abgehen und ankommen, und auch das steigen oder fallen des Preisses der Guter, und was sonst zu wissen dienlich bekandt zu machen.

Advertissemente oder Bekant machungen, welche man an mich schicken möchte, sollen das erste mahl vor 3 shill. 3 mahl aber vor 5 shil: hinein gesetzet werden.

Und weil ich nutzlich erachte die gantze beschreibung der aufrichtung dieser provintz, mit allen derselben privilegien, rechten und gesetzen, bey ermangelung genugsamer Neuigkeiten, darinen bekandt zu machen; solte nicht undienlich seyn, dass ein jeder, zumahl wer kinder hat, diese Zeitungen wohl bewahre, und am ende des jahres an einander hefte; zumahl da solche dann gleichsam als eine Chronica dienen können, die vorigen Geschichte daraus zu ersehen, und die folgende desto besser zu verstehen.

Auch wird anbey zu bedencken gegeben, ob es nicht rahtsam wäre, in jeder grossen Township einen reitenden Boten zu bestellen, welcher alle woche einmahl nach der stadt reiten und was ein jeder da zu bestellen hat, mit nehmen könne

So bald nun die obgemeldte anzahl der Unterschreiber vorhanden, welche so bald als möglich ersuche in Philadelphia

Title page of the first edition of Franklin's German-language newspaper, 1732.

Sabbath, he never worked on Saturday." In 1730, Franklin bought out the newspaper *Pennsylvania Gazette*. After this began the publication of a long series of books and almanacs, many of which he wrote himself.

Paper was as much a problem for Franklin as it was for the German printers, since all paper had to be imported from England. Wilhelm Rittenhuysen, later Americanized as Rittenhouse, met this problem. He had been apprenticed as a youth to a papermaker near Mülheim-an-der-Ruhr, his birthplace. In America he was spurred on by Franklin and Sauer to build the first papermill in North America. After operating it for some years, his son Klaus took over the papermill, which became known far and wide.

Rittenhouse paper was generally used by Christopher Sauer, now the most active printer in the colonies. Sauer had been born (1693) in Westphalia. He arrived in Pennsylvania in 1724 as a member of the Seventh Day Brethern and settled in Germantown, where he established himself as a clockmaker, apothecary, and bookseller. In 1738 he resolved to become a printer and publisher and brought his presses and his type from Germany with his own capital.

In 1739 he printed the *Hoch Deutsche Amerikanische Calender*, wherein one could read, beside the calendar for the year, astronomical observations, rules for bloodletting, dates of fairs and markets, and the goings and comings of the European nobility. The Sower (Sauer) Press was to issue one hundred and fifty titles, produce a religious magazine and a German-language newspaper. But his most important bibliographical achievement was the printing of Luther's German Bible (1743), the second Bible printed in America.

About the same time New York was filling up its Indian territory as rapidly as Pennsylvania. It became British policy to fill up her colonies with German Protestant immigrants to counter the French, who were filling Canada with Catholics. By 1703 news of the Germans' success began to drift back to the old country, which was caught in a new disaster. The winter of 1708–9 was so unseasonably cold that vines and fruit trees were destroyed. In the spring mass migration began gathering momentum until the Palatine Germans began to arrive at the rate of a thousand a week.

Robert Livingston, adviser to the governors of New York, was authorized to feed the newly arrived Germanic emigrants at the public expense, and in return the more hardy of the immigrants were given over to the Royal Navy and set to cutting masts for ships and producing tar. But as these farmers knew nothing of extracting tar pitch the operation failed, and so they were allowed to settle in New York state along the Hudson. There they laid out over a hundred towns and villages, while others scattered along the fertile Schoharie River Valley and the Mohawk. In 1713 the Palatinate Germans dragged their humble belongings on sleds, walking waist deep in snow. Seven villages were hastily set up to contain five hundred settlers, but the quick onset of winter left them completely destitute. The poverty was appalling, and yet in the spring, with borrowed cattle and horses, they made teams and plowed the land. By the following year their perseverance had prevailed and they gained a foothold. Eventually a tidy row of German towns appeared in the valleys.

German Jews appeared in New York about the same time. In colonial times the first to appear were of the Sephardic communities, Portuguese Jews who had first settled in Brazil. When the Dutch won a victory over parts of Brazil, Peter Stuyvesant, then governor of Curaçao, forced the Jews out of Brazil. They went to New York. The German Jews who followed them there in the eighteenth century were Anshai Mayriv, "the people of the West," speaking Yiddish among themselves, though they always thought of themselves as German and retained the German language for ritual, cultural, and daily purposes.

Religious persecution drove the German Jews to America. Records show that they came from southwest and northwest Germany, but unlike the other Germans few gave them a helping hand. Individuals were sent out as forerunners; often brothers such as Simon and Joseph Dreyfous, who hailed from Alsace, traveled together. By the time of the American Revolution the German Jews numbered two thousand in North America.

The Jesuits' Holy Experiment VIII

It was the Holy Experiment of the Jesuits that permitted the Germans to reside once again in that portion of the Americas from which they had been excluded for almost a century. The Jesuits were building "cities of God" throughout Argentina, Uruguay, Peru, the Amazon Valley, and Mexico. All qualified Jesuits, no matter what their national origin, were allowed to take part in the experiment. In this way, Germanic peoples—Bohemians, Silesians, Bavarians, Württembergers, Prussians, Austrians—were once again allowed in the Americas from which they had been excluded since the days of the Inquisition.

Long before the pronouncements of Jean-Jacques Rousseau, the Jesuits were acting on the principle that "Men are born good and happy, that society alone had made them unhappy and wicked." They declared that the white colonists throughout the southern Americas were so thoroughly corrupted by power and avarice that there was no chance for the Indians to receive decent Christian treatment at their hands. Therefore, the Jesuits would enter Indian-held territory and turn South and Latin America into cities of God.

There is a certain truth in the statement that the Jesuits had been founded in order to counteract the rise of Lutheranism (the founders of both were roughly contemporaneous), yet, like many an emotional movement, it achieved something quite different.

Ignatius Loyola was born Iñigo de Oñez y Loyola in the Basque country. Wounded during the seige of Pamplona (1521), while his wounds mended he turned to reading the lives of the saints. Inspired by what he read, he left the army, made a barefoot pilgrimage to Jerusalem, and then began studying at the universities of Alcalá and Salamanca. He then left Spain and went to Paris, where, in 1534, he founded the Society of Jesus.

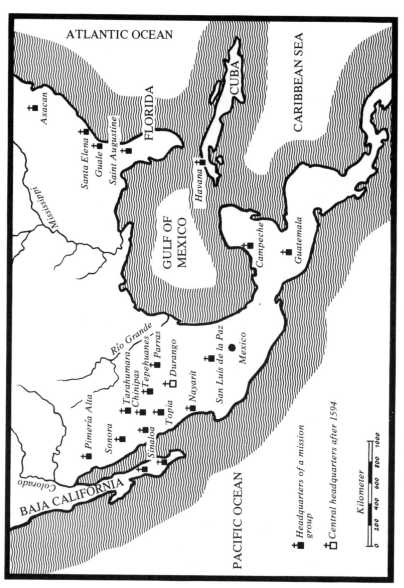

Jesuit missions in Spanish North America from 1566 to 1767.

Toward the beginning of the seventeenth century the Jesuits began their "reductions," or enforced communities, in many places throughout Spanish America—Quito, Peru, Chile, the Amazon Valley, and Mexico—but mostly they centered about the regions of the "purple land," principally in what is now Paraguay. In the early seventeenth century these lands were almost devoid of white settlers. The Spanish principle of *conquistar y popular*, "conquer and populate," had not been carried forward. Spanish cities hung upon the coast and rivers, but the vast treeless pampas were a wilderness—sparsely occupied by either animal or man. Paraguay was a violent land of contrasts, with a skein of tropical rivers; the pampas were succeeded by scrub forest and jungle, much of it populated by the Guaraní Indians, the most aggressive as well as the most intelligent of all the tribes. This is precisely the area of Paraguay the Jesuits chose.

The region was no paradise; it was a desolation of jungles, rivers, and swamps. One began at the Río de la Plata, an estuary so vast that the river seemed, at Buenos Aires, to be an arm of the sea. Above this and beyond it, when the river narrowed and became the Río Paraná, the main river bifurcated to the right into the northeast. The Paraná continued as a turbulent stream of cataracts which, far higher up, broke into the river falls of the Iguassu. The other branch was the Paraguay, which went in a more or less northerly direction until it was eventually lost as rills and streams in that huge land massif known as the Mato Grosso of Brazil.

White civilization, when it existed, hugged the shores of the main rivers; the rest of the interior was in undisputed possession of the Indians. The coastal-dwelling Tupís, who had posed so many problems for Hans Staden in 1545 when he was their captive, were now extinct. But those Indians who had pursued Ulrich Schmidel when he lived for twenty years in the jungles and pampas in the middle of the sixteenth century were still very much in evidence. In addition to the bow and arrow, which they wielded so well that they could "transfix a white man even in two skin armours and a coat," they had added to their arsenal of weapons copper-tipped spears, axes, clubs and slings, and the bola, an ingenious weapon made of rawhide and weighted with three heavy copper balls which, when thrown, could entwine animal or man in the same manner that fabled Laocoön was

Father Florian Paucke in his report, "Back and forth, back sweet and content, forth bitter and despondent," gives a complete picture of life in the Reducciones *of the Jesuits. His illustration shows how the missionaries crossed rivers.*

wreathed by the serpents. In addition, they had added the white man's weapon—the gun.

As soon as the general plans were laid down, the Jesuits began to move into the areas assigned to them. It must be stressed that they were not backed by armed support. By 1600 they had persuaded whole kin groups and tribes to gather into *reducciónes*. No white man and no other missionaries but the Jesuits were permitted into these areas; no white trader was allowed to enter into trading. The monopoly was Jesuitical.

The Indians were taught to become carpenters, joiners, painters, masons, sculptors, tanners, and masters of many other crafts. They were taught how to use the plow, grow wheat, and cultivate such foodstuffs that they would not know famine again. Animal husbandry was carried out on a systematic basis.

Eleven *reducciónes* had been planned for Paraguay alone. Good roads connected each self-supporting community with the other. The natives were armed and taught by the militant Jesuits how to use modern weapons to defend themselves, principally against the Portuguese Brazilians (there were no fixed borders, in the geographic-political sense, between the Spanish and Portuguese colonies).

The ground plans for such a Guaraní *reducción* are well known because the Jesuits left a huge archive of architectural drawings. There were, as well, many artists among the Jesuits, and they have left panoramic drawings of many such communities. The church building dominated a huge plaza, about which were the warehouses and other buildings of the Jesuit administrators. Arranged about the plaza were houses, laid out as neatly as the conformation of the land allowed. The Indian dwellings were stone-built and grass-thatched.

"We were," remembered a Spanish Jesuit, "a polychrome of nationalities, French, a few English, an occasional Irishman, Spaniards in dominance, Flemings, Italians, then Austrians, Silesians, Bavarians, and Württembergers. There was Inocencio Erber from Laibach, Josef Unger from Eger, Joseph Brigniel of Klagenfurt, Thaddeus Enis came from Bohemia, Father Klein, who first saw the light in Graz, Karl Tux of Peterswald, Strobel came from Bruck-an-der-Mur. . . ." And so the lists extended. Over two hundred Jesuits came from the Germanies during the one hundred fifty years of their existence (1588–1767).

Andreas Feldman, called Father Agricola because he was a farming expert, was one of the first Germans to arrive (1604). Soon many others joined their brothers. In the late 1600's came Wencelaus Christman, who had been Cura de Loreto in Prague. One of the most outstanding was Antonio Sepp who developed the musical life of the missions. German padres each brought their own specialty: Heinrich Peschke, physician and pharmacist; Juan Krauss, architect; Asperger, medico; Martin Dobrizhoffer, the great apostle of the Abipóns; José Oberbacker, apostle of the Indians of the Gran Chaco. Among the German Jesuits, Adel was a weaver; Thalhammer a surgeon; Mayr was a carpenter; Franck, an ironmonger; Mayer, a watchmaker; Haffner was an iron founder; Klausner, a tanner; Wolff was not only a musician, but a violin and harpmaker as well. The list of names and professions is long and impressive.

One result of this extraordinary experiment was that the Guaraní built churches of the most advanced baroque architecture, the Indians themselves being the masons and carpenters. They were taught to make and then play the harp, violin, contrabassoon, cornet, and guitar, all instruments which were made in the missions.

They also produced a native art. The Guaraní, Jose-Maria Kaibuy, was famed for his portraits and woodcarvings. Many were trained as architects, their names carved on their church façades. Engravings for books published in the missions were executed by a German-trained Indian who signed himself Juan Yaparl.

The Indians had no sophisticated culture that could be used as a starting point on the road to Christianity. If they were to be taught the Christian religion, it had to be taught from the beginning. The main obstacle to conversion was not a lack of willingness on the part of the Indians to accept Christianity, but the appalling contrast between the behavior of the nominally Christian colonists and their code of conduct. The contrast was such that it was difficult to persuade the Indians that the Christians seriously believed their own religion. To the colonist, the Indian existed only to be exploited and enslaved. The question was whether, in face of the white man's onslaught, the Indian would survive at all. The task of the missionary in such a position was to fight the battle for the Indian and protect him as far as possible. Consequently, the Jesuits were inevitably drawn into bitter conflict with the white colonists. This pattern was repeated throughout Spanish America.

We know more about Father Antonio Sepp of Ingolstadt and his travails because he wrote and was published. His *An Account of a Voyage from Spain to Paraguay* was so famed that it was published in Churchill's *Collection of Voyages* (London, 1732).

In his letter of April 15, 1691, Sepp explained that he was the oldest of the missionaries and had the "advantage of a cabin six foot long and three broad," but the rest were herded in the forecastle among chickens and chicken dung. Ten persons died every day. He and forty other Jesuits lived by God's peculiar (meaning "special") mercy. Installed at one of the Paraguay missions, Sepp was at pains to tell his brother how the priests dressed: "Our leather shoes are fasten'd with a leather bottom, without heels; and our stockings are likewise made of black fashion as we wear in Germany, except that it

Under the direction of the Jesuits the Indians built splendid churches, enriching the baroque style of their teachers with their own decorative elements. The church of Tepoztlán is valued as one of the most beautiful examples of this pretentious architecture.

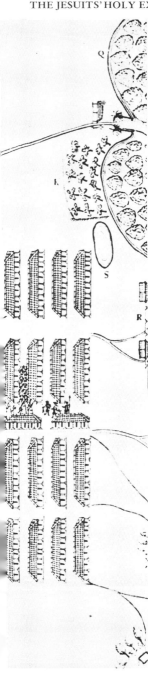

The map of the Reducción *of San Juan, drawn by Father Antonio Sepp, shows the orderly arrangement of individual buildings inside a settlement.*

is not open, but has a seam down to the bottom, without lining, pockets, or border; it is made out of black linnen cloth."

Sepp wrote of the new aspects of a land that differed so much from his native Ingolstadt: "Hereabouts there are no trees, such as our elms, firs, or such-like." The lands—the pampas—were vast and capable of holding immense herds of cattle, but Sepp averred: "It may be truly said of these Indians, that they follow our Saviour's rule, not to be concern'd for the next day; for, if I happen to allot a cow to a family, enough to serve 'em three or four days, they will often eat her in one. . . . The Indians were 'lazy' they had to be beaten to conform (instead of a birch we use a scourge). . . . The correction being over they kiss the missionary's hand."

Antonio Sepp also was a musician, a violin and harpmaker, which arts he taught to the Indians. He wrote to his brother of his routine in this City of God. First he attended the hospital and then the school, "where boys are instructed in reading and writing, and the girls in spinning and needlework. I also visit my musicians, the singers, trumpeters, *Chorknaben*, etc. Some days I instruct certain young Indians in dancing. . . . After these, I go among the workmen of divers sorts, to the brick and tilemakers, the bakers, smiths, joyners, carpenters, painters, but above all, the butchers, who kill betwixt fifteen and twenty oxen every day."

The baroque churches raised by the Jesuits in the jungle and on the plain came easily to the Germans. It was precisely the architectural form that appealed to the Indian masons, who brought to its florid design motifs of their own variation. Among the Jesuit architects were Lucas Meyferhofen, architect of the mission of San Miguel; Hans Wolff, violinmaker and architect; Bernardo Nusdorffer, a native of Bavaria who built the *reducción* of San Carlos, where he also died.

Many of the Jesuits wrote their "relations" (personal narratives), but the difference was that the Germans published theirs while few of the others were published during their lifetime. One who became famed because of his book was Martin Dobrizhoffer. He was born in Vienna, studied theology in Graz, and lived eighteen years among the Abipóns, whose territory lay along the west bank of the Paraná-Paraguay River, across from the Guaraní. He wrote his book in Latin, apologizing for the style: "The judicious reader will pardon any

Color Plates

Hernán Cortés (1485–1547), Spanish conqueror and governor of Mexico.

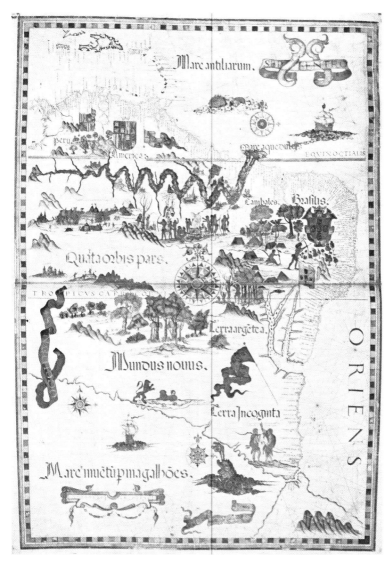

Map of the east coast of South America by Hieronymus Köhler, 1534.

"Jungle scene in Brazil," oil sketch by wor.

veler and painter Johann Moritz Rugendas.

RHEXIA speciosa

Rexia speciosa, *from a hand-painted engraving from the gigantic collection of Alexander Humboldt, who discovered the plant in the mountains of Quindiu in Colombia.*

Title page of the travel account by Robert Hermann Schomburgk,
Views in the Interior of Guiana, *1841.*

rusticity of expression in an author who has passed so many years amongst savages in the woods of America."

No contemporary account of the region of the Abipóns was as complete as his, with descriptions of the country and its inhabitants, the geography of Buenos Aires, of Tucumán, Córdoba, and the Andean areas. He wrote of the missions, of the incredible multitudes of sheep, horses, mules, and oxen raised by the Indians, of various "Temperatures of the Air," of animals and plants—in short, as encyclopedic a work as would be found in the century. He was careful to name all of the Jesuit martyrs—and there were many, including himself. "Father Martin Dobrizhoffer," he wrote of himself, "whilst defending his own house and the chapel against six hundred savages in the town of the Rosary . . . had one rib wounded by a savage Toba, at four o'clock in the morning, on the 2d of August, in the year 1765."

As they had been in Mexico and North America, the Germanic peoples were also pioneers in printing and publishing in South America. The first South American printing press was established in Peru in 1596; after that the next and most remarkable was the press in Paraguay.

In 1632 the Jesuit mission asked official permission to print books, as the Indians had been taught to alphabetize the Guaraní language. Padre Juan Baptista Newmann, from Bohemia, brought type faces to Paraguay, and a printing press was constructed in the missions. Type was cast in the Guaraní language and books in this language were issued from the mission presses. They now rank as some of the great typographical rarities in printing. Newmann became the second German to print books in the Americas.

There were other literary Jesuits. Padre Juan Eusebio Nieremberg published a book on the difference between life on earth and heaven, illustrated with copper engravings made by a Guaraní artist and printed in Paraguay. Europeans could also read of the bloody battles which occurred in Paraguay in 1759 between the Portuguese and the Spanish colonists, which of course involved the Indians.

Padre Florian Paucke was less fortunate with his book. Two hundred years were to pass before his encyclopedic work was published. Its 1,112 pages with hundreds of illustrations is an ethnographic masterpiece. It is true that the illustrations are naïve, almost childlike in their execution, but they explicitly detail the lives of the Guaraní

Indians capturing horses, from the travel report of Florian Paucke.

…dr mit keingt kbinern faugen
…inor mchor mrchkigen, und
…n rinjagen und faugen

Indians with whom he lived for twenty-one years at the San Xavier mission up the Paraguay River.

Florian Paucke, who was born in eastern Prussia in 1719, joined the Jesuits, and volunteered for the Paraguay missions. In 1748 he moved to Lisbon where, with other Jesuits, he took one of the Portuguese–West Indian fleet ships to the Americas. He landed at the Río de la Plata on New Year's Day, 1749, and was moved first by ox cart, then by horseback, and finally by canoe to the San Xavier mission, thirty-four miles north of Santa Fe, on the Paraná River. San Xavier was built in the same style as the other *reducciónes*, and Paucke made a graphic watercolor of it. The church dominated the administrative houses and the usual cluster of dwellings, in this case housing 452 families. Paucke's account is an incomparable record of a people's gradual emergence from the most primitive conditions into a collective life made better by animal husbandry, systematic agriculture, and the creative crafts of woodcarving, painting, and the writing and printing of books. The Guaraní were then perhaps the most advanced of any of the primitive cultures in the Americas. Paucke's own interest reflects what was accomplished. His study of the language, with grammar and vocabulary, alone would have ensured his ethnographical immortality, but with the countless illustrations of the now-vanished daily life of the Guaraní, it stands as one of the great records of the Americas.

It is well that Paucke had the manuscript completed by 1767, for in that year the end came. For years rumors had drifted from one European court to another. The Jesuits were a state within a state; they loaned money to the Crown; they owned vast, inviolable lands. The Marquis de Pombal, prime minister of Portugal, in 1759 expelled the Jesuits from the Portuguese mainland and all its colonies. Voltaire began his attacks on the Jesuits and after 1762 was in correspondence with Count Aranda, the powerful Minister of State for Charles III of Spain. Because the Jesuits, with ample justification, were suspected of undermining the king's authority, Charles III decided to expel them everywhere from the Americas. The decree was signed and sent out from Spain by emissaries of the highest rank. They carried sealed orders to all the vice-royalties and captains-general of the Americas. The decree was not to be opened until August 20, 1767, on pain of death. Then, simultaneously in all parts of the Americas, wheresoever

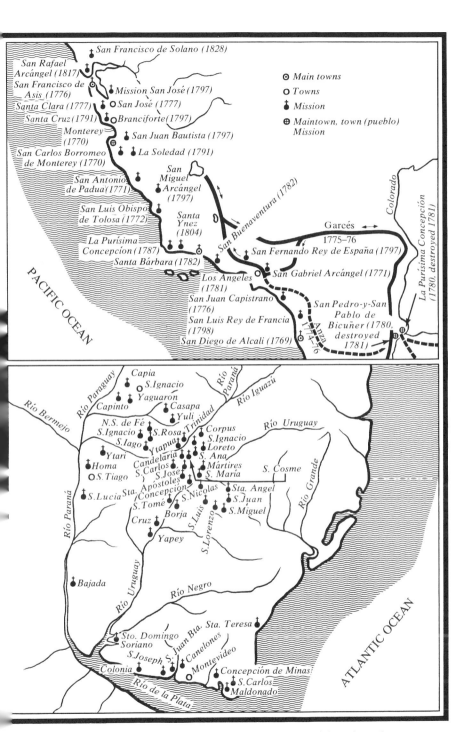

Eighteenth-century Jesuit missions in California (above) and in Uruguay.

there were Jesuits, the armed forces were to seize and exile them. That was the end of the Jesuits' Holy Experiment.

A century earlier the Holy Experiment had been brought to the Valley of the Amazon. It seemed incredible that it could be carried out, yet the plan was to organize all the Indians into *reducciónes* within this immense area. As elsewhere, the Jesuits were to bring the Indians into communities and teach them the crafts of civilization. In 1686 the Society of Jesus turned their efforts toward "civilizing" the entire Amazon Valley. Only a few men, led by Padre Samuel Fritz, were to organize a hostile area comprising millions of square miles into a semblance of order that nature had never given it.

It was only when Fritz arrived, in 1686, and saw for the first time this immense green world that he realized the immensity of this task. Two million square miles of forest, so titanic that Fritz's mind could not at first grasp its magnitude. So warm and luscious was the embrace of the Amazonian earth and its effect on plant growth that the mind had to be reoriented to size. Grasses were bamboos, sixty or more feet high; milkworts were stout woody twiners; periwinkles were trees exuding a deadly poison; and violets were the size of apple trees.

Fritz was born in the village of Trautenau (Trutnov) and educated at the Jesuit college in Prague, from which, at the age of twenty-nine, he departed for the Americas. He left the ship at Cartagena, the huge port that was then the entrance to the Spanish Americas. Then in slow stages he traveled overland by foot and horse through the length of Colombia, going over the Inca road to the viceroyalty of Quito (now Ecuador).

As soon as he adjusted himself to the climate, he left Quito in the company of two Indians. He went from tribe to tribe by canoe, journeying down a thousand miles of rivers to Yurimaguas, where he built a church. Fritz was tall, had a healthy, ruddy complexion, with blue eyes and a curly beard. He walked in sandles made of hemp. His cassock was of coarse weave. His familiar figure, walking the jungles, using his cross of black wood as a baton, would be known and respected by all Indians for the next eighteen years.

Samuel Fritz was put in charge of the Omaguas. This was the tribe, it will be recalled, who was attacked by Philipp von Hutten and

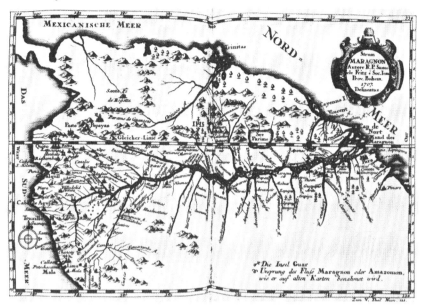

The first detailed map of the Amazon region, which was drawn according to exact measurements, came from Father Samuel Fritz, who labored as a missionary in this enormous region from 1886.

Bartolomäus Welser in 1545, since they believed that the Omaguas lived at the site of El Dorado. History was turning back the clock. Where before the Germans had come with blood and iron, now they appeared with nothing more lethal than a cross of wood. In the years allotted to him, Padre Fritz was to set up twenty-eight communities and make the Amazon so safe for travel that one could come from high-placed Quito (9,300 feet) and be escorted from one Indian settlement to the other without any noticeable contretemps.

In his journeyings up and down the Amazon, Fritz carefully kept a series of journals and began to lay down his observations for the first systematic map of the Amazon:

For better knowledge and general information concerning this great river Marañon or Amazon, I have made this geographical map with no little toil and exertion, having navigated it in the greater part of its course as far as it is navigable. Although up to now so many maps have appeared, without prejudice to any one, I say that no one of them has been drawn with the proper survey of levels, since they neither saw nor took the levels of this great River, or they extracted them from authors, whose writings left them confused. With this new exploration of the whole of this river Amazon, that I have made and brought to light.

The object was, of course, to put all of the various tribes into *reducciónes*—a difficult undertaking for a jungle people whose agricultural methods of slash-and-burn demanded constant use of new lands. Yet Fritz was able to so organize it that he and his fellow missionaries made the Amazon safe through its entire three thousand-mile length, each strategically placed mission acting as a silvian waystation. It was the route used by the French academician Charles Marie de la Condamine on his return from Quito to Europe.

The Amazon map was Samuel Fritz's memorial. But neither he nor any other Spaniard ever saw his map, for the engraved matrix of the first map of the Amazon was captured on its way back to Spain by Vice Admiral Charles Wager, when, in June, 1708, he attacked the armada commanded by Conde de Begaflorida.

By March 16, 1723, Samuel Fritz was dead. The eighteen years he spent in the jungles had demanded their toll.

In 1600 the Holy Office of the Inquisition in Mexico disposed of its last German "Luterano," the carpenter Andreas Paul of Danzig. Then the process of bringing Germans back into Mexico began all over again. With the establishment of Jesuit *reducciónes* in Mexico, as elsewhere in Spanish America, national origins were overlooked so long as the priests were Catholic. Once more German-speaking Bohemians, Austrians, Swiss-Germans, as well as many from the other Germanies were permitted to come to the Americas from which they had been proscribed since 1570. As in South America, the German Jesuits were in the minority; nonetheless, they would be pioneers in opening up the raw lands of northern Mexico, the southwestern United States, and the two Californias. They would leave behind, as well, an impressive array of publications.

Padre Josef Neumann was the first German Jesuit to arrive, in 1678. He was followed three years later by Padre Eusebio Francisco Kühn, called Kino. In time he would become one of the greatest of the missionary-explorers and geographically prove that "California was not, as long supposed, an island."

Father Kino, one of the most famous mission-aries, founded twenty missions during his twen-ty-five years of service in South America.

Since Kino was so historically important in the opening up of the western domains, the fact that he was born near Trento means that he is also claimed by the Italians. It should be remembered, however, that the border lands then were fluid and unfixed and that Germans abounded in the region controlled by Austria. The one pertinent fact of Kino's origin was that he spoke German, attended the universities of Ingolstadt and Freiburg in Breisgau, studying mathematics, theology, and geography, and finally that he studied and took his novitiate in Landsberg (Bavaria). When he arrived in Mexico in 1681, he was listed as Eusebio Francisco Chini (i.e., Kühn-Kino) (from) Germanum.

Kino moved north, traveling on horseback or foot, and over a period of twenty-five years made explorations in Alta Sonora, southern Arizona, Lower California, and into California itself. He was precisely what his biographer called him, "Padre on Horseback," establishing missions among the tribes of the Sierras and the Pimas at Guaymas. At the Mission of Dolores (now the city of Magdalena), he introduced cattle raising, brought in horses, mules, and sheep, and tried to establish advanced agricultural methods among these Indians. In twenty-five years he established twenty missions; thus twenty western cities owe their origins to his indefatigable travels. Kino was also observant in geography and ethnology:

My Indians [he wrote in his journal-diary] are affectionate and friendly, of good stature and health. The men wear nothing, except headgear. The women cover themselves with clothes reaching from breasts to their feet. They are whiter than the Indians in other parts of New Spain. They eat fish and other products of their country. The arrows are unpoisoned. The chieftains wear reed pipes around their necks but are blown only in battle. They are eager for knives and other iron objects. Women and children are shy.

Although he did not live to actually see the Pacific, Kino had such a grasp of geography that he stated emphatically that California was not an island, which ran contrary to all the published maps of his time. He was the first to surmise that Lower California was part of the mainland. Later, after his death, his theory was confirmed. Kino spent his last years in peace among his converted Pimas, dying there in 1711.

Of the fifty-six Jesuits assigned to Lower California and Sonora—Mexicans, Italians, Spaniards, and one Scot—fifteen were Germans. It was these men who wrote of their experiences, most of which were published in their lifetime, making a considerable contribution to the knowledge of unknown areas. Joseph Och, who came from Frankengau, wrote of his travails between 1757–67; Ignaz Pfefferkorn of Mannheim wrote a precise geographical description of Sonora which he published at his own expense. Jacob Sedimeyer, a native of lower Bavaria, was a linguist who toiled in the mission of Sonora and authored the first dictionary of the Pima language. Joseph Gasteigger, born in Leoben in Austria, wrote before his expulsion about his mission at Guadalupe. But he died in California in 1775 before he could see it in print. A friend of Kino, Marc Anton Kappus, who claimed Steundbühl as his birthplace, authored in Spanish a religious book about his travels in the Pima country.

The Visitator, inspector of all missions, was a German: Ferdinand Konsag of Warasdin. Juan de Esteyneffer, who came from Silesia and lived in Sinaloa, was able to see his medicinal book printed in Mexico City in 1729 while he still lived. This *Florilegio medicinal* was one of the earliest eighteenth century herbals. Among these self-effacing padres was Johann Jakob Baegert. His pioneer publication, *Nachrichten von der Amerikanischen Halbinsel Californien*, published in 1772, was the result of firsthand exploration and observation.

The baptismal registry in the church of St. Georg in Schlettstadt, Alsace, under the date of December 3, 1717, shows that Johannes Jacobus Baegert, son of Michaelis Johannes Baegert, maker of gloves and leather goods, and Maria Magdalena (Schiedeck) Baegert, was baptized on December 23, 1717. In time, turning to the priesthood, Baegert took his novitiate, left for Spain, studied languages, and waited to be shipped to Mexico. The ships, protected by two Spanish men-of-war, eventually reached Mexico on June 16, 1750. Two months later he was informed he was to go to California.

Father Baegert left Mexico City on November 16, 1750. He gave a detailed account of his trip to San Luis Gonzaga in letters to his brother. On May 26, he left Loreto accompanied by a soldier and several Indians. After a ride of thirty hours he arrived at San Luis on May 28, 1751, where he found "a tiny church which had collapsed during a recent storm" and two small huts, also in need of much re-

The plaza of Chuquisaca: a large plaza, dominated by a monumental church, always formed the center of a Reducción.

pair, which were to serve as his living quarters. About his parishioners he wrote that he found "no more than three hundred and sixty souls, children and adults of both sexes. Several missions have even less." "The roads in general," he found, "are still as they were in the year 'one' after creation of the world. From Guadalajara to Yaquí one sees fewer villages, houses, or people than in the open country in Alsace, one half a day's ride on the mailcoach."

When he arrived at his post in 1751, Baegert was thirty-three years old. He spoke French, German, Latin, Spanish, and added to these the languages of the Guiacuras. He was the only white man within thirty hours of travel. During his seventeen years there he had the company of only three soldiers and his semiwild Guiacuras, "who never wash, never work unless one stands behind them. They are human in nothing but shape." His observations were of the fullest: the material culture, habits, and language of the Guiacuras; the geography, plants, and agriculture. He had lived so long in isolation that although he wrote in German, he had forgotten many words. His own possessions were meager, consisting of two copper vessels for preparing his chocolate, two or three earthenware pots, a small oven which he sometimes did not use for half a year, some cow bladders for storing water, a crucifix, some paper pictures on his walls, a couple of bare wooden chairs, a rough table, a plank bed and a cowhide for the floor, besides his treasured china plate.

Baegert remained at his lonely outpost for seventeen years, until suddenly, in 1767, a governor appeared with sealed orders and arrested the German Jesuits, of which there were eight, along with the others.

The Mexican Jesuits suffered the same penalty; not a single one was allowed to remain in the country. In 1767, royal officials entered the Jesuit missions, seized the members of the order, and sent them to Veracruz. In Mexico the Jesuits had controlled 103 Indian missions and 23 colleges. Their activities in both fields were irreplaceable.

The expulsion of the Jesuits was in many ways a disaster to all the Americas. Once again the Germans were expelled from the soil of Mexico. Yet within ten years (1788) the Holy Experiment would be changed into a "geological experiment," and the Germans would return once again, this time as experts in mining and mineralogy.

C harles III, the first Bourbon king of Spain, was one of those pro-
gressive, liberal rulers during the Age of Enlightenment who
reacted favorably toward new inventions and the application of the
new sciences for the betterment of society. While the liberalizing
trend of the Enlightenment was a pertinent factor in bringing down
the Jesuits, it also had the effect of opening the New World to the
natural scientists.

In the field of commerce, new trade channels were opened up in
Spanish America for competing nations; new ideas were allowed to
filter into the colonies, especially in the field of mines and metallurgy. Charles III ordered the latest German mining innovations to be
introduced into Spanish America.

Fausto d'Elhuyar, born in 1755, gave promise of possessing great
talents in geology. He was sent by the Spanish Crown, along with his
brother, Juan, to study mining at Freiberg. After completing their
studies, the two brothers made extensive journeys to mines in Scan-
dinavia, Hungary, and Austria, along with additional studies of mine
management in Saxony—all this so that d'Elhuyar could furnish
Mexico and parts of the other Americas with the latest methods of
mineralogy, metallurgy, and mining management. On his return,
d'Elhuyar established in Mexico the Colegio Real de Mínera,
which still exists. He also brought to it plans, drawings of mining
techniques, and German mining equipment. In addition, he arranged
for Spanish translations of German books on mining. (The first professors at the Colegio de Mínera were German.) In addition, Fausto
d'Elhuyar was charged by the Spanish court to contract with the
Saxon regime at Dresden for a group of technicians to go to Mexico
and a geological mission to Peru.

On arrival in Mexico, the German miners—Freidrich Sonnen-

*Timotéo Leberecht, Baron von Nordenflycht (1752–1815), intro-
duced silver mining in Peru in 1788. For almost a century thereafter
the family furnished German consuls in South America.*

schmidt, Louis Leutner, and Franz Fischer among the group—were
assigned to the rich silver mines in Guanajuato, Zacatecas, and
Taxco, where, said Humboldt, "there are rich veins of silver . . . at
average land heights from 5,520 feet to 6,500. The mines are surrounded by cultivated fields and villages; forests crown the neighboring peaks, and everything here facilitates the subterranean wealth."
    All, or almost all, these German mining experts remained until

they were either killed or exiled during the revolution against Spain. The operations in Peru were directed by Baron Tadaëus von Nordenflycht, who had been the director of the mines of Miczanagora in Cracow. He was descended from a Swedish nobleman who had married a German countess living in Kurland. The elder Nordenflycht had the formidable title of Oberbergdirecktor of mines as well as being Rittergutsbesitzen in Ostsee-Herzogstümern. It is small wonder, then, that he named his son, born in 1752, Fürchtegott Labrecht von Nordenflycht. When the Spanish emissaries arrived in Dresden to arrange his contract they found Fürchtegott ("fear God") such a fearful rush of consonants that they took only the last part of his name, Tegott, which eventually developed into Timoteo and, in Spanish, as Tadaëus Baron von Nordenflycht.[1]

Nordenflycht studied mining in Freiberg, then in Sachsen, went on to the University of Leipzig, and finally rose to be director of the mines in Austrian Poland. He set off for Peru with his group in 1788. Had the Baron any inkling of what this would lead to, he probably would have stayed in the European mines. The difficulties he encountered in Peru were so great that the mission was known thereafter as "Nordenflycht's conflict." While other groups departed to reside in Uruguay and Chile, another important part of the Nordenflycht group arrived in Argentina on the way to Peru.

Anton Zacharias Helms' first task was to be no less than a geomorphic survey of South America from Argentina to Peru. His other task was to bring into Peruvian mining the new amalgamation techniques. Anton Helms took his assignment with good will. He was then thirty-nine years old, having been born in Austria in 1751. He had seen service with the Poles in Chemnitz, and it was while here that he was selected to go to Peru. Upon landing with his group in Buenos Aires on October 29, 1788, he had only to display the king's edict and was given horses, pack mules, and Indians to begin his trek toward Peru.

Helms' ride of eighteen hundred miles to the Peruvian mines is

---

[1] A cousin of Nordenflycht married a General von Kaltenborn. His son migrated to Milwaukee in 1868, and there Hans von Kaltenborn, known as H. V. Kaltenborn, was born (1878–1965). Famed as a reporter on the old *Brooklyn Eagle* and during World War II as a radio commentator, much of this genealogical information is drawn from his autobiography, *Fifty Fabulous Years*.

The immigrants to the New World tried even in their dress to pre-serve the customs and habits of their old homeland.

noteworthy because he thought to keep a diary. When it was published he prefaced it thus: "This diary was not written out of any vanity or desire for literary glory, but only to furnish useful information of little known places; it was mainly written because of the encouragement given me by friends in order that those interested in my Peruvian voyage would have an idea of the natural riches, the landscape and the extended mountainous areas of these countries."

Helms and his German miners journeyed across the pampas, which were then awash with the cold Antarctic wind known as the *pampero*, all of which he describes in one of the rarest panoramic peregrinations in the eighteenth century. They crossed the pampas to the rising foothills of the Andes and into Tucumán, an ancient Inca site, then on to Salta, where the salt leeches began, and into the Indian town of Jujuy. They then climbed up to Tarija and on to Potosí, at an altitude of 13,600 feet.

Francisco de Carvajal had discovered the silver mines of Potosí in 1541. There the Spaniards had built one of the world's highest cities, and here the Spaniards built their mint, La Casa de la Moneda. Helms inspected the mines and noted how the Indians were forced to go underground with only pickaxes to break off the pieces of silver ore, which was mixed lead and copper pyrites. Brought up to the surface, these sulfides of silver were transformed into chlorides and then treated with mercury. The amalgam was heated and the result was silver.

A Frenchman, Amedée Frezier, who visited the mines in the same century as Helms, wrote of them: "To safeguard themselves against the bad air that they breathe in the mines, the Indians continually chew coca, and they claim that they could not work there without it. Only the Indians are fit for this work, on which it is impossible to employ negroes, because they all die."

"La Paz [anciently Chuquisaca] is nicely constructed," Helms wrote, "and very clean, possesses many nice and rich churches and cloisters, more than 4,000 fireplaces and 20,000 souls and filled with the very rich, and slaves. . . . The wealth of this town is due to the commerce of the coca leaf. The Indians chew it all the time and mix it with lime slack in order to release the cocaine. No Indian can work without his coca."

Anton Helms found the mines and miners a remarkable contrast compared to the Old World. There mining was an honorable profession, with miners' guilds and uniforms in which to parade on feast days. It was different in Peru. Here everything—gold, silver, copper, tin, lead, mercury, salt, plaster, stone, transparent alabaster for windows—was mined with Indian slave labor.

Helms thought little of Spanish metallurgical techniques and said so openly, which, coming to Spanish ears, did not go well with Spanish pride. When the conquistadors arrived in Peru they preferred placer mining in a wash trough. Once washed free of the dross, the impure gold was bathed in boiling sulfuric acid, which dissolved all the metals except gold. This was refining.

Later the Spaniards extended their methods of extracting gold. Thousands of natives were employed in hollowing out mountains, extracting sulfides with picks, crushing and pulverizing the ore by hammer. Washing and refining followed. So arduous was this work that the Indians preferred to live and die between the cyclopean walls of the Casa de Moneda at Potosí rather than go down into the mine.

It was these techniques which the Nordenflycht mission was

De re metallica, by Georg Bauer, called Agricola, was still valued in the 18th century as the basic work on mining. The German miners in Chile and Peru still mined according to the methods which these two woodcuts from the 16th century show.

supposed to change. Helms' journey took him along the edge of Lake Titicaca, the highest navigable lake in the world. He passed the famous Jesuit-built churches of Juli and Pomata, came to Chucuito ("mountains rich in gold and silver"), reached Puno ("much destroyed because of the last Inca revolution of Tupac Amaru"), and so moved down the valley to Cuzco.

After looking at the mines in upper Peru, Helms moved his caravan across the flooded plain of Zurite and the raised road which ancient Inca engineers had fashioned into a causeway and came to the

gorge of the Apurímac. Here they reached the bridge called by Thornton Wilder "The Bridge of San Luis Rey." Built about 1350 by the Inca Roca, the bridge was situated on the Inca road running between Lima and Cuzco. Over a strongly built masonry tower on either side, the Indians wove and hung huge rope cables out of coarse agave fibers. Two main cables—"as thick as a man's body," wrote one of Pizarro's soldiers—were suspended from the two towers. From the suspended cables rope supports hung down, and to these the bridge proper, made of wooden planks, was attached. Since the bridge rocked with the wind coming up from the canyon, two guy ropes held the bridge to prevent swaying.

When Helms arrived at the bridge in December of 1788, he wrote: "Soon after leaving the Uripa, we again climbed to the summit of a vast ridge and consumed much time in the descent toward a rapid river, crossed by a dangerous hanging bridge, about one hundred and twenty feet in length and suspended by badly made hemp ropes. Here we were obliged to stop until the bridge was repaired, and passed the night in a dark mountain cave. Here, besides suffering from excessive heat, we were so dreadfully stung by mosquitoes that we scarcely recognized each others' faces the next morning."

Once across, they traveled on the ancient Inca road, in many places still intact. All along the way Helms examined the geology of the land. His notebooks are filled with geological observations: "Covered with flesh-colored sandstone . . . the entire field covered with small pure quartz crystals. . . . From the town of Abancay to Cochcajas . . . clay-slate mountains, lime, gypsum, hornblende, green phosphorus stone."

Helms then turned west and went over and down the Inca road to the Cañete Valley. "During this day's journey we were frequently in the greatest danger, since the path which leads down the steep side of the mountains toward the river is in many places scarcely a quarter of an ell broad; and if the mule should make a single false step, both he and his rider would be precipitated into the abyss and dashed to pieces." They came to the sea, turned north along the coast, "walking in deep sand along the Pacific sea" to Lima.

There Helms met Baron von Nordenflycht and his group of Saxon miners. "Lima," Helms reported, "is a large city; but on account of the frequent earthquakes the houses are only one storey high and very flimsily constructed. From the outside they have a mean appearance, but within they are magnificent and well appointed. The streets are very regular; straight, broad, clean and well paved; and on almost all of them are the palaces of the rich nobles. . . . Thirty years ago, Lima was one of the richest and most flourishing cities in Spanish America. The population was then estimated at seventy thousand. At present [1790], owing to the total decay of trade, the population is said to have sunken as low as fifty thousand Spaniards, people of color and negroes."

The Viceroy of Peru, Teodoro de Croix, a Netherlander, had requested of his king that he send to Peru skillful Saxon miners with the requisite talents and knowledge. In the meantime, he had inaugurated, at the expense of its proprietors, a Supreme Council of Mines on the model of a similar tribunal in Mexico. "On my arrival in Peru, however," Helms observed, "I found that the members of this supreme court were entirely destitute of mineralogical knowledge."

Helms and his group stayed only three weeks in Lima, during which time he had several private interviews with the Viceroy. At the request of the governor of Huancavelica, he was ordered to proceed to that city as director of the royal quicksilver works for the purpose of introducing new furnaces in place of the ill contrived and wasteful variety which were then in operation.

The lands that Anton Helms and his miners crossed had, he said, "three faces." First was the desolate coast, over a thousand miles in length, a fierce desert broken every forty miles or so with streams, large and small, which came down from the Andes. The second "face" was the Cordilleras, covered first, with cactus, then with trees, and higher up with ichu grass. This region is called the *ceja de la montaña*, "eyebrow of the mountain."

Helms left Lima accompanied by his family and five other German miners and found that "the sudden transition from the hot climate of Lima to the cold mountainous regions threw my wife, servants, and miners into an intermittent fever." The Helms party arrived by mule in Huancavelica in May, 1790. He was aware that the Viceroy took a great interest in the area since there were the mercury mines of Peru, which were important for the extraction of silver ore. The working conditions at three miles above sea level were arduous enough, but worse, he noted, was the fact that "the malignant fumes caused by the

Teodoro de Croix became viceroy of Peru in 1776.

Francisco José de Caldas (1770–1816), a versatile explorer.

particles of mercury . . . not only put out the lights with which the Indians work in the depths, but also shorten the life span of these wretched workers."

After a seven months' stay in Huancavelica, he made his way, in July, 1791, to Cerro de Pasco, now one of the great copper, lead, and silver mines in South America. Then it was only a small town "where the sub-delegate, the officers who superintend the refining house and collect the king's duties, and where some wealthy proprietors of mines, reside. Most of the other proprietors live near their mines on the great silver mountain of Huariaca, distant about six miles from Pasco."

After additional months spent in the Andes on a survey of the mines and mining methods, Helms wrote a long report to the Viceroy, pointing out the manner in which the mines could be made more productive to the owners and accordingly advantageous to the King's treasury. "I proposed to the Viceroy plans for the erection of machinery for pounding and washing the ore and proved that sixteen of my Idrian furnaces would produce as much as the seventy-five ones in use. These plans were rejected by the Viceroy, on account of the cost, which I estimated at 100,000 piasters, though the king annually lost

more than 200,000 piasters on the mines owing to bad management."
The Viceroy was unwilling to consider the funds needed for this reform and "categorically refused" to go further with the plan. "Thus
all I could obtain," wrote Helms wearily, "was a commendatory letter
in praise of my zeal. I therefore decided to quit Peru."

Meanwhile, the head of the mission, Baron von Nordenflycht, was
having a continuous flow of problems. He was then thirty-eight years
old, worldly, quite handsome, with blue eyes—a rarity in Peru—
exceedingly well groomed, and envied by most Limeños since his
plumed-colored coat was of the latest European cut, whereas their
clothes were two seasons behind. Behind his façade of lace and ruf-
fles Baron Nordenflycht was of proven ability. He had, after all, the
edict of Charles III and had been commissioned by his Saxon king to
lead a party of thirteen mineralogists and experienced miners to Peru
in an attempt to increase silver and gold production. The group had
guarantees of religious freedom, pensions, expense money, and material aid in Peru. Some forty pages of documents, including royal
cédulas, contain exact details of the negotiations in Germany, in
which figured the distinguished director of Mexican mining, Fausto
d'Elhuyar, and Luis de Onís, future minister to the United States
(1810–18). A lengthy contract was negotiated between Onís and nine
of the German miners, setting terms of service; some of the Germans
labored in Peru for nearly twenty years.

Shortly after their arrival, Nordenflycht became involved in local
conflicts. According to one source, the miners were victims of
calumny; their mining methods were branded impractical; and they
were accused of heresy and Judaism. Their machines, it was said,
would cause wide unemployment. They became imbroiled in several
lawsuits, and Nordenflycht and members of his family were several
times denounced to the Inquisition.

To make Nordenflycht's life even more miserable, he had the
misfortune of having interminable legal difficulties with Micaela
Villegas, known far beyond Lima as La Perricholi.[2]

[2]In 1825, Prosper Mérimée published a collection of short plays, one of which was
La Carrosse Saint Sacrement ("Coach of the Holy Sacrament"). It is not certain where
Mérimée got the material for his version of the Perricholi legend. Perhaps it came from
officers of the French ship that stopped in Lima in 1778, loaded with rich merchandise,
for La Perricholi went aboard and stayed there, it is rumored, for several days. In 1868,
Halevy and Meilhac adapted Mérimée's play for Jacques Offenbach. This opera bouffe,

Micaela Villegas was born in Lima on September 28, 1748, of a Creole family (that is, a Spaniard born in the colonies). At an early age she became adept at the guitar and dancing and in time developed a good singing voice. By the age of fifteen she had appeared on the stage, and at seventeen she became the mistress of the bachelor viceroy, Manuel de Amat. Aged sixty, he was well born—"a gentleman on all four sides." Amat built much of Lima in the style of the French, constructed a new bullring, the Coliseo de Gallos, established a lottery, and built a new theater. He also built in this hot, rainless land a rococo Paseo de Aguas, detouring a branch of the Rimac River to pass over an arch and drop like a plunging waterfall to the city below. All of the splendid Lima residences date from this period. He had the streets paved, public lights installed, built the church of Las Nazarenas and reorganized the provincial army. He also expelled the Jesuits and began the redevelopment of Peru's mining industry, making the suggestion that German miners should reorganize it. He sired one of Micaela Villegas' children, bestowing on his son a sword and a royal sash and attached a letter to his silk underwear saying "Es voluntad del Rey." He left Peru on the eve of the first American revolution in 1776.

Thus ended Micaela Villegas' influence. As soon as she lost her protector, social storms broke about her. She lashed out at her enemies, turned sour within, and became intensely bitter. "When a soul," the philosopher warned, "knows that it is unloved, and does not itself love, it betrays its sediment; its dregs come up." And the dregs poured all over Baron von Nordenflycht.

Water was of the utmost importance in this rainless land. Lima was, in fact, a riverine oasis, receiving additional water channeled down from brawling Andean streams. The German water war was brought on over the excessive amount of such channel-conducted water used by Nordenflycht's metallurgical laboratory.

Micaela Villegas owned the Casa Molina in the Alameda, across the river from Lima, which was where the German mining commission had installed its machinery since a constant flow of water made

La Perichole, was recently revived in New York and played for two seasons at the Metropolitan Opera. Micaela Villegas briefly enters Thornton Wilder's *Bridge of San Luis Rey* in the letters of the Marquesa de Montemayor, supposed to have been written about 1790: "The public still idolizes its Perichole; it even forgives her years. . . ."

Note the spelling. Méimée wrote it Perichole, although the correct spelling is Perricholi: *Perra*=bitch; *Chola*=half-caste.

cheap power possible. There was a constant conflict, legal and social, between La Perricholi and Baron von Nordenflycht and the German miners.

But Baron Nordenflycht's problems were somewhat soothed by love. On November 4, 1796, in the Church of Santa Ana, he married María Cortes y Azúa of a notable Chilean family who had settled in Lima. Of this union was born a son, Pedro, who remained in Peru, rose to be a captain in the army, and was eventually shot by the Spaniards during the revolution. Another son, Dionysio, was left to carry on the Nordenflycht name, his grandsons seeing service in Mexico in 1865.

By the time he was ready to leave Peru, after twenty-five years residence, Nordenflycht had completely forgotten the German language. Baron Nordenflycht died in Spain in 1815 in the odor of sanctity—he had become a Catholic in order to marry a Catholic—in the year when the second American revolution was beginning.

The First American Revolution   X

J acob Leisler was certainly not one of those "bemused supernumeraries" which the Germans were purported to be in the history of
the Americas; neither was his role "theoretical and speculative." He
had, in fact, led the first stage of the revolution against British exploitation of the colonies. Fifty years before the Boston Massacre,
Jacob Leisler was hanged. Thus it was that a German became the first
American martyr for independence.

Jacob Leisler had been born in Frankfurt-am-Main about 1640 and,
as many a German before him, had taken service with the Dutch East
India Company. Captured by Tunisian pirates, he somehow found the
means of ransoming himself and thereafter, by a concatenation of
events, he found himself in New Amsterdam soon after the British
takeover from the Dutch. Since he spoke German, Dutch, and
English and knew his way about, he emerged as the leader of the re-
sentful Dutch-English colonists. Leisler's rebellion lasted three years.
In the end the rebels were overcome by a greater force; nine were
tried and two hanged, one of them being Jacob Leisler. His grandson
would be Gouverneur Morris, one of the signers of the Declaration of
Independence. The trapdoor was sprung at high noon, May 16, 1691.

John Peter Zenger took up where Jacob Leisler left off. Zenger
was the second publisher-printer in the colonies. He had been one of
a company of three thousand Palatinate Rhinelanders who had emigrated to England and were sent out, in 1710, by Queen Anne. The
trip had its Dantesque horrors—four hundred seventy died in the
five months' transit, including Zenger's father. At the age of thirteen
Zenger was apprenticed to the printer William Bradford. By 1734 he
was a printer with an office on Broad Street near the Long Bridge.
"As there was but one Printer in the Province of New York that
printed a publick News Paper," he wrote, "I was in Hopes . . . I might

German John Peter Zenger became the champion of American freedom of the press. In a lawsuit the journalist and publisher (standing between the court and his counsel for the defense) was finally acquitted. Zenger had dared to accuse the authorities of dishonest intrigues.

make it worth my while." His press also issued a number of early books, including one on arithmetic, the first such published in the American colonies. In 1733 he started his newspaper the *New York Weekly Journal*.

The paper waged war against an administration that most agreed was foully run. To the astonishment of his readers, he wrote, "On . . . the Seventeenth of this instant I was Arrested, taken and Imprisoned in the common Gaol of this City, by Virtue of a Warrant from the Governor. . . ." And later, "The Liberty of the Press is a Subject of the greatest Importance, and in which every individual is as much concerned as he is in any other Part of Liberty."

The trial of Peter Zenger for the freedom of the press and a legal definition of libel became famous throughout the colonies and in England. Zenger himself printed the history of the trial: "The Jury . . . being ask'd by the Clerk whether they were agreed on their Verdict . . . they answered . . . 'Not Guilty' . . . and the next Day I was discharg'd from my Imprisonment." Zenger's trial and the verdict was widely published. Five editions were printed in London in a single year and it became one of the important events of prerevolutionary times.

By the time of Zenger's death in 1746 the seeds of dissent were emplanted which would lead to revolution and independence—a war in which Germans, serving on both sides, were to play a conspicuous part.

In the year 1775, Britain's troubles in North America came to the fore. The British-owned plantations provided admirably protected markets for British industries. The colonies produced raw materials— sugar, tobacco, furs, fish, and timber—and at the same time they created a market for slaves, as well as absorbing some of the more undesirable elements of English society—whores, criminals, and bankrupts. This so angered the usually amiable Benjamin Franklin that he published an "Open Letter to the King" in his *Pennsylvania Gazette* on January 13, 1763, writing that he was sending the King an equivalent number of rattlesnakes.

Since George II was the Elector of Hanover, he had such a natural affection for his native Germany that when disagreement spread across Europe his ministers needed little encouragement to enter into the Seven Years' War. Never since Marlborough's day had England enjoyed such victories. Wolfe, gambling with his little army, surprised the French and won Canada. The rich sugar and spice islands— Martinique and Grenada—fell into British hands. Dakar, in Africa, and the French slave trade also went into the British maw. And in India, Robert Clive won Bengal.

Few men came to the throne at a moment of greater exaltation than George III. He was twenty-two years of age when, in 1760, he succeeded his grandfather as king. He married Charlotte of Mecklenburg-Strelitz, produced sixteen children, changed ministers as he changed clothes, and went gently but permanently mad.

No one then in England, or even in the colonies, discerned North America's possibilities or its future greatness. For most in Britain the

George I of England (1660–1727) (left) underestimated the value of the colonies, and George III (1760–1820) lost them in the Revolution.

colonies were remote, full of Indians, and these "Americans," a mixture of German, Irish, Scotch, and Indians, seemed to them to be a testy lot, captious and irascible. They were always protesting about something, with committees, petitions, and confrontations. Moreover, they seemed to lack a proper sense of their responsibilities: without the British army they would have been overrun in the French and Indian wars; without British credit their economy would be ruined; and without British consumption of their Virginia-grown tobacco, where would they be? For the majority of English politicians the first stages of the struggle with the American colonies were merely irritating. George III's American policy was emphatically simple: the colonists must respond to absolute obedience. Since his own viewpoint was so obvious, the King took royal umbrage when opposed.

The American Revolution began as a simple protest. Molasses, from which rum was distilled and drunk in prodigious quantities, was to be taxed—the famous Stamp Act. Coffee from the British West Indies, indigo from India for dyeing, and Madeira wine from Portugal also were to be taxed. There were, in addition, the Currency Act and then the Quartering Act (billeting of troops in colonists' houses at their expense). The result of this "taxation without representation" was violence. In 1771, British troops fired on menacing colonists. It was called the Boston Massacre, though only five people were killed. This led later to the Boston Tea Party, in which a disciplined group of men, dressed as Mohawk Indians, raided the sailing ship *Dartmouth*, anchored in Boston harbor, and dumped 342 chests of tea into the sea.

With the possible exception of Samuel Adams, no one in America thought that this would lead to war, and none believed it would end with American independence. Benjamin Franklin was then in London attempting reconciliation and feared that "an accidental quarrel or a personal insult might lead to open hostilities."

On April 19, 1775, the skirmish at Lexington took place, followed by the affair at Concord. War was on, and by June 17 the Battle of Bunker Hill was joined. More than one German took part. David

This contemporary illustration by the German C. M. Sprengel shows the American protest to the Stamp Act, 1765.

The Boston Tea Party (1773) was the stimulus for the American War of Independence. Boston settlers, dressed as Mohawk Indians, tarred the British vessel Dartmouth *and threw its cargo of tea overboard to protest the oppressive taxes.*

Ziegler had been born at Heidelberg and served in the Russian army. He changed this uniform for the blue regimentals of the Continental Army. He was commissioned a lieutenant and took part in the Siege of Boston.

As in the beginning of all wars, most believed that it would be over in a matter of months, but as the months did not produce victory the British realized that their world victories had spread thin the red line of their soldiery. They also had to take into account that if the rebellion lengthened, they would be confronted by the intervention of their erstwhile enemies, France and Spain.

The British made an overture to Catherine of Russia for troops, but she would have none of an involvement in such a war. The Prussians, then the best troops in Europe, were approached, but Frederick the Great turned the offer down, and in doing so had harsh words for the German princelings who would send their troops to shoot down Americans and other Germans.

Since George III was himself the Elector of Hanover, he then turned to his royal German cousins. And why not? The Germans and Britons had recently fought as allies in the Seven Years' War. Moreover, many Germans held positions of trust and importance in England. War then was international; officers changed from country to country and fought constantly under different flags. In the period from 1700 to 1800 nations formed countless short-lived alliances, often for the pursuit of transient goals. It was almost impossible to foresee, if war broke out, who would be ranged on which side and who on the other. Even more difficult to predict was the side upon which those who had entered the war as allies would be found at the end of it.

German soldiers recruited for America were offered liberal promises; twenty dollars and one hundred acres of land were guaranteed every private and noncommissioned officer. While the thirty thousand German troops were generally called Hessians, less than half came from the duchy of Hesse-Cassel. There were Brunswickers and troops from Hesse-Hanau (not to be confused with Hesse-Cassel); the Duke of Waldeck furnished contingents of Waldeckers; Ansbach-Bayreuth

The Battle of Bunker Hill, 1775, in which the British defeated the American militia.

Embarkation of German soldiers to America. Sold by their rulers, they had to fight with the British troops against the American settlers.

sent troops; Frederick Augustus of Anhalt, who controlled a population of no more than twenty thousand was able to scour up six hundred officers and men for American duty.

After Britain had tested the quality of American resistance at Bunker Hill, the King sent over to Germany Colonel William Faucit to finalize the treaties. On January 9, 1776, Elector Frederick II of Brunswick signed. For the sum of Ł750,000 he was to furnish four thousand troops: dragoons, light infantry, and two companies of Jäger sharpshooters.

The treaties were printed at Frankfort and Leipzig in 1776 and appeared in the Parliamentary Transactions. For each man Britain agreed to pay thirty marks hard money; for every man killed, wounded, captured, or made unserviceable by wounds or sickness, a like sum was to be paid; but for deserters no compensation was to be made.

The King of England also agreed to pay levy money. "According to custom," the treaty detailed, "three wounded men shall be reckoned as one killed; a man killed shall be paid for at the rate of levy money. They were to take an oath of service to the King of England, thus putting them under double allegiance to their own sovereign and to that of Great Britain."

The one upon whom most opprobium fell was Elector Frederick II of Hesse-Cassel. Then fifty-six years old, he was not unpopular in his country, for he had enriched it by many educational institutions and patronized the arts and sciences. He is unjustly reproached with avarice, a charge that belongs more to his son, but since he gave the largest contingent for the allied army sent across the Atlantic and derived the greatest pecuniary benefit, he drew down upon himself the most reproaches.

For the most part, the German "auxiliaries"—or, as they wished to call themselves, *Hülfstruppen*—were volunteers. There were desertions, as there are in all wars, yet General von Riedesel, commander of the four thousand Brunswickers who served in New York, wrote to his wife on the eve of embarking for America, "I have not had a single deserter and everyone is content." Captain Johann von Ewald, who served through the whole eight years in America and rose to be a general in the Danish Army, wrote: "No one found fault with our going into the British Service for pay and none of the officers or men complained, and in letters and officers home there was no complaint." Which was generally true, and for good reason, since letters adverse to the American war were not printed in Sprengel's *Yearbook* in which articles on the war, as well as letters and parts of journals, were published. Complaints were suppressed, yet much of the German reporting was objective. The Stamp Act that set off the conflict was clearly reported; the first clash between colonist and soldier, entitled "Das erste Bürger-Blut," was objective; and an eyewitness account of the Battle of Bunker Hill was also printed. However, all of the letters in Schlözer's *Briefwechsel*, the foremost German periodical of the day, printed at Göttingen in the Hanoverian domains of George III, were printed in favor of Britain.

In moving to their port of embarkation the armies avoided large towns where they might encounter dissent. Johann Gottfried Seume, a theological teacher at Leipzig who rose to local prominence later as

*Uniforms of German soldiers in the War of Independence: the Hessian
Rifle Corps of General Riedesel.*

a writer, wrote in his autobiography of his particular adventures as a recruit:

I was brought under arrest to Ziegenhayn where I found many companions in misfortune from all parts of the country. There we waited to be sent to America in the spring. . . . I gave myself up to my fate, and tried to make the best of it, bad as it might be. . . . The story of those times is well known. No one was safe from the grip of the *Soldatenhändler*. Persuasion, cunning, deception, force—all served. No one asked what means were used. . . . Strangers . . . were arrested, imprisoned, sent off. They tore up my academic matriculation papers, as being the only instrument by which I could prove my identity. At last I fretted no more. One can live anywhere. . . . My comrades were a runaway son of the Muses from Jena, a bankrupt tradesman from Vienna, a fringemaker from Hanover, a discharged secretary of the post office from Gotha, a monk from Würzburg, a steward from Meiningen, a Prussian sergeant of hussars, a cashiered Hessian. . . .

In his regiment there were mutineers who received the usual punishments of the time—running the gauntlet, sometimes hanging—confirming the apothegm of Frederick the Great that soldiers should fear their officers more than the enemy. The people of Germany—still a patchwork of three hundred city-states, electorates, duchies, bishoprics, margraves, landgraves, and free cities—were not all docile. Comte de Mirabeau, then a fugitive in Holland, published a pamphlet addressed "To the Hessians and other nations of Germany, sold by their Princes to England," an eloquent protest against the rapacity of German princes and a splendid tribute to the patriotism of the Americans.

Frederick the Great, in a letter to Voltaire (June 18, 1776), expressed his contempt for the *Soldatenhändeler* and found occasion, at a somewhat later time, to throw impediments in the way of their troops. "Had the Landgrave come out of my school," he wrote, "he would not have sold his subjects to the English as one sells cattle to be dragged to the shambles. . . . I pity the poor Hessians who end their lives unhappily and uselessly in America."

The poet-playwright Friedrich von Schiller was appalled to think that German soldiers would go to America to fight against German pioneer immigrants. The son of an army surgeon attached to the service of the Duke of Württemberg at Marbach, Schiller was trained as a surgeon and served in the same corps as had his father. When he turned to writing, he disclosed a violent, dissenting nature. Arrested at the age of twenty-two after the performance of his first drama, *Die Räuber*, he was censured and forbidden to write anything other than medical treatises. He then went into hiding and wrote *Kabale und Liebe* (1784), a ringing protest against the war in America.

The Americans, however, then fighting for their lives, did not make any distinction between the volunteer or dissenter. The Germans were lumped together as "Hessians" and their presence on American soil, fighting in a war that was not their concern, immortalized them in a paragraph of the Declaration of Independence: "He [George III] is at this time transporting large Armies of foreign Mercenaries to compleat the works of death, desolation and tyranny, already begun with circumstances of Cruelty & Perfidy scarcely paralleled in the most barbarous ages, and totally unworthy the Head of a civilized nation."

Yet what has been overlooked in the battle of words is the importance of these troops in the histories of both countries—the Americas and the Germanies. Of the thirty thousand sent, a little less than half returned. They were, after all, "volunteers," said the Hessian Major Pfister, "and they were allowed to remain in America if they wished." A number of these thousands helped to populate North America and Canada.

Captain Johann von Ewald, born in Kiel, had lost his left eye in a duel and would fight the whole eight years of the American war, eventually emerging as a lieutenant general. In addition, he would author several important books on the outgrowth of the war. In 1789 he wrote: "Few people know the brilliant part played by our Hessian corps in America, and history has failed to do them justice. The outcome of that war was the result of the bad management of the British government, and not the fault of British soldiers, or their allies, the Germans."

Many of the famous names of European history were part of the German forces on both sides. General Martin von Schlieffen, the Hessian ambassador to London and destined to become commander in chief, was the ancestor of Count Alfred von Schlieffen, famous in World War I for the "swinging door" plan through Belgium. Count August von Gneisenau, one of the most brilliant soldiers Germany

*Augustus Neithardt von
Gneisenau, later Prussian
general field marshal,
participated in the siege
of Yorktown.*

has ever produced, was a young subaltern who fought and surrendered
at Yorktown. He would be later chief of staff to Blücher at the Battle
of Waterloo and, as field marshal, reorganize the Prussian army.
Claus von Stauffenberg, the hero of July 20, 1944, was a direct
descendant of Gneisenau through his mother, Countess Üxküll-
Gyllenband. A certain Sergeant Küster fought in these wars and
remained in America; his descendant would be General George
Custer. There were Bohlens who remained behind, and a Wöllwarth,
whose name, Anglicized into Woolworth, laid down the beginning of
the family who produced four generations of American millionaires.

Captain Baron von Münchhausen was appointed aide-de-camp to
Sir William Howe, general of the Anglo-German armies. He was the
nephew of that Baron von Münchhausen who made the collection of
marvelous tales of ridiculously exaggerated exploits. Both Howes,
the admiral and the general, were half-German through their mother,

Countess Sophia Charlotte, who was the sister of General von Kiel-mansegg.[1]

Some of the finest German officers—Domberg, Langen, Yorck, and the aforementioned Gneisenau—developed out of the American experience. Lieutenant Johannes Hinrichs, who fought as a Jäger in the first battle of Long Island, was later wounded and cared for by an American family; he became a Prussian lieutenant general, as did Schuler von Senden, who fought through the whole war. Many of the famous names of Germany, who in later wars fought for what they conceived to be right, took part in the American war, such as Captain Leopold-Franz von Plessen, of the well-known Holstein family, who married into the Fugger-Babenhausen.

Not quite a few who had their own idea of honor and loyalty fought in this war and would pass it on to their descendants. Of those who fought in the Americas quite a few would leave descendants who would be involved in the attempt to overthrow Hitler on July 20, 1944. Yorck, a relative of Yorck von Wartenberg, was one of those who surrendered at Yorktown. There was a von Stein, an Ehren-krooks, a Pöllnitz, a Rantzau, and von Giemars; three von Hagens fought under General von Wurmb, and their descendant, Albrecht von Hagen, would be one of the first to die with Stauffenberg, condemned and hanged by the Volksgericht. The Hessians and others of the German states who fought in the Americas made a great impact on history within the Americas, yet comparatively little attention has been paid them.

The American Revolution was one of wide division; the British were divided on the issues and the remedy, and the colonists were no less divided (over one hundred thousand went over to the loyalists' cause). Their dilemma was expressed by a naturalized American citizen named Jean de Crèvecoeur: "If I attached myself to the mother country, which is three thousand miles from me, I become what is called an enemy to my region. If I follow the rest of my countrymen, I become opposed to our ancient masters . . . how should I unravel an argument in which reason herself has given way to brutality and bloodshed."

The Germans were divided at home as well as in the Americas.

[1]The former commanding officer of NATO ground forces in Europe, General Johann Adolf Count von Kielmansegg of Sigmaringen, is a direct descendant.

British and German troops disembark at the harbor of New York.

Baron von Ottendorf served with the American army as a captain and deserted with Benedict Arnold. Captain Andreas Emmerich, who had fought bravely in the Seven Years' War, later settled in America, but left for Europe at the outbreak of hostilities and raised a volunteer corps for service against the Americans. Later, in 1809, he took a leading part in a conspiracy against Jerome Bonaparte, King of Westphalia, and was executed. German fought German, and more than once a German soldier surrendered to his own kinfolk, resident citizens of America.

The first contingent of German troops arrived on August 15, 1776. They had survived a horrendous voyage mostly on salt pork, dried peas, and sea-biscuits "so hard that I had to break [them] up with a cannon ball," wrote the poet-soldier Johann Seume. On arrival they were quartered on Staten Island and were struck at once by the comfortable houses of the inhabitants and the appearance of wealth and plenty they found there. It seemed extraordinary to the Hessians that people would revolt against a government under which they enjoyed such bounty.

The Germans were as surprised about the Americans and their professions as the Americans were about theirs. A diary published in one of the German newspapers gives a graphic account of the first military operations. "We found no professional soldiers," Colonel von Herringen wrote. "Among the prisoners are many so-called colonels, lieutenant colonels, majors, and other officers, who however [in daily life] are nothing but mechanics, tailors, shoemakers, wigmakers, barbers, etc. . . . ."

On August 22, 1776, the British with their German mercenaries landed on Long Island. They fought desperately over sparsely settled lands known as New Lots, Flatbush, Bedford, and in less than a month they had pursued the retreating colonists to Brooklyn Heights and then followed them onto the island of Manhattan, which the troops of General Washington had evacuated.

General William von Knyphausen became commander of the German troops in Manhattan. A good soldier and an excellent administrator, he was a tall man with a florid face set off by a full-bottomed periwig which he always wore faultlessly powdered. Knyphausen was well connected in London, where his brother, Dodo, was the Prussian minister. He had seen long service in the Seven Years' War, he spoke and wrote English, and he was to play a part in the defection of Benedict Arnold.

On October 28, 1776, the Hessians and the British gathered for an assault on Fort Washington. The fort had a commanding position on a hill that rose 238 feet above the plain and overlooked the Hudson River. Knyphausen himself led the attack ("Wonder," says an eyewitness, "that he came off without being killed or wounded"), and his Hessians sustained the greater number of casualties since they had the honor of leading the attack. Among the two hundred fifty wounded was Captain Wilhelm von Hagen, who died several days later. Having lost the fort, the American garrison of twenty-five hundred men walked out, laid down their arms and battle flags. The Hessian general complimented them for their resistance. In honor of the capture the fort was renamed Fort Knyphausen.

The British-Hessian army now moved into New Jersey. Their plan was to march on Philadelphia once the Delaware River had frozen over. The Hessians were quartered in Trenton, their march being delayed so that the troops could celebrate a German Christmas. George Washington decided to attack at this time, for he had been told by German-born Americans serving in his army that it was the German custom to celebrate Christmas for two days.

Trenton lay close upon Assumpink Creek, which emptied into the Delaware River. The Hessians were quartered in the hundred and one houses that made up the township. Colonel Johann Rall, their commander, usually a strict disciplinarian, had shown much bravery when he served under the Russian General Orloff as a volunteer against the Turks, but in America he showed disdain, saying that he took no more notice of the Americans than a handful of flies. Consequently, Colonel Rall took few precautions. His picquets were inadequate; earthworks were suggested, but rejected since the ground was frozen. His subordinates thought this rejection of military stance improper and went over his head to appeal to the commanding officer in New York City. But it was too late.

Washington crossed the ice-choked Delaware on Christmas night of 1776. He had numerous German-born Americans under his command; Colonel Nicolaus Hausegger commanded the German-speaking Maryland Line, which included old Colonel Rall, a cobbler when he was not a colonel and a cousin of the Colonel Rall who commanded the Hessians.

The surprise was complete. Rall was in bed when the Americans attacked. He emerged quickly enough and resisted in vain, but was severely wounded and surrendered to his cousin, the other Rall, whereupon he died. The Americans, at a cost of none killed, four wounded, and two frozen to death, had captured twenty-three officers and eight hundred eighty-six soldiers. The battle's importance was not the number of prisoners taken, but its psychological effect. It showed that an untrained and unskilled people, if they believed in a cause, could stand up to battle-tried veterans. The Landgraf of Hesse-Cassel was furious; his regiment had lost fifteen stands of flags and he vowed that none would be reissued until his troops took an equal number from the enemy. The Hessians were marched to prison quarters in Virginia and Maryland, where there were already many German-born settlers. One of the prisoners, Corporal Reuber, remembered in his diary that "Little and Big, young and old looked at us sharply. An old woman cried out that we ought to be hanged for coming to America to rob them of their Freedom."

Hessians, ambushed by General Washington on December 25, 1776, at Trenton, are marched into Philadelphia as prisoners of war. (From a contemporary engraving by Sprengel).

General Washington, however, posted notice that the Hessians had been forced to fight by their princes and asked that they be treated with kindness. Some of them were paroled to German families living in Fredericksburg, Maryland, and were put to work on farms. Others were sent to Lancaster, Pennsylvania, where the much-needed Conestoga wagons were manufactured. There they were put to work with their fellow Germans. The Americanization of the Hessians had begun.

The British reacted fiercely to this victory at Trenton. As soon as their lines of communication were open they undertook to follow Washington's small army to Philadelphia. Throughout the summer of 1777 the bulk of the army moved across New Jersey. At Brandywine (a transmogrification of the German *winebrant*, brandy), close upon Philadelphia, the Americans fought a delaying action. In the forefront of the attack were Hessian sharpshooters, trained marksmen drawn from the hunters and gamekeepers of Germany and formed into a regiment of about a thousand troops under the command of Lieutenant Colonel von Wurmb. One who played a prominent part was Captain Johann von Ewald, whose textbook on light-infantry tactics was written out of his experience in the American wars. Brandywine was a costly battle in lives. The American Congress had beaten a forced retreat when, on September 26, 1777, the British marched into Philadelphia. Two battalions of Hessian grenadiers were posted at Germantown. There, in the first days of October, German would again fight German.

A battle within a battle began when loyalist (American) was pitted against patriot (American). The British had taken advantage of this split by offering land to all who would join the loyalist provincials: two hundred acres to each noncommissioned officer and to each private "fifty acres of land, where every gallant hero may retire and enjoy his bottle and lass."

The Americans in turn made an appeal to the Hessians. Congress, acting on the report of a committee that included Jefferson and Franklin, resolved to offer immediate rewards to Hessians who would "choose to accept of lands, liberty, safety, and a communion of good laws and mild government in a country where many of their friends and relations are already happily settled, rather than continue to be exposed to . . . a long and bloody war." Hessians, if they would desert from the British army, would be accepted as American citizens "and be invested with their rights and privileges . . ." and Congress would provide "for every such person fifty acres of unappropriated lands."

Washington had busied with such offers written in German within days of the invasion. One promised "fifty acres of land to every soldier who will come over, and any captain who brings forty men with him shall receive eight hundred acres of woodland, four oxen, one bull, two cows, and four sows." Deserters would not be obliged to serve on the American side, but might devote themselves at once to the improvement of their estates. Such officers, however, as would accept service in the army of the United States would receive a rank higher than that which they had enjoyed in the army they were leaving, and would be appointed to a corps *composed of Germans* or be employed on frontier or garrison duty exclusively.

"These promises were not entirely without result," wrote a German historian. "In August, 1778, two Hessian lieutenants came to Washington's camp and held out hopes that other officers would follow them. These hopes were illusory." In turn, General von Knyphausen made an appeal in German to all Germans "who were American settlers" to join the swelling ranks of loyalists.

There was no conflict of loyalties in Brigadier General Peter Mühlenberg. His father had emigrated from Germany in 1742 and became pastor of the Lutheran church in Philadelphia. Peter, who had been born in Germantown in 1746, returned to Germany, attended the University of Halle, and was forced to spend a few years in the German army, where he was known as Devil Peet for his hell-raising. He returned to North America, became a pastor, like his father, and was widely known for his passionate sermons. He rallied sentiment against British rule among the German-speaking settlers, and was one of the signers of a resolution stating that "it is the inherent right of British Subjects to be governed and taxed only by representatives chosen by themselves." He attended the Virginia convention in March, 1775, where Patrick Henry gave his "Liberty or Death" speech, and there agreed to raise a regiment to be known as the 10th Virginian Riflemen.

After the Hessians landed, Mühlenberg suited his actions to his words. In the last of his sermons, in January, 1776, he delivered an eloquent speech on personal duty, ending the peroration with: "There is a time for preaching and praying and there is also time for battle. That time has arrived." He threw off his ministerial robes and revealed himself in the silver-blue uniform of a brigadier in the American army. Off he went to battle and there he remained until the last trumpet had been sounded.

New book was being taken at the ultrafashionable Brooks Club at London in 1775, and members crowded about to watch a floridly handsome man record the first wager. That entry read—and still does—"John Burgoyne wagers Charles Fox one pony [fifty guineas] that he will be home victorious from America by Christmas Day, 1777."

The operation that was to end the war in three months was initiated by "Gentleman Johnny" Burgoyne, who arrived in Canada on May 6, 1777, aboard H.M.S. *Apollo*. The ship dropped anchor at Quebec, then possessed of only ten main buildings, all built by the French (and recently acquired by the British) surrounded by less than one hundred houses and a windmill. Burgoyne then proceeded to outline

General John Burgoyne, supreme commander of the English troops in the War of Independence, had to surrender in 1777 at Saratoga.

his "Thoughts on conducting the War" which would end the rebellion by Christmas, 1777.

Burgoyne was a wit, a poet, and a playwright, whose first effort, *The Maid of the Oaks* (1775), had been produced in London by no less a theatrical luminary than David Garrick. He was also, *en passant*, a general. Burgoyne epitomized the eighteenth-century gentleman, successful in words, politics, and arms. After completing his education at the Westminster School, he entered the army in 1740, but sold his commission in 1746 and retired to France. He reentered the army in 1756, when the Seven Years' War broke out, and was sent to Lisbon in 1762 as a brigadier general to aid England's ally, Portugal. He entered Parliament and from 1768 to 1774 showed great ability as a speaker and a politician.

Burgoyne's plan was, on paper, simple and expedient. The army would move down to Albany along the upper Hudson River, pushing aside what he assumed would be feeble American opposition. Another prong of the attack would come down from Lake Ontario, reduce the forts along the Mohawk River, and join forces in Albany. The combined British forces under Sir Henry Clinton would advance from Manhattan up the Hudson and join forces with Burgoyne in Albany, which would effectively cut New England off from the rest of the rebellion.

By the time Burgoyne arrived in Canada, Sir Guy Carleton (whom he would replace), with the aid of Brunswickers and artillery men from Hesse-Hanau, had repelled the attack of General Benedict Arnold on Quebec, December 31, 1775.

Major General Friedrich Adolph von Riedesel had arrived at Quebec in 1776 with a contingent of Brunswickers and elements of the Hesse-Hanau artillery. He was born in Lauterbach, Hesse, on June 3, 1738. His father sent him to the University of Marburg to read law, but while there he was cajoled into entering the army. His birth rendered it easier for him to rise in his profession than it would have been for a commoner. At the outbreak of the Seven Years' War, after considerable apprenticeship, Riedesel was made staff officer to the Duke of Brunswick and fought through the whole of the seven years. He was an excellent officer, cool and discreet in danger, swift in action, unceasingly active in his study of the battle terrain, and equally unceasing in the care of his men. At the time of his arrival in Canada he was thirty-eight years old. He was strongly built, with a somewhat large head, and a florid face with large and expressive blue eyes.

Aside from the war itself, the Brunswickers' presence had after-effects on American history. It was the beginning of the German movement en masse to Canada, starting the waves of migration that has given Canada five hundred thousand people of German blood. More, it bequeathed to literature the Letter-Memoirs of the Baroness von Riedesel, an unmatched autobiography of a wife's devotion to her husband, so timeless in its appeal that after two centuries five new editions have recently been published.

The Brunswickers were not well provided for the Canadian winter. Fortunately, the first winter was so mild that people called it the "German winter." From his winter quarters at Trois-Rivières, near

The commanding general of the Brunswich Auxiliary Corps with the British Army, Baron Friedrich Adolph von Riedesel (left), played a leading role in the American War of Independence. His wife, Baroness Frederika Charlotta Louise von Riedesel (right) was painted as "Spring" by Tischbein the Elder in 1762. The ancestral home of the Riedesels, Castle Eisenbach in Lauterbach in Hesse (opposite), today is still in the possession of the family.

Montreal, Riedesel traveled by sleigh over eighteen hundred miles, visiting his outposts. Upon observing that the American militia were better riflemen than his own, he kept at their training all through the winter, doing for his troops what his counterpart, Baron von Steuben, was doing for the American army at Valley Forge.

In the beginning, General von Riedesel was swept along by Burgoyne's ill-founded optimism. "These rebels," he wrote in a letter home, ". . . are only a few dozen ambitious people who direct this whole affair . . . they do not even know how to fight. They are unpaid, they lack everything. . . ." In September, 1777, he thought it "almost certain that the whole affair will be soon over and in 1778 we will be back in the Fatherland."

Riedesel kept up a lively correspondence with his wife—the "Generalin" he called her—for he expected her to join him in the Americas. Friedericke, Baroness von Riedesel, was a daughter of Hans Jürgen von Massow, one of Frederick the Great's Prussian generals. She was married at sixteen to Baron von Riedesel. As painted by Tischbein, she appears to have been a delicate, fragile woman, dark eyes set in a cameo face as exquisite as a piece of Dresden china. Her fragility was deceptive, however. Poised and charming, she had much inner strength and a strong concept of duty. If she feared, as she must have, coming to a land of vast emptiness, of Indians and war, it did not prevent her from taking the long ocean voyage with her three children, several maids, and "the honest Röckel," her gardener, an old family retainer. She sailed on April 16, 1777.

On June 23, in what had been a Jesuit church in Montreal, Burgoyne called his war council. It included the chiefs of six Indian tribes, fine, tall warriors under the charge of Colonel Barry St. Leger. Riedesel and his officers were astonished at their Indian allies, who "to show their fiery tempers . . . had painted their eyelids red and smeared their new uniforms with red ocher as a sign that they were to fight for life or to the death. They were armed with long-shot guns and sharp knives for use in taking scalps."

The British intended to use the principle of "frightfulness" *(Schrecklichkeit)* as a weapon. The Indians were to be paid two guineas for each rebel scalp they brought in. "Warriors," said Burgoyne, "go forth in might and valor of your cause—strike at the common enemies of Great Britain and America—disturbers of public order, peace and happiness, destroyers of commerce. . . . I positively forbid bloodshed when you are not opposed in arms. Aged men, women, children, and prisoners must be held sacred from the knife or hatchet, even in actual conflict."

Edmund Burke, an Irish M.P. who disapproved of the British role in America, scathingly criticized Burgoyne in the House of Commons. He imagined a riot on Tower Hill, where the royal menagerie was kept. "What would the Keeper of His Majesty's lions do? Would he not fling open the dens of the wild beasts and then address them thus? 'My gentle lions—my humane bears—my tender-hearted hyenas, go forth! But I exhort you, as you are Christian and members of civilized society, to take care not to hurt any man, woman, or child!'" Lord North, the prime minister who had sanctioned the employment of the Indians, laughed at Burke's riposte until tears ran down his cheeks.

During the French and Indian wars and at the time of Chief Pontiac's rebellion, Lord Jeffery Amherst, the commander of the British military, "despised red men," wrote the historian Ray Allen Billington,

as he did the beasts of the forest; "could it not be contrived," he wrote to Bouquet, "to send the Small Pox among those dissatisfied tribes?" And Bouquet replied that he would try to distribute germ-laden blankets among them, adding, "as it is a pity to expose men against them, I wish we could make use of the Spanish method, to hunt them with English dogs . . . who would, I think effectually extirpate or remove that vermin."

But now, in 1777, the same Indians the British would have destroyed were to be used in terrorizing the rebels.

Riedesel kept up appearances, although to his mother he wrote bitterly in May, 1776: "I am surrounded only by Englishmen who are drunk with haughtiness. With these people, I *have* to get along;

but if something happens you may be sure it will be my fault."

Riedesel was firm enough with his own troops, but Burgoyne gave him other troubles. The Brunswick dragoons, who were to have obtained horses in Canada, found there were none and they were serving unmounted. Consequently, they were singularly ill equipped for the fighting that lay ahead. Their thick Prussian-blue coats were too tight for the heat, their leather pants too stiff, their high-spurred, above-the-knee jackboots weighed twelve pounds each, their long broadswords, designed for cavalry action, dragged close to the ground when they walked, and their rifles, designed for close action, were short-ranged.

The campaign to end the war by Christmas began in June, 1777. St. Leger and his contingent of British, Germans, and a thousand Iroquois, under the famed Indian leader Joseph Brant, moved out first. They went by ships to Lake Ontario, where they took the small fortress at Oswego, and then moved quickly to capture Fort Stanwix. This fort had been built in 1758 to dominate the portage, the "great carrying place" as the Indians called it, on the upper Mohawk River. By July 25, Barry St. Leger had reached Fort Stanwix and began the preliminary stages of the siege.

On the first day of July, 1777, the main army, a vast flotilla of Anglo-Brunswicker troops, conveyed on frigates, pinnaces, sloops, ketches and an uncounted number of open flatboats—*batteaux*—including four hundred Indian "scouts and scalpers," set off to carry out Burgoyne's plan.

They pushed on to Fort Ticonderoga. A British artillery officer, who spotted an unfortified hill dominating the fortress, observed, "Where a goat can go a man can go, and where a man can go he can drag a gun." Suiting this amazing deduction to action, a cannon was hauled to the top of Mount Defiance, thereby putting an end to the siege of Fort Ticonderoga. At night, the Americans abandoned it, leaving behind vast military stores.

General Riedesel, while thumbing through his dog-eared copy of Burgoyne's *Thoughts for Conducting the War from the Side of Canada*, had noted a tactical departure. The plan of the campaign was to ferry down all heavy guns and troops on flatboats. This now had been changed at the suggestion of Philip Skene.

A loyalist and proprietor of a royal patent of thirty-four thousand acres of land at the head of Lake Champlain, Skene had founded a colony, which he called Skenesborough, of houses, forges, lime kilns, sawmills, and even a shipyard. When hostilities began, General Benedict Arnold captured Skenesborough and held Skene's family captive. Skene was a large person, "pleasant and with affable deportment," the sort of man whom Burgoyne could trust. Skene therefore suggested his township for use as Burgoyne's headquarters. Thus, instead of going easily by the water route, they now had to drag siege guns through the forest; the oozily soft lakeside trail had to be corduroyed with logs, a costly, time-consuming business. All of Riedesel's military recommendations were brushed aside. Burgoyne settled himself at Skenesborough and brought up "Mrs. Commissary," his mistress, the military commissary's wife.

"It is very true," wrote the Baroness von Riedesel, "that General Burgoyne liked to make himself easy, and that he spent his nights in singing and drinking, and diverting himself with the wife of a commissary, who was his mistress. She was as fond of champaign as himself."

The wives of other officers and soldiers also came along. And there were many. Baron von Riedesel's wife appeared with her three daughters (Gustava, age six, Fredericke, age three, and the youngest, Caroline, who had her first birthday in America) along with her maids and "the honest Röckel." They were installed in a house near Fort Anne on Woods Creek, a few miles from Skenesborough. There the Baroness settled down as a soldier's wife, and from there she began to write long letters to her family at Wolfenbüttel, telling about the Indians, the vast forests, and how she had eaten bear meat ("I tasted it for the first time and found it delightful and loved it"). She would be an eyewitness to the making of American history.

Whenever Baron von Riedesel could break away from his duties, he would spend the night with his wife and children. They talked often over the leaks to the enemy. "I observed," she wrote home, "with surprise that the wives of officers were beforehand informed of all the military plans. I was so much the more struck with it as I remembered how much secrecy there was in the armies of the Duke of Brunswick during the Seven Years' War." It was precisely this lack of secrecy that led Lieutenant Colonel Baum and seven hundred Brunswickers to defeat.

This famous painting by John Vanderlyn shows the killing of Jane McCrea, the fiancée of a British officer, by British Indian auxiliaries.

Burgoyne had promised the Baron horses for his dragoons. Now he had "intelligence" that great military stores were to be had in Bennington, Vermont, with an uncounted number of horses. This should have been a swift raid of lightly armed men, but Burgoyne turned the honor over to the Germans, along with a "cloud of Indians" and "Tory spies." On August 11, Lieutenant Colonel Friedrich Baum took off with his men. Bogged down with two canoes, they were over-armed and overextended. Each carried, in a pathetically hopeful gesture, a halter to secure the soon-to-be-captured horses. The Indians, instead of acting as scouts, killed cattle for their cow bells, so terrifying the people that soon the whole countryside was aroused. Then they went on a scalping spree and took the long-tressed scalp of Jane McCrea. Actually she leaned toward the king; her fiancé, a loyalist, was serving with Burgoyne's army. Her death was given wide publicity and was to have sweeping repercussions, for it provided the Americans with a rare propaganda item. It caused Burgoyne to call a meeting to explain the rules of "selective scalping." The next day the Indians had gone, and with them went the scouts who were Burgoyne's eyes and ears.

The American militia formed their battle companies under General John Stark. The German commander, Baum, made a quick estimate of the situation and sent off a runner for reinforcements. Soon the Brunswickers were surrounded and overwhelmed. The munition wagon exploded, leaving them without shot, and then Baum gave his last order. His men unsheathed sabers and began to cut their way out of the siege. They had made good progress when Baum took a ball in the chest.

The Americans had killed, wounded, or captured seven hundred "solid" Germans and a mass of military matériel. Colonel Breymann, who came to aid, also lost heavily, although he was able to bring back the bulk of his men. Burgoyne rode out and met the men, besplattered and wounded, and gave a florid speech complimenting them on "their very pretty success."

On the other end of the spectrum were the troops of Colonel Barry St. Leger, still standing before Fort Stanwix.

St. Leger, who had spent twenty of his forty years in the army, was, as portrayed by Sir Joshua Reynolds, a handsome officer. His force consisted of Royal Greens, a company of Tory Rangers, three hundred fifty Hesse-Hanau Jägers, and one thousand Indians under Joseph Brant. Out of range of the fort, Barry St. Leger paraded his men in a gay display. More impressive to the defenders of the fort, who knew what the fate of their families would be if the fort surrendered, were the Indians. It made them all the more determined to resist. The American commander of the fort, Colonel Peter Gamesvoort, had meanwhile sent off a runner to warn the militiamen of the Mohawk Valley, and soon the relief party, composed mostly of German settlers, were moving to its relief under the command of General Nicolaus Herkimer. A German emigrant from the Palatine, Herkimer had gained experience in the French and Indian wars and was the leader of the Committee of Public Safety and organizer of four battalions of infantry, mostly German-speaking, ranging in age from sixteen to sixty. These he marched off to relieve the fort.

On August 6, despite a screen of friendly Oneida Indians who moved ahead on his flanks, Herkimer's battalions fell into a well-laid ambush, and in the melee Herkimer had his knee smashed by a bullet. He was dragged to a tree and there, sitting on his saddle, coolly pulling on his pipe, he directed the operation of the grim battle.

The alarm sent off to Albany brought General Benedict Arnold, who swept together a relief force. He managed, by a ruse, to magnify his numbers, and so fearful was the name of Arnold that Barry St. Leger's force promptly evacuated and the threat ended. Herkimer, as he lay dying, believed he had failed. In General Washington's judgment he had not. Herkimer's stubborn stand against the force of St. Leger was one of the principal factors leading up to the British debacle at Saratoga.

Under a magnificent autumn sky, Burgoyne's army was in full advance along the banks of the Hudson. Albany lay only twenty miles away. Baroness von Riedesel had at first been told that she would have to return to Canada. She demurred, won out, and thus, children and all, followed behind the army. "I would have purchased at any price the privilege granted of seeing my husband daily." She sent back everything but light summer dresses, for she had little doubt that they would reach Albany—"the promised land." "My dear Baroness," oozed General Burgoyne in confirmation, "you must know that we British never retrograde."

"In the beginning all went well," she wrote. Then strange sounds began coming out of the forest: the eery nerve-twanging, gobble-gobble of a wild turkey. This particular wild turkey turned out to be Daniel Morgan, a veteran of Quebec and a trained forest fighter, talking to his men. Shots came out of the wood, men fell wounded and dead. Burgoyne split his army into three sections. Riedesel went to the left bank of the Hudson, Fraser to the right, and Burgoyne remained in the center. As soon as they had contacted the enemy and battle was joined, a cannon shot would be the signal for uniting the three units.

The weather grew colder. The first flock of geese flew by, urgently honking their way south from Canada. For those who knew, it was the prelude to a frigid winter. At night wolves unearthed the half-buried bodies, and bears went about berry-gathering in late harvest. At Freeman's Farm, a cleared area where wheat had been recently threshed, the Anglo-Germans advanced toward the American fortification at Bemis Heights. Suddenly the wheat field whirled with bullets. Within minutes every cannonier had been shot by the Americans; six hundred men were lost the first day. The British threw up breastworks and that old veteran, Captain Pauch of the Hesse-Hanau artillery (who left a personal narrative of the battle), brought up his guns and poured a lively barrage of grapeshot into the American ranks. But behind British lines the Americans were cutting off their escape.

One September evening Riedesel dined with his wife at the Taylor house, a few yards from the Hudson River and a quarter of a mile from where the battle raged. "Burgoyne assured us," wrote the Baroness, "that our troops had been victorious . . . but my husband told me everything went badly and to be prepared to depart."

Burgoyne still believed that Sir Henry Clinton would make contact with him. Early in October there had been action up the Hudson River where Scotch and Irish brigades, reinforced with German Jägers, were making slow progress. Burgoyne called a staff meeting. Riedesel's estimate of the situation was that they should leave the heavier guns behind and make a strategic retreat *now*. They should shorten the lines of communications and await new supplies and reinforcements from Canada.

Burgoyne, reasserting that Britons "never retrograde," ordered another assault in an attempt to turn the enemy's left flank. It began badly. Many officers were killed or wounded. Burgoyne insisted, in the middle of battle, on giving a formal military funeral to General Fraser. "Many cannon balls," wrote Baroness von Riedesel, "flew close to me, but my whole attention was engaged by the funeral scene. . . ."

The strategic retreat that Riedesel had suggested was now too late. They were completely surrounded. The army had to "retrograde" in the rain. Still Burgoyne lingered, putting the army on half rations. "Pork, pork, pork," complained a German soldier in his letters. "Pork at noon, pork at night, pork cold, pork warm. Friends! . . . you would have looked with loathing at our pork, yet pork was to us a lordly dish, without which we should have starved. . . ."

The Riedesel house was turned into a hospital and was immediately an object for bombardment. "We were at last," the Baroness said, "obliged to descend into the cellar, where I laid myself in a corner near the door. My children put their heads upon my knees. . . . On the next morning, the cannonade began anew, but in a different direction. . . . Eleven cannon balls passed through the house, and made a tremendous noise. A poor soldier, who was about to have a leg amputated, lost the other by one of these cannon balls. We heard his groans and lamentations during the whole night. . . . I endeavoured to dispel my melancholy by continually attending to the wounded. . . ."

On October 13, Burgoyne asked for surrender terms, and on October 17, 1777, the "Convention of Saratoga" was signed. The Baroness did not hide her fury at Burgoyne's ineptitude. Later she brought formal charges against him in the House of Commons.

Saratoga was a stupendous victory for the Americans. Two lieutenant generals were captured, along with two major generals, three brigadiers with their staffs and aides, 299 other officers, ranging from colonels to ensigns, chaplains, and surgeons; 389 noncommissioned officers, 197 musicians, and 4,836 privates passed out of the armed forces of Great Britain in America. The matériel captured was of vast importance; it included twenty-seven guns of various calibers, five thousand stands of small arms, great quantities of ammunition, and military stores and equipment of all kinds.

But the Baroness maintained her spirit. She sewed the colors of their regiment into their mattress, got into her "dear calash," and rode off through the American lines to a troubled capture. First they went to Albany, then Boston, and later to Cambridge, where they were put up in a two-storied house on Brattle Street, known as Tory Row because so many loyalists had lived there. But the American Congress found them too costly, and the German troops were eventually marched down to Virginia, where, at Charlottesville, Thomas Jefferson watched their arrival.

The Riedesels were soon very friendly with Jefferson, who allowed the Baroness a piano. As usual among the Germans, there were several musicians, and they accompanied the Baroness when she sang Italian arias. Jefferson was sorry to see the Riedesels go when the General was finally exchanged for an American officer of equal rank. Riedesel sent Jefferson a farewell note of "heartiest thanks for every mark of Friendship which you have so kindly testified to me from the first moments of our acquaintance. . . ."

In March, 1780, in New York City, the Baroness gave birth to another daughter. "My husband had wished for a son, but the little one was so pretty that we were reconciled over its not having been a boy. We had intended naming the boy 'Americus,' but the name now had to be changed for the little daughter into 'America.'"[2]

General von Riedesel was gazetted to Canada again, where the Baroness gave birth to another child, whom she called Canada. Her spirited narrative became such a part of American history that, two hundred years later, it is still being read. It is as fresh and human as it was when it was first written.

---

[2]America von Riedesel in time married Ernest Count von Bernstorff. In 1914 a descendant, Johann Count von Bernstorff, became the Imperial German ambassador to the United States of America. In a touching gesture, Count von Bernstorff visited the Schuyler house in Schuylerville, New York, where the Baroness von Riedesel had taken refuge during the battle, and there left reproductions of the five Riedesel daughters.

Distribution of Germans in North and South America.

The World Turned Upside Down XI

The victory at Saratoga became the catalyst for two events. France signed a treaty for participation in the war, and Baron von Steuben was dispatched to America. General John A. Palmer, his American biographer, states that, "in evaluating our debt to France, we should not forget that one of her greatest services was to send us this Prussian expert."

France was, in a sense, digging its political grave by participating in a war which proclaimed as its ideal "liberty and justice for all," yet most of the courtiers who frequented the Court of Versailles were enthusiastic about entering the American war. Not so Louis XVI. If he entered the American contest at all it would be not to set up an American republic, but to discomfort the British, hoping thereby to allow France to retrieve its West Indies islands—source of sugar, rum, and spices—which had yielded to British sea power.

To aid the French in getting off the political fence, Benjamin Franklin had been at the Court of Versailles since 1776. There he joined the other American representatives seeking credit, supplies, and commitment to their cause. They had already achieved one success; the Marquis de Lafayette, aged twenty, had secretly equipped two ships and had already gone to America where, to the astonishment of everyone, including himself, he was made a major general in the Continental army.

Even though the revolt of the American colonies was a challenge to absolutism, the American war was enormously popular in the French court, which leaped at the chance to strike a blow against England and at the same time test the theories of Rousseau and the other *philosophes* about the nobility of natural man. The French government was interested in "the intentions of the [Americans], their resources and plans for revolt to determine whether they are

Beginning in 1777, Colonel von Steuben (1730–94) drilled the American militia according to Prussian methods. He was finally appointed inspector general of all the troops. Here he is shown inspecting the troops.

worth helping." Before 1778 the government involved France in the American war by setting up Hortalez et Cie, into which funds were channeled to purchase supplies, especially a potent new gunpowder perfected by the chemist Antoine Lavoisier, who would later fall victim to another revolution.

There were still many Germanies, a bewildering patchwork of dukedoms and fiefs; only Prussia was at that time a political entity in itself. There were Germans, such as the royal houses of Hesse and Brunswick, who gave, or sold, their troops to England for use against the Americans. On the other hand there was Frederick the Great and the Prussians, who stood away from it and admired the American effort—a feeling which, as Henry A. Pochmann points out, America returned. Then there were Germans serving in France, such as Baron Ludwig von Closen, aide to Count de Rochambeau; and others, such as the House of Pfalz-Zweibrücken or, as they preferred to call themselves, the Royal Deuxponts.

Zweibrücken—Deuxponts—which lay in the coal-rich areas of the Saar on the French-German border, had shifted so often back and forth between speech and rule that it was as much French-German as German-French. All higher culture in the eighteenth century was European, and most of its nobility spoke French. And because Versailles was attractive to these princelings, they gravitated to that court. Thus the Royal Deuxponts.

Countess Forbach of Zweibrücken knew Benjamin Franklin so well that she gave him a walking stick. He, in turn, gave it to George Washington. "My pretty walking stick," he wrote, ". . . I bequeath to my friend . . . General Washington. . . . This stick was given to me by an extraordinary woman, Madame Forbach, the Duchess-widow of Zweibrücken." She had two sons, Wilhelm and Christian, who were to lead their regiments to final victory at Yorktown.

On February 6, 1778, Benjamin Franklin, in a simple suit and wearing his hair unpowdered (Franklin claimed he could not afford court dress and his hired wig did not arrive in time), joined Silas Deane and Arthur Lee, the other American representatives at the Court, and signed a treaty of alliance with France. At the ceremony Louis XVI said, "I hope that this will be for the good of both nations."

One of the good things was Baron Friedrich Wilhelm von Steuben, who was to turn a rabble into an army and, by the sheer drive of his personality, help forge a fighting force. He was also to write its first military manuals (still a force in the American army), becoming in the process one of the most popular and picaresque figures in American history.

When Benjamin Franklin interviewed von Steuben in Paris, he knew that the name of Frederick the Great was a talisman to literary Americans. Yet the fact that von Steuben had served in Frederick's army was not sufficient. Franklin knew the feelings of the American Congress toward foreign adventurers seeking commands.

Benjamin Franklin as American envoy to France in 1783.

General Palmer, von Steuben's biographer, leaves no doubt that Franklin himself tutored the Prussian officer in what he must *not* say to Congress in order that they might both attain their ends. Franklin knew men and he knew the world. He had visited Göttingen University, the first American to do so, was a member of the prestigious British Royal Society and a founder of the American one, and was rightfully proud of the range of his experience.

Von Steuben was not, as he styled himself (and as time and documents have proven), "Baron" von Steuben, lieutenant general in the Prussian army, possessor of vast estates, and an intimate of Frederick the Great. German scholars have found documents at Karlsruhe showing that von Steuben was a descendant of one Augustin Steuben, who emerged, through the assistance of an accommodating genealogist, with the sonorous names and titles by which his grandson became known to America.

Yet von Steuben had been an officer in the Prussian army, had served with distinction in many battles, had corresponded with Frederick the Great during the Seven Years' War, and was an aide-de-camp to the king, who recommended von Steuben to Franklin. His conceits were many, but so were his talents. When he appeared before Benjamin Franklin in 1777 he was only a Prussian captain, forty-seven years old, and out of service.

Von Steuben arrived at Boston on December 14, 1777, and was made a guest of the nation. He changed into the uniform of a major general of the Continental army and set off to meet the members of the American Congress. "Only fancy to yourself," said the chatty Peter Stephen (née Pierre Duponceau), von Steuben's secretary and aide, "an old German baron, with a large brilliant star on his breast, three French aides-de-camp, and a large, spoiled Italian dog. None of all that company except [myself] could speak a word of English."

Following the advice given him, von Steuben kept a singularly aloof attitude about money or rank, explaining that having been obliged to relinquish his income in Germany to come to America, all he would ask was that Congress defray his expenses should his services be of value. Thereupon a verbal agreement was made. Should he effectively contribute to the success of the American cause, he would be entitled to reimbursement for the expenses of his journey to America and to indemnification for an income of about six hundred guineas from the summer of 1777 until the date of his discharge from the army. Thereafter he would be entitled to the same income until the end of his life, or to the capital value of such an annuity.

He arrived at Valley Forge on February 23, 1778, where George Washington's welcome was cordial and sincere. It was then the nadir of the revolution. The American army had lost the battles of Brandywine and Germantown, the British were occupying Philadelphia and New York, and another huge expedition was gathering in Canada (happily to be diverted by the victory at Saratoga). The American soldiers were ill clad, ill shod, and the regiments were depleted because enlistment time had run out. There were many desertions. Yet von Steuben recognized in this ragged soldiery a spirit as good as any he had ever seen. "No army in Europe," he told Washington, "would have held together under such deprivations."

On March 19, Carl Vogel, the Baron's valet, dressed the General's peruke and powdered his wig while von Steuben drank coffee and smoked his clay pipe. Then, with his dog Azor running alongside, von Steuben mounted and rode out to see the American army. "Never before or since," said an American officer, "have I had an impression of the ancient fabled God of War as when I looked on the Baron: he seemed to me a perfect personification of Mars—the trappings of his horse, the enormous holsters of his pistols, his large size, and his strikingly martial aspect. . . ."

Language was the first and immediate problem. Von Steuben spoke French and German, but no English. Washington turned over to him two military aides, John Laurens and Colonel Alexander Hamilton. In order to prepare drill regulations von Steuben would dictate in French, Hamilton would translate in polished English, and, since there was no time to print the drill regulations, one for each battalion had to be written in holograph. The result was that once the instructions were in English, von Steuben could neither read nor understand his own text. As the regulations were being written out, von Steuben took to learning his own drill regulations in English. He did it by rote.

The indefatigable von Steuben, toiling from reveille until taps, relied mostly upon pantomime; each of the infantry movements he illustrated himself over and over again until it had sunk into the brains of those who attended—his "School of Soldiers," as he called them. He progressed from detail to squad, from squad to platoon, from company to regiment, then on to entire brigades and, in time, the whole army. "A new American army was forged by Steuben on the bleak, windswept plateau at Valley Forge."

The perseverance of von Steuben turned the language handicap into success. At first the soldiers were understandably amused by his broken English—wonderfully rich in profanity under stress. He quickly used up his English *wortschatz*, lapsed into French, and then exploded in German. From that time forward, writes General Palmer, "Steuben became one of the most popular figures in the affections of the plain soldiers of the Continental Army."

The immediate result of von Steuben's training was the somewhat pyrrhic victory at Monmouth, New Jersey. With France now active

in the war, their first feint by sea had been at the lightly held islands in the West Indies. This immediately changed British strategy. London ordered its fleet to the West Indies along with five thousand troops, which meant that Sir Henry Clinton must move out of Philadelphia because of the scarcity of British ships. The bulk of his army had to move by land across the whole of New Jersey.

At three o'clock in the morning, June 18, 1778, the Anglo-German troops crossed the Delaware River and began their long, exposed march. Von Steuben believed it was a chance to crush their forces; they had fifteen hundred wagons strung out for miles. It was a killing march for the Germans and the British. The weather turned suddenly tropical, with fierce, wind-driven rain; the innumerable bridges crossing the bogs and creeks of the New Jersey flatlands had

*Colonel von Steuben in-
structing recruits at
Valley Forge.*

been broken by the American partisans, so that vital hours were
consumed in repairing them. General von Knyphausen had not only
to face American bayonets, but the attacks of mosquitoes as well.
"My soldiers' faces," he wrote, "were so swollen by the bites of mosquitoes that they were beyond recognition." Two hundred thirty
Hessians deserted on the march.

On the plains of Monmouth the British formed a line and gave
formal battle. Von Steuben, out of range, sat proudly observing
through his telescope the battle of his "sans culottes," as he affection-
ately called them. "I thought that my children moved up with as much
precision as an ordinary parade and with . . . the intrepidity of veteran
troops." The army was responding to von Steuben's training in field
discipline.

While the Battle of Monmouth raged, it produced, among other things, America's first heroine—Molly Pitcher. She was born Molly Ludwig in Trenton, New Jersey, the daughter of German immigrants who were indentured servants. She married a native American named John Caspar Hays, who enlisted in a colonial artillery company in 1775. Herself employed as a servant to a family in Pennsylvania, she returned to New Jersey to visit her parents and be near her soldier-husband when she learned that Washington's Continental army was on the way. During the battle she carried water from a nearby spring to the thirsty troops, thereby earning her nickname, Molly Pitcher. When Hays collapsed from heat prostration, she manned his gun and was dubbed "sergeant" by the soldiers. George Washington, reviewing troops after the battle, personally complimented her.[1]

Monmouth was a standoff victory; the Anglo-German armies, although they suffered severe losses, slipped away during the night and boarded transports which took them to New York. It was a tactical victory for the Americans, "but the forger of that victory," writes General Palmer, "was done in the bellows (and bellowing) of Steuben. This new birth of the Continental Army as a trained fighting machine is Steuben's contribution to the history—and victory—of the War of Independence."

In 1779 the war moved south. Lord Charles Cornwallis (the only British general who seemed to know how to handle an army) moved across wide frontiers, attacking cities, conquering many and burning others. He forced the Americans to be constantly on the defensive; with command of the sea, the British freely moved their troops anywhere.

Charleston, South Carolina, was put under siege. Its fifteen thousand inhabitants were the richest and gayest in the American colonies, among them quite a few German Jews, many of whom were doctors. Down the coast the marauding armies went, along with the Waldeckers and Hessians, marching through Georgia into Florida. The Waldeckers even found a German-speaking Indian; he had deserted

---

[1]Molly lived with Hays until his death in 1789, after which she married George McCauley. In 1822 the Pennsylvania legislature awarded her an annuity for life: "Act for the relief of Molly M'Kolly." She died in Carlisle, Pennsylvania, on January 22, 1832.

the Waldeck regiment and after many adventures had become an Indian.

Everywhere, again and again, American troops were beaten, yet they displayed an awesome resilience. Finally, at the Battle of Camden, South Carolina, the Americans lost General de Kalb.

"Baron" de Kalb, as he styled himself, was in all honesty born simply as Johann Kalb. The son of a Bavarian peasant, he left home at sixteen, joined the army, and fought his way up the hard way. By 1743 he appeared in the army lists as Lieutenant Jean de Kalb, and after four years he was listed a captain. In the Seven Years' War, when he fought against the Germans, he became a major, and after the peace (1763) he rose to be colonel. After that he took for himself the title of Baron, married Anne van Robais, daughter of a wealthy French manufacturer, and inherited vast estates in Courbevoie. His participation in the American war was the most disinterested since he lacked neither money nor fame. De Kalb spoke English, French, and German, and, since he rose from the ranks, was one of the most capable officers. Over six feet tall, with hazel eyes that always seemed to be laughing, he bore hardships with good grace and could walk thirty miles a day. Now he was fighting his last fight.

The Americans gave way under a bayonet charge at Camden. The German-speaking Maryland and Delaware troops, under the command of General de Kalb, fought off all attacks, rallying about de Kalb's figure as one would about a standard. "Long after the battle was lost," says John Fiske, the historian, "the gigantic form of de Kalb fighting on foot, directing the Maryland German troops could be seen." His head was laid open with a saber cut; he had taken eleven bayonet thrusts when Chevalier du Buysson, a friend of Lafayette, tried to cover his body from further attacks. Bleeding to death from his wounds, de Kalb held on to a cannon wheel, fending off British troops who were trying to tear off his regimentals. Three days later, de Kalb died in Camden.

The continuous defeats were especially galling to the Americans, who had expected, after the French declaration of intentions, that they would participate actively. There was, as yet, no visual form of support, and more, there had been a mutiny among the soldiers at Morristown and it had spread to Pennsylvania. The British hastened to take advantage, until they found that the mutiny only had to do with the failure of Congress to pay a year's wages. The mutiny seemed to cause Baron von Steuben no anxiety, but other news arriving at the same time did: Benedict Arnold had defected to the British. An accomplice, the British Major John André, was captured and von Steuben was ordered by Washington back to West Point to sit on André's court martial.

This event shattered von Steuben, as it did many Americans, for General Arnold was an excellent field officer. Above all else, he was a warrior with a good tactical instinct, a natural leader of men, and a good fighter.

Born in Norwich, Connecticut, in 1741, the great-grandson of a Benedict Arnold who had once been governor of Rhode Island, he had been apprenticed at fourteen to a firm of druggists. While still young he left home to enlist in a New York regiment to fight against the French. Later "Dr." Arnold, as he was called, moved to New Haven, opened a pharmaceutical shop, prospered as a merchant, bought ships, and captained them himself to the West Indies. He was proud, arrogant, highly sensitive, and easily slighted. A good warrior—by far the best in the American army—he was often passed over for promotions. He had been wounded at Quebec and Saratoga, and to allow his wounds to heal he was placed in charge of strategic West Point on the Hudson River.

In May, 1779, Arnold began his overtures to the British. While Sir Henry Clinton was away, the correspondence of treachery devolved on Lieutenant General von Knyphausen. Under the sobriquet of "Mr. Moore," Arnold began to feed him top army secrets.

Thus were two Germans involved in the drama of Arnold— Knyphausen and Steuben. Both were highly placed in opposing armies: each known to the other; each related by strong ties to their native land; yet each at opposite ends of the political spectrum. Yet both would do their duty, for each had sworn fealty to the cause he served.

Von Steuben was, with Lafayette, the only non-American on the court-martial board. The old Baron knew his duty. He, along with the others, signed the verdict: "Major André, adjutant general to the British army, ought to be considered as a spy from the enemy; and . . . suffer death."

Colonel David Franks of Pennsylvania, one of the German Jews who took an active part in the war, found his life hanging in the balance; he had been an aide-de-camp to Arnold, but it was shown that he had no connection with the treason. He later became an aide to Washington, and his home in Germantown was for a time used as Washington's headquarters.

There were then no more than fifteen hundred German Jews in the North American colonies. The oldest synagogue in New York, dating from 1654, had a member, Colonel Nathan Myers, in command of a brigade stationed in the city. The Jews who were established in Rhode Island and those in Maryland had begun to join their German confreres quite early. In Baltimore the colony of Germans and German Jews had increased to such an extent that they formed a substantial part of the Continental army, known as the Maryland Line. By a convention, four regiments of soldiers were set up only for Germans; the rolls of those who formed these regiments are still preserved.

Baltimore was also divided in its sentiments; some Germans were involved in the Tory conspiracy. Seven were condemned to death and executed in a manner reminiscent of the Middle Ages. One who perished was Caspar Fritchie, father-in-law of the famous heroine Barbara Fritchie.

William Hoffmann, who began the paper industry in Maryland, was given large printing orders by the Continental army. He had been born in Frankfurt-am-Main in 1740, trained as a papermaker in the Old World, and followed the same trade in the New. He settled two hundred German papermakers in an area he called the "Papermills," and there was printed the first paper money for the Continental Congress.

The German Jews of Baltimore were also active in the American cause. Jacob Hart loaned General Lafayette $7,256 for his American troops, and Congress thanked the "exertions of the merchants of Baltimore." South Carolina, too, had its complement of Jewish patriots—the Cardozas, Cohens, Isaacs. Further, the Jews fought under their commander Abraham Seixas, who formed a corp of volunteer infantry.

In Georgia there was a small colony of German Jews who had appeared when the Salzburgers arrived. One of the earliest was

Mordecai Sheftall (as his name was Anglicized). He was involved in a court martial because he had charge of the American army stores in that area when the British occupied Georgia in December, 1788. He was regarded by the British as a "Great Rebel," held in a common jail, and would have perished had not a Hessian officer named Zeltman, "finding he could speak his language," allowed him to communicate with his family.

At long last, in 1781, the French were arriving in force. The very day of his arrival the French commander, Comte de Rochambeau, wrote to Washington defining his own status and that of his troops: "Sir: The commands of the King, my master, place me under the orders of Your Excellency. I come, wholly obedient. . . ."

The British now feared an attack on New York City. Sir Henry Clinton dispatched an urgent message to Lord Charles Cornwallis, who, with his generals (Benedict Arnold among them), was in the act of turning the southern states upside down. Clinton ordered Cornwallis to drop back on a seaport with all his troops and be prepared to dispatch part of his army to reinforce New York. This is the reason that Cornwallis and his victorious army slowly moved into the little tobacco port of Yorktown at the estuary of the York River in Virginia. No one had the slightest idea that Yorktown would be the scene of the last formal battle, or that it would end in America's independence.

With the British troops there were 1,725 Hessians, Waldeckers, Ansbachers, and Bayreuthers under the command of Lieutenant General von Bose. These Germans had fought in every engagement in the American war, even into Florida and Louisiana, where the English colonel capitulated and the Germans passed into Spanish captivity. Now they were concentrated in Yorktown. At the smaller fortress of Gloucester, across the river, the British command placed Captain Johann von Ewald and his Jägers. He had fought against German-speaking American troops, but he had given strict instructions that Baron von Steuben was not to be fired on no matter what the circumstances.

The developing Yorktown battle was well chronicled by German soldiers. Lieutenant Stephan Popp of the Jägers, serving with the Ansbach regiment, wrote in his diary of the labor they had to endure

Uniforms of the Third Regiment of the Guards of the Margrave of Ansbach, who fought on the side of the British.

in trying to fortify Yorktown. Johann Conrad Doehle of the Bayreuth regiment told how guns had been removed from warships to be placed in the fortress: "This Yorktown . . . is a small city of approximately three hundred houses; . . . [with] considerable circumference. It is located on the bank of the York River, somewhat high on a sandy but level ground. It has three churches . . . but without steeples, and two Quaker meetinghouses, and a beautiful court or meetinghouse, which building, like the majority of the houses, is built of bricks. Here stood many houses which were destroyed and abandoned by their occupants. There was a garrison of three hundred [American] militia-men here, but upon our arrival they marched away without firing a shot."

Also present at Yorktown was Roger Lamb of the 23rd Welsh Fusiliers. He had served with Burgoyne, was captured and escaped, journeying fifteen hundred miles to rejoin the army. It was his memoirs that Robert Graves used as a basis for his book *Proceed Sergeant Lamb*. Lamb showed a complete indifference to the thirty thousand German troops in the British army, a force which amounted to about half of the fighting force. Sergeant Lamb mentioned Hessian Jägers only in passing and only rarely their "regularity and bravery." Yet in Yorktown the Germans comprised one third of the British force.

Cornwallis, meanwhile, was directing the building of redoubts at Yorktown. Doehle left a detailed account of the early days of the siege. He told of his "unloading duty," bringing ashore munitions and provisions for a protracted siege. He also noted the vast number in sick bay: "September 12. We get terrible provisions now, putrid ship's meat and wormy biscuits." Many of them were down with the "bloody flux" or diarrhea. The fever was spreading "and we had little rest day or night, partly because of the poor food."

The war of words among the British commanders then was far deadlier than the war of bullets. Cornwallis was dueling with his commanding general, Sir Henry Clinton, as to the strategy to be adopted. Clinton thought that the meeting between Washington and Rochambeau meant an attack on New York; therefore he wanted to dispatch transports to remove Cornwallis' army to New York.

On August 18, Lieutenant Colonel Ludwig von Wurmb, the commander of the Hessian Jägers, informed General Clinton that he was certain the Americans would attack Yorktown. He had learned that a French officer had sent his mistress to Trenton, which could only mean that the Franco-American army would be going southward. Too, his scouts had reported seeing depots of food and forage staked out all across the face of New Jersey, which could only mean an advancing army. General Clinton brushed aside all of von Wurmb's intelligence.

On September 28 the Anglo-German patrols heard sounds of the American army advancing for the siege. Once again German soldiers were noting in their diaries details of the opening battle. The French were attacking the outposts and von Bose's regiment was taking the brunt of the attack. "Private Zeilmann," wrote Doehle, "was killed at

An American soldier as a Bavarian officer saw and drew him: "They have long rifles and bayonets and are very hardy and healthy."

Americaner Soldat.

his post"; another comrade was wounded and Doehle sat on him while the surgeon extracted a ball from between his shoulder blades. "Today over thirty men were shot and wounded on detached outposts." The outposts were now pulled out and fell back to the Yorktown fortress. Stephan Popp wrote: "The regiments in the line moved back to the city because the enemy always came nearer and stronger. . . . In the night three of the men of our company deserted."

Lord Cornwallis had been assured of support. A cutter running the blockade had brought a letter from Sir Henry Clinton: "My Lord: At a meeting of the General and Flag officers held this day, it is determined that above five thousand men, rank and file, shall be embarked on board the King's ships."

Cornwallis was an experienced soldier. He had fought in the Seven Years' War, commanding a division at the Battle of Minden. He had always been foremost in British victories and now, at forty-three, he was in his prime. But he was sustained by two illusions: that reinforcements would arrive in time, and that the British fleet would overcome the French.

The siege lines about Yorktown were now completed. On October 9 the battle for the first redoubts began. This was to be Rochambeau's fifteenth siege, and his movements were followed by a young Bavarian, Baron Ludwig von Closen. As Rochambeau's military aide, von Closen tells in his journal how each morning at dawn he would inspect the position of the remaining British ships, accompanied by Count Wilhelm von Forbach of Zweibrücken.

Baron von Steuben was the only officer on the American side who knew the ritual of the siege, and he was determined to show that his American "sans culottes" were just as professional as the French. Baron von Closen said: "It is really painful to see these brave men, almost naked, with only trousers and linen jackets, most of them without stockings, but, would you believe it? very cheerful and healthy in appearance."

As so often in this war, Germans faced Germans, von Bose on the British side and von Steuben on the American. Their troops fought with gallant fierceness, while both sides faithfully recorded the incidents of a war that was not in the least their concern.

There was no doubt now about the outcome. Cornwallis was outgunned; cannon balls rained down on his redoubts. Captain von

Ewald was standing by a parapet when a British officer, in the act of firing a cannon, looked up to see its effect. A ball from the American side completely carried off his head. Nor were the American generals immune. Baron von Steuben was standing with General Anthony Wayne in a second parallel trench when a shell crashed only a few feet from them. Von Steuben dived into the trench and General Wayne fell on top of him as the bomb exploded. Said the Baron to Wayne: "I always knew you were brave, General, but I did not know you were perfect in every point of duty. You covered [my] retreat in the best manner possible."

On October 11, Doehle wrote in his diary about the "stupendous cannonading, during these twenty-four hours, thirty-six hundred shots were counted from the enemy, which they fired at the town, our line, and at the ships in the harbor. These ships were miserably ruined and shot to pieces. Also the bombs and cannon balls hit many inhabitants and Negroes of the city, and marines, soldiers, and sailors. One saw men lying nearly everywhere who were mortally wounded and whose heads, arms, and legs had been shot off. . . . I saw with astonishment . . . how cannon balls of twenty-four and more pounds flew over our whole line and the city into the river, where they often struck . . . ships. . . . The fragments and pieces of the bombs flew back again and fell on the houses and buildings where they . . . robbed many a brave soldier of his life or struck off an arm or a leg."

On the American side the honor of leading the first French assault was given to Count Wilhelm von Forbach. "On the 14th of October . . . at the assembly of the regiment . . . for duty in the trenches, the Baron de Viomenil ordered me to come . . . and gave me command of the battalion that he had just formed, telling me that he thought he gave me by that proof of his esteem and confidence."

Every leader who had fought from the beginning was there— Wayne, Greene, Hamilton, Lincoln, Mühlenberg, Knox—so that there was a natural fascination when, on October 17, a British officer stood on the parapet beside a diminutive drummer, waved a white flag, and held up a despatch. An excited red-faced aide burst into the command tent. Washington broke the seal and read: "Sir, I propose a cessation of hostilities for twenty-four hours, and that two officers may be appointed by each side to . . . settle terms for the surrender. . . . Cornwallis."

Lord Carnwallis surrenders at Yorktown to George Washington (from the painting by John Trumbull).

The surrender on October 19 was described by the victors. Although Christian von Forbach probably did not even fire a shot, he was present at the surrender and appears in John Trumbull's huge contemporary painting, *Surrender of Lord Cornwallis at Yorktown*. Cornwallis was indisposed, therefore he gave the actual surrender

over to Brigadier Charles O'Hara, the Irish-born general known less for his knowledge of warfare than for his fabulous uniforms.

Both forces were drawn up for the ceremony. It began when the American drum and fife corps played "Yankee Doodle"; the British came on with their bands playing "The World Turned Upside Down."

Never has so important an historical event been introduced with so pitifully banal a tune, thereby illustrating the ironical apothegm of Voltaire, who said, "When a thing becomes too stupid to say it, you sing it." The verse was:

> If butter cups buzzed after the bee,
> If boats were on land, churches on sea,
> If ponies rode men, and if grass ate the cows,
> And cats should be chased into holes by the mouse,
> If mamas sold their babies to the gypsies for half a crown,
> If summer were spring, and the other way 'round,
> Then all the world would be upside down.

The cat *was* chased into the hole by the mouse! Rank by rank the British grounded their weapons in front of the Americans. The Scotch wept and the British swore. The Americans observed that only the German contingents seemed to have performed with dignity. American observers were struck by the precision and polish with which the Germans marched out. The English were unable to match it; several American observers noted that many of the redcoats were thoroughly drunk and marched "most irregularly."

Among those whom General von Bose led out would be some of the best German officers in future wars. Dömberg, Langen, Senden, von Ewald were to apply the lessons in European wars that they had learned in America. All along the way Germans broke ranks to greet those who came from the same *heimat*. No one attempted to prevent German fraternization.

Washington sent his victory despatch to the American Congress at Philadelphia, but they knew of it two days before the official notice arrived. A Virginian officer had copied Cornwallis' request for surrender terms and sent it by pony express toward Philadelphia. The following day, October 23, Benjamin Franklin's newspaper told how "an honest old German, the official *wachtmeister* for Philadelphia Towne, had conducted the despatch rider at two a.m. to his Excellency the President of Congress, then continued his watch duties by calling out: 'Basht dree o'glock und Gornvallis ist gedaken!'"

It took several weeks for news of the surrender to reach London. Lord North, the prime minister, had it on the morning of November 25. "Oh God," Lord North exclaimed, pacing up and down in his offices at 10 Downing Street. "Oh God. It is over. It is all over."

And so it was, but not for the German contingents. Several years elapsed before many of them returned to their homelands. Of the 29,867 who were sent out, 4,626 were killed and one hundred twenty-seven unaccounted for—a surprisingly low mortality rate for eight years of service. Of those who came over, 12,554 chose to remain. Many remained with the consent of their officers, and the American Congress offered them every advantage.

It is astonishing [wrote Johann von Ewald] what stuff deserters often tell in order to please their new friends and obtain a good reception. After I had been taken prisoner at Yorktown and had made the acquaintance of several officers, a French general, then chief of the Deux-Ponts Regiment, asked me quite in confidence whether the Hessians were not very discontented with the English service. . . . I could not help laughing at his stories, and assured him that not a single word of all this was true, but quite the contrary, whereupon the general was very much astonished, for every deserter had assured him that it was so.

Quebec, before 1740, had attracted mostly Swiss Catholics and German-speaking Catholics from Alsace-Lorraine. The Germans who settled in Nova Scotia after 1750 did so for the same reasons they settled in America—religious persecution or the search for a *kleine Freiheit*. The British were then less concerned with nationality than with an emigrant's religion. They wanted Protestants in Canada to offset the dominant French Catholics. "In order to counterbalance the numerous and very prolific Acadians, it seemed a good policy," wrote a Canadian historian, "to bring Protestant settlers into the country, who owing to the difference in religion would not join the French party in cases of emergency. British settlers would have been best liked, of course, but from Great Britain there was little emigration at that time. . . . Therefore the British Government decided to attract Protestant settlers from Germany, France and Switzerland."

The British published invitations in Germany to settle in Nova Scotia. Between the years 1750–53, some twenty-three hundred immigrants settled in Halifax, a number of French and Swiss families among them. The French came chiefly from Montbéliard, a small district in the east of France not far from the border of Lorraine. It was known as a stronghold of the Reformation. The Germans came mostly from the electorate of Hanover, which at that time was under the English Crown; many came also from the Palatinate and the upper Rhineland.

They settled a town and called it Lüneberg after their old city in Hanover. As late as 1767 there were two hundred fifty German families in Lüneberg, while the French did not count more than fifty families. In schools English was taught in the morning, German in the afternoon.

After Yorktown, Canada became a haven for loyalists who had fled their native states. Maxwell Sutherland writes:

Among the loyalists and disbanded troops who thronged the environs of New York in 1783 was a small group of discharged soldiers and officers from the various German regiments. These natives of Hesse, Anhalt-Zerbst, Brunswick, Waldeck, and Ansbach-Bayreuth shared little in common with the human tide that flooded into the last British stronghold except their ultimate destination. Some were to find their way into Canada by the overland route from New York, but the majority, caught up in the prevailing enthusiasm of the Loyalists, intended to take passage to Nova Scotia, where they were to settle at Halifax, Shelburne, and near Annapolis Royal.

The British made generous offers of land. The governor of Nova Scotia was ordered to divide lands for twenty-six soldiers of the 3rd Waldeck Regiment who were "valuable tradesmen and . . . farmers."

Once they found themselves in Halifax, German soldiers sent for their wives and children in Germany, "by which time there were twenty-four Waldeckers, fourteen Ansbachers and Bayreuthians, five Brunswickers, at least forty-eight Hessians." The over-all picture was a little Teutonic island afloat in a sea of British loyalists, a babel of German provincial dialects surrounded by the loud murmur of colonial English.

The year 1796 brought another wave of Germans from the United States. A land speculator was sent to New York state looking for land on which to settle emigrants from Hamburg, but as Canada's terms were better it was decided to settle there instead, even though officials claimed that the immigrants from Germany were "the refuse of the streets of Hamburg." They came from the Old World as well as from New York and Pennsylvania, moving through the difficult land into the wilderness, their Conestoga wagons holding all their worldly possessions. German-American settlers seeking land in Canada moved up the Mohawk, Delaware, and Susquehanna rivers, made their rendezvous in what would become the city of Buffalo, and then moved into the raw wilderness east of Toronto and on into the Waterloo district. When the forests were too thick to make a good road, they poled up the rivers in their flat-bottomed boats until they came to a place which they called German Mills.

Philip Eckardt, millwright, carpenter, and ancestor of a distinguished line of Toronto businessmen, built the first sawmills there. In 1799 two young men, Joseph Sherp and Samuel Betzner, out of Franklin County, Pennsylvania, set out for upper Canada along the Grand River. One of them founded the village of Doon, the other Betzner, now the village of Blair. The land was excellent, their work was rewarded, news traveled, and soon they were joined by more settlers from Pennsylvania. They prospered. A century later their descendants erected a memorial at Doon. On top of the tower is a weather vane showing a copper Conestoga wagon drawn by six copper horses.

The Amish were not far behind. Members of the sect were joined by new arrivals from Germany. To make sure that there would be no misunderstanding, their leader, Christian Naffzigger, waited upon George IV in London, who gave him willing audience. He wanted to make certain that the offer of fifty acres for the head of each family could be carried out. Assured by the King that it would be so, Naffzigger returned to Germany, gathered his coreligionists together and, in 1824, took possession of the land.

Fifty thousand German-speaking immigrants came into Ontario between 1830–70. By 1871, 158,000 Germans were listed, one tenth of the entire population of Canada. The 1941 census listed 464,682 Canadians of German origin, 37,715 of them from Austria.

The German Explorers   XII

The German veterans of the American wars had scarcely adjusted themselves again to civilian life when the people of Paris stormed the Bastille. In 1789 the French Revolution began, and soon all Europe was drawn into its orbit.

Those German intellectuals who had maintained a lukewarm or negative attitude toward the principles of the American Revolution now enthusiastically embraced the revolution in France. Christoph Martin Wieland and Friedrich Gottlieb Klopstock wrote stirring odes on it; the philosophers Kant, Herder, Fichte, and many others turned to Paris as the mecca of freedom. Even Georg Forster, who had traveled around the world with Captain Cook, went to Paris to celebrate the *Quatorze Juillet*, the first year of political liberty.

In the beginning the German nobility took a neutral stand. They did not mind seeing France, which had bullied the Germanies for two centuries, taken down a peg or two. But when the August Declarations demanded a classless society, the friendly mood began to change. When the French National Assembly abolished the privileges and prerogatives of the nobility, and when German princes found their vast estates in Alsace confiscated, there was much blue-blooded hue and cry.

In August, 1791, Frederick William II of Prussia issued his Declaration of Pillnitz, which called for the restoration of the French monarchy "in the common interest to all sovereigns of Europe." Duke Ferdinand of Brunswick issued a proclamation directed to the French people in which he announced his intention to reestablish the legitimate French throne and end the anarchy in France. Many Germans who had been sent to America to put down the striving for liberty were now used to restore the bankrupt society of France. But France was not in dissolution. She became rejuvenated by the first

Austrian botanist Baron Nikolaus Joseph von Jacquin explored the lands of the Caribbean Sea in 1755.

foreign invasions, war began in deadly earnest, and for five years heads rolled. "Your revolution is a bore," Anatole France has Jean Blaise say in *Les Dieux ont Soif*.

It lasts over long. Five years of enthusiasm, five years of fraternal embraces, of massacres, of fine speeches, of *Marseillaises*, of tocsins, of "hang up the aristocrats," of heads promenaded on pikes, of women mounted astride cannon, of trees of Liberty crowned with the red cap, of white-robed maidens and old men drawn about the streets in flower-wreathed cars; of imprisonments and guillotinings, of proclamations . . . of cockades and plumes, words and *carmagnoles*—it grows tedious!

While these armed conflicts went their inevitable ways, many Germans were doing pioneer work in Alaska, California, Columbia, Peru, and Chile. To these unexplored places went a long succession of navigators, geologists, botanists, zoologists, and geographers.

In 1756, when for a brief moment external pressures had lessened, Austria was able to send a botanist to the lands about the Caribbean Sea. Baron Nikolaus Joseph von Jacquin was born in 1727 in Holland and lived to be ninety years of age. When he was thirty, armed with the usual royal patents, he was allowed by the Spaniards to collect plants around the rim of the Caribbean lands and its isles. His short, still unpublished autobiography, in the National Library in Vienna, shows that he moved freely around and into what is now Colombia; he also collected widely in Jamaica, Cuba, and Florida (then held by the Spanish). His collections were remarkable; even more so the illustrations of his "selected American plants," which were wholly different from the rigid botanical illustrations of the period. About the time that the Waldeckers were invading Florida in the last battles of the American war, Jacquin was publishing in Vienna his second work on American plants, embellished with 264 hand-colored plates, in execution and presentation some of the finest watercolors in botanical history. Charles III, the King of Spain who had given Baron von Jacquin royal sanction to travel in his realms, was himself unable to procure a copy because of its rarity. Jacquin's son continued his father's studies with a publication on American birds, of equal rarity and beauty.

It was in the north, however, around the Arctic, where the Germans became the first scientific explorers. The Northwest Passage

Explorer Georg Forster (1754–94) with his father, Johann Reinhold Forster (1729–98). The two became famous through their world trips with the Englishman Cook.

had dominated British interest for centuries, almost, in fact, as soon as the discovery of America. British literature is full of narratives of heroic, albeit fruitless, attempts to find a passage from the Atlantic to the Pacific across the frozen north. In 1725, Peter the Great of Russia put his head to it; he wanted to know more of the Siberian lands that stretched over the top of the world to Alaska.

A Danish navigator, Vitus Jonassen Bering, had been born at Horsens, fought in Russia's New Navy (much of which he helped to build), and as a reward received command of the expedition. In 1728 he set off to discover whether Asia and North America were connected. The following years were frigid and long. In 1741, on his third voyage from the Siberian port of Okhotsk toward the American continent, he faced a succession of storms, scurvy, and sickness. These followed him until he was wrecked and killed on the island which now bears his name. One of several Germans who served on these expeditions was Georg Wilhelm Steller (originally Stöhler). Steller is credited with the discovery of several species of fish and plants.

Captain James Cook, accompanied by the father-and-son team, Johann Reinhold and Georg Forster, between 1768 and 1779 explored the waters of the southern hemisphere to the Antarctic Circle. J. R. Forster's *Observations* (1778) was a landmark in scientific recording. Georg Forster's *Voyage Around the World* (1777) stimulated Alexander von Humboldt to undertake his own geographic explorations. "My *philosophe aimable*," Humboldt said of him, "my most distinguished teacher and friend, whose name I can never mention without a feeling of the most heartful gratitude. Through his influence a new spirit in exploration was born."

The prospects of controlling the mythical Northwest Passage now excited most of the maritime nations. The English laid claim to all northern lands between the Atlantic and the Pacific, including the Bering Strait. Spain, soon to enter the contest, claimed the northern lands as an extension of her California possessions. And then the Russians claimed them on the basis of Bering's pioneering explorations.

Admiral Adam Johann von Krusenstern, of German origin but in the Tsar's service, commanded a new expedition (1803–6) which was to eventuate in the first Russian circumnavigation of the globe. Born in Estonia, Krusenstern served six years in the British navy before he joined and was raised to captain's rank in the Russian army. On these voyages, serving in varied capacities, were a number of Germans, many of whom would reach fame by making a contribution to the history of the Americas.

Otto von Kotzebue, son of the well-known German dramatist, was also born in Estonia. Specializing in natural science and oceanography, he first accompanied von Krusenstern and later, under his own command, explored the coast from Alaska to California, stopping in 1817 at Yerba Buena, an island in San Francisco Bay. He discovered some four hundred islands in the South Seas, and on sailing north through

Poet Adelbert von Chamisso gave a masterful description of his Trip Around the World, *1815–18.*

the Bering Strait discovered and explored the bay called Kotzebue Sound. Participating also in these voyages was Adelbert von Chamisso as botanist and Johann Friedrich Eschscholtz, who collected many animal specimens and for whom the genus *Eschscholtzia*, the California poppy, is named.

Adelbert von Chamisso was born of French parents in Champagne in 1781. His parents fled to Germany during the French Revolution, which explains why Chamisso wrote exclusively in German. On his return from von Kotzebue's first voyage (1818), he was made curator of the botanical gardens in Berlin. In that year he discovered what he called "alternation of generations," the recurrence of the life cycle of two or more forms in certain animals. He is little remembered for his botanical explorations and scientific experiments, however. Mostly he is recalled as the author of *Peter Schlemihls Wunderbare Geschicte* (1814), the humorous story of a man who sold his shadow to the devil.

Baron von Langsdorff was another of the young scientists who went with von Krusenstern. Although Langsdorff belongs more to

Georg Heinrich von Langsdorff made a name for himself primarily through discoveries in California and Alaska.

the history of Brazil, his pioneer researches were important to the knowledge of Alaska and the California coast as well. Georg Heinrich von Langsdorff was born in 1774 in the lovely village of Wöllstein in Rheinhessen. Later, upon receiving his parchment as a *medicus*, he traveled to Portugal, where he was assigned as surgeon to the German army under Prince Christian of Waldeck. He took part in the peninsular campaign of 1801, and afterward was offered the post of physician-naturalist on the Krusenstern voyage. He became, in effect, the historian of the voyage. Their ships touched at many parts of Brazil, then moved about Cape Horn, where Langsdorff collected specimens and plants. In 1803 the expedition touched at many parts of California and Langsdorff made the first known illustrations of the Indians of San Jose. In Alaska he made the first detailed illustrations of the Eskimo kayak, which he observed on Kodiak Island, and illustrated as well other historical details of the first settlements in an area soon to be hotly disputed by three nations.

One of these pioneers—and there were many in this period—was Thaddäus Haenke, the greatest German-speaking explorer to appear

*Thaddeus Haenke, one
of the most important
explorers of the New
World, was so fascinated
by it that he remained
there.*

in the Americas before the advent of Humboldt. Haenke came to the
"New Lands" neither by reason of gentle birth nor by the purity of
his blood. He was sought out for his botanical knowledge and because
he met the requirements set by the King of Spain for those who
would travel in the expedition then forming: he must be Catholic; he
must be young and able to sustain the adversities of the expedition;
and he must travel from Prague to Cádiz by his own means. In such
manner did Thaddäus Haenke become a member of the great exploratory expedition captained by Alessandro Malaspina.

One of ten children, Haenke was born in Bohemia on December
6, 1761, into a middle-class family that could trace its presence in
Bohemia since 1453. His father held a judgeship, which gave Thaddäus a slight toehold on his upward climb. He was educated in Latin
and music in a Jesuit seminary at Prague. There he found a place with
the *Sängerknaben*, and at the same time learned to perform on the
organ, piano, and oboe. In 1780, at the age of nineteen, he began the
study of mathematics, astronomy, and botany. In 1788, as a consequence of the Spanish government asking a botanist to accompany
the Malaspina expedition, Jacquin, under whom Haenke had studied,
wrote the Austrian ambassador in Madrid: "Spain will hardly find
another young scholar as qualified as Thaddäus Haenke. Moreover,

Naval captain Alessandro Malaspina in the commission of the Spanish kings explored the west coast of America in 1789. German physician and botanist Thaddeus Haenke was in his entourage.

there is hardly another person more deserving this opportunity than he."

Haenke betook himself to Cádiz, but arrived after the frigates of Captain Malaspina had departed. The king, Charles IV, ordered him to sail quickly with the first frigate to Buenos Aires or Montevideo at the Crown's expense. His ship, the *Santa María*, was caught in a fierce offshore wind and capsized at the mouth of the Río de la Plata. Haenke lost almost the whole of his luggage and instruments, and when he was rescued and dried out he discovered that he had again missed Malaspina, who had left for the Pacific by way of Cape Horn, rounding it on December 23, 1789. The only way left to Haenke was to ride across the pampas and climb the Andes, a distance of seven

Malaspina's expeditionary ships Descubirta *and* Atrevida *in a South American harbor during their five-year exploratory trip.*

hundred fifty miles, in an attempt to meet Malaspina's ships when they docked in Chile.

Haenke went by horse from Buenos Aires to Chile. "I started out alone on my long, dubious, land voyage through the entire center of South America. One comes out of this roadless land, this uninhabitated world, to the city of Mendoza." He reported also: "My collection of plants from the top of the Cordilleras are certainly one of the strangest and rarest collections that a botanist has ever found in the Andes. . . ."

Arriving at long last in Chile, Thaddäus Haenke came aboard the three-masted flagship *Atrevida* and met Captain Alessandro Malaspina. Malaspina was tall, erect, and gray-eyed, descendant of a noble Italian family. Alessandro Malaspina di Mulazzo studied navigation first in Rome and then in Naples. As the King of Spain was also then the King of the Two Sicilies (Naples), Malaspina followed, like many other Italians, Charles III to Spain when he became king. As a reward for his services, Malaspina was given command of a fleet: the *Atrevida* with twenty-eight guns and the *Descubierta* of similar size and tonnage, along with a number of smaller vessels. It was to be a scientific voyage with political overtones and lasted from 1789 until

1794. The fleet was to proceed along the entire length of the American coast from Cape Horn to Alaska, cross the Pacific, visit the Philippines (one of the colonial jewels in the Spanish Crown), and then return via Cape Horn to Spain. They were to map the American coast, taking soundings and carrying out astronomical and hydrographic observation while making geomorphic observations of the land. They were also instructed to collect the fauna, flora, minerals, and natural products as well as study the languages and customs of the natives. The ships' roster included Spanish botanists, linguists, and, fortunately, three excellent artists.

The expedition set sail soon after Haenke's arrival in Chile, going along the arid coast from Chile toward Peru. The sea was motionless, "like a great blue-gray lake," and the ships were smoothly propelled by the wind and the strong coastal currents. At night Haenke watched the golden arms of the Southern Cross gleaming in a star-studded sky.

Finally they anchored under the great fortress guarding the Callao, the port of Lima. "In Lima," Haenke wrote, "I watched the splendid entry of the Viceroy, a very remarkable solemnity in a city where luxury is at home more than in any other part of the world."

By March, 1791, they were in Mexico, anchoring under the great fortress of San Diego at Acapulco in time to see the arrival of the great silver-bearing armada from the Philippines. These treasures would be transported across Mexico to the port of Veracruz, and from there on to Spain. "As for myself," Haenke wrote, "I am still alive and now traveling through Mexico and nations inhabited mostly by Indians and where everything languishes and fades under the burning sun." When Haenke landed in California, it was a land of missions and docile natives. The isolation was so complete that the Indians and their missionaries had scarcely heard of the American Revolution, let alone the French. Thaddäus Haenke made the first systematic collections of plants in California's history.

By the end of August, 1791, they were in Alaska, where Malaspina and his staff carried out extensive surveys and laid down, politically, the Spanish claim for Alaska. This claim collided at once with those of England and Russia. To consolidate the Spanish claim, Malaspina set up a colony and called it Valdéz in honor of a Spanish minister. It was during this operation that the seeds of suspicion fell upon Malaspina that would eventuate in a calumny and end in his being imprisoned.

Thaddäus Haenke continued with the expedition to the Philippines, Australia, New Zealand, and other islands, and then, at his request, he was dropped off again in Peru, in 1794, to continue his scientific explorations.

Haenke realized the chemical importance of Chile saltpeter, the sodium nitrate deposited on the vast, rainless coast of Peru and Chile. Working under the most primitive conditions, he was able to treat crude saltpeter and thus make it usable for gun- and blasting-powder; from it he also obtained nitric acid to be used at the royal mint. The next step, the conversion of saltpeter into agricultural fertilizer, was only hinted at.

By 1794, Thaddäus Haenke wrote home: "You will doubtlessly be surprised that I have decided to travel again through the lands of South America in order to enrich our knowledge of natural science." In Cochabamba (Bolivia) he installed a native woman as housekeeper (she must also have been his mistress, since she gave birth to his only known child, Francisco), yet his soul felt a great emptiness because of the lack of music. He asked his shipping agents in Cádiz to "please be so kind as to obtain for me one of the best pianofortes from Germany, as well as a harmonium of the latest type . . . along with Bach's published music. . . ." There were only mule roads to Cochabamba, so the piano had to be carried on the backs of Indians.

While Europe was being devastated by Napoleon, Thaddäus Haenke carried on his work, oblivious of the wars. In a letter dated February 15, 1800, he wrote enthusiastically about the beauties of the Spanish colonies in South America: "Europe would be depopulated if its inhabitants would have a clear idea about the happiness, beauty, the abundance, and the undisturbed peaceful realms of these lands." He kept on working and collecting around Cochabamba until the winds of revolution swept him and all his collections under the debris of war.

Yet even the wars and distance did not conceal his passing. He was mourned in Prague, and London newspapers noted his death: "All friends of science and those personal friends of Thaddäus Haenke will learn of the news of his death with deep emotion. . . ."

Humboldt's America

By 1799 the French Revolution had spent itself. During the short reign of the Directory (1795–99), Napoleon had been victorious almost everywhere. After the Italians and Austrians were overwhelmed, the Treaty of Campo Formio (1797) unloosed a martial avalanche. It covered France, it rolled on Italy, on the whole of Europe. Universal conscription was being proclaimed to the sound of snare drums. Everywhere there was war, chaos, misery, and a rain of blood.

In this war-torn epoch, two Germans appeared in the Americas; one was born a peasant, the other an aristocrat. The lives of both would have a far-reaching effect on all the Americas—and beyond. The peasant, John Jacob Astor, was born John Jakob Ashdour at Waldorf in the Duchy of Baden on July 17, 1763. The aristocrat, Baron Alexander von Humboldt, was born in Berlin on September 14, 1769. Each man, in his own way, would place his mark on the history of the Americas and leave them irrevocably altered.

North America at this time had acquired a minor flood of émigrés, mostly French, along with a sprinkling of French-speaking Germans from Alsace. Baron Frédéric de la Roche was one such. He had landed in New York in November, 1792, and then went on to Philadelphia, where he became a silent partner in the Wm. Louis Sonntag Company, a firm of German Jews long settled in Philadelphia. There he was joined by Élie Charles de Talleyrand, Beaumetz, Comte de Volney, and Frédéric de la Rochefoucauld, descendant of the famous writer and himself author of *Voyage dans les Etats-Unis d'Amérique*. They included among them Anthelme Brillat-Savarin, author of *Physiologie du Goût*, an elegantly witty compendium on the art of dining. He took up employment as a flute player in a New York City orchestra to earn his keep while finishing his famous treatise on gastronomy. Joining this group of émigrés in Philadelphia and New York was Médéric Moreau de Saint-Méry, whose detailed journal gives a good idea of the state of German settlers and their milieu at the end of the eighteenth century.

Saint-Méry was born on the isle of Martinique in 1750. He had been left money by his father, and so journeyed to Paris, where he became a lawyer and an ardent champion of the French Revolution, from which he was forced to flee in 1794. Saint-Méry's American journal found that "All the northern section beyond the city of Philadelphia, beginning with this street [Cedar], is peopled by Germans. . . . The population here includes many foreigners, especially Germans. . . . Their peaceful character, their love of work, the similarity of their language to English, which easily lets them be understood— all these things bring them in great numbers to the American continent. . . ." Saint-Méry noted that "the construction of the houses which one sees between Frankfort [Pennsylvania] and the Red Lion still retains some flavor of the German character, which is reflected particularly in the spacious barns, built of stone like the houses."

In the United States census of 1790 there were 3,929,214 people, of which more than 250,000 were German-speaking distributed thusly: New England, 1,500; New York, 25,000; Pennsylvania, 110,000; New Jersey, 15,000; Maryland and Delaware, 20,500; Virginia, 25,000; North Carolina, 8,000; South Carolina, 15,000; and Georgia, 5,000. The German Jewish population was less than 15,000. There is a legend that Congress defeated by one vote a movement to have German replace English as the official language. There never was such a proposition put forward and there was never such a vote.

It seems that in 1795, Frederick Augustus Mühlenberg had been called upon to cast the deciding vote upon a very important matter. Congress had appointed a committee to question the Jay Treaty, which was exceedingly unpopular because it was considered too favorable to England. Chairman Mühlenberg, on April 30, 1796, cast the deciding vote in favor of the treaty, thus incurring some of the disfavor which the unpopular treaty carried with it. The tenacity with which the Pennsylvania Germans clung to their native tongue may have given rise to the legend that a struggle for language suprem-

John Jacob Astor, former butcher journeyman, became the "King of Manhattan" through his business abilities.

acy existed in Congress. A search of the records, conducted by Thomas L. Montgomery, State Librarian, Harrisburg, Pennsylvania, showed that Mühlenberg was never put in the embarrassing position of deciding for or against the language of his fathers.

Until he was sixteen, John Jacob Astor worked in his father's butcher shop. Then he went to London to join his brother Georg, who owned a musical instrument shop. In 1783 he left for New York.

New York City, at the time of his arrival, was encompassed at the tip of Manhattan Island, well below the current City Hall. The population of New York in 1784 was forty thousand free people and twenty-five hundred slaves. There were twenty-two churches.

In 1794, Saint-Méry found that "New York's streets are not particularly clean, and it is not unusual to see animals of all sorts wandering about. . . . Although windowpanes and sidewalks are washed on Saturday, nobody bothers to remove the dead dogs, cats, and rats from the streets." He found that the butcher shops "in New York are inferior to those of Philadelphia." It was to one of those "inferior" butcher shops that John Jacob Astor came to work with his brother, Henry, in the autumn of 1784.

During his early months in New York, Astor was employed as a butcher. There was nothing wrong in starting life as a butcher, but later, when Astor was "Mr. Manhattan" and owned much of its real estate, he was still dismissed in certain circles as "that German butcher," which is ironic considering that a bare hundred years later the wife of a descendant would rule New York society through her famous set of "The Four Hundred," which was the limit her ballroom would accommodate.

But then, perhaps, not so ironic after all, for it was the vagaries of fashion that started John Jacob Astor on his rise to fame and fortune. Sensing the times, Astor invested his savings in the fur trade. The beaver hat had become *de rigueur* for gentlemen of taste and fashion. The beaver, a quiet, inoffensive rodent, was of the utmost importance in the discovery, exploration, and settlement of America's northwest territory. In the search for their skins, men pushed back the frontier. It was the lowly beaver that gave Astor his first working fortune; the American Fur Company, founded in 1808, was an outgrowth.

By 1811, Astor was pushing his fur-trading stations westward. Trappers in the Far West were worried about the incursions of Canadians into their territory. It was then that Astor—that "German-born financial genius," as the American historian Ray Billington writes of him,—"set up a breathtaking scheme." His plan not only opened up the West unofficially, it was the first shot in the war for the United States' claim to territory in the Pacific northwest, then disputed by Spain, Russia, and England. At his own expense Astor fitted out the sailing ship *Tonquin*, which included among its passengers thirty-three trappers. They sailed around the Horn and moved up to the Columbia River in what is now the state of Washington. There, on the banks of the Columbia, they built a fort which they used as a base for trapping. They called it Astoria. Astor also opened up commerce with China, receiving in exchange for his furs the luxury trade of Peking.

Astor, a stocky man with brows that partially hid his piercing blue eyes, was a businessman—and only that. He continued to speak German at home and made no pretense of hiding his peasant manners. "Just think," said Albert Gallatin, then Secretary of the Treasury, "he dined here last night and ate both ice cream and peas with his knife, and he actually wiped his fingers on the sleeve of my sister's white jacket." Still, Astor often played Mozart and Haydn on the flute, which was more than most businessmen in New York could do at that or any other time.

When Astor felt that the fur business had reached its zenith, he turned to real estate. At one time he owned half of Manhattan Island. At the time of his death, in 1848, he was worth $20 million, the richest man in America—not bad for an enterprising German butcher. Astor made no great pretense to culture, but he left $400,000 to form the Astor Library, now part of the great New York Public Library.

John Jacob Astor's great-grandson, William Waldorf, after twice running for Congress, left for London in 1890, and purchased the estate Cliveden from the Duke of Westminster. In 1899 he became a British citizen, and in 1916, after generous gifts to the English war effort, he was made a baron. The following year he was created a viscount. On his death in 1919, his son succeeded to the title and was forced to relinquish his seat in the House of Commons. The Second Viscount Astor's wife, née Nancy Langhorne of Virginia, ran for and was elected to his seat, thus becoming the first woman ever to sit in the British Parliament. Not bad for the offspring of a butcher's son.

The emergence of Alexander von Humboldt was one of the most important events in the history of the Germanic peoples in the Americas. He devoted his lifetime of ninety years to publishing the

The fast-growing city of New York was almost completely devastated by a fire on October 19, 1776.

results of five years' exploration in the Americas. He stimulated and awakened the interest of Americans in their own lands, provided the geographical background for the building of the Panama Canal, inspired Simón Bolívar to lead the second American revolution, and aided Thomas Jefferson in securing Louisiana for the United States. "Humboldt," said Bolívar, expressing the general feeling of Spanish America, "did more for the Americas than the efforts of all the conquistadors." In the United States, John B. Floyd, then Secretary of War, wrote: "The name of Humboldt is a household word through our immense country, from the shores of the Atlantic to the waters of the Pacific. We have honored ourselves by its use in many parts of our territory, so that posterity will find it everywhere linked with the names of Washington, Jefferson, and Franklin."

Humboldt was well-born (his father was on the staff of Frederick the Great), his education wide, generous, and humanistic. His interests leaned toward the natural sciences, so that it was not unusual

The ruins of the Inca palace of Huayna Capac in Ingapirca, Ecuador, greatly impressed Alexander von Humboldt. The German explorer and his friend Bonpland are shown at the lower right.

to find him, at twenty-three, Inspector of the Royal Mines in the Fichtel Mountains of Franconia. His enthusiasm, coupled with an extraordinary energy and staying power, caused him to undertake many reforms and innovations. In the meantime, he privately undertook investigations in geology, botany, and physiology. By the age of twenty-nine he was author of three well-received books on these subjects.

In 1799, Humboldt followed the road to Paris. Upon hearing that Vice Admiral Charles de Baudin was to circumnavigate the globe, Humboldt sought him out and was given a place on the scientific staff. As war delayed their departure for a year, Humboldt turned to Spain. He planned, if possible, to go to the Americas and there join the Baudin expedition when it touched at one of the American ports on its worldwide itinerary.

One should never discount the value of accident—or, for that matter, coincidence. Since Humboldt was buoyed up by the hope that he would meet Admiral Baudin in either Caracas, Cartagena, or

Aimé Bonpland (1773–1858), friend and companion of Alexander von Humboldt on his exploratory trips through South America.

Lima, to each of these ports he made his way. In the end he failed to meet Baudin. His misfortune became his fortune, for on the way he widely explored the American lands.

Since his birth rendered royal introductions easy, Humboldt, upon coming to Madrid with the French botanist Aimé Bonpland, immediately had an audience with Baron von Forrel, the Saxon ambassador to Spain (an important post since Saxon miners were all over the Americas). Forrel, in turn, presented Humboldt to Charles IV on March 17, 1799, before whom "I explained the motives that led me to wish to undertake a voyage to the New World and the Philippines." On June 5, 1799, the ship that was to carry Humboldt to South America weighed anchor. After eighteen months of exploration in Venezuela, they spent four months in Cuba and then returned to Colombia, where they expected the arrival of Admiral Baudin. The expedition did not arrive. Humboldt wrote to Baudin:

Cartagena, April 12, 1801
Citizen! Just as we were starting from Havana for Mexico and the Philippines, the gratifying news reached us . . . we felt sure that you would touch at Valparaíso, at Lima or Guayaquil. We changed our plans . . . we started to look for you in the South Sea. . . . I will wait for your arrival at Lima.

Humboldt journeyed to Lima by moving through Colombia, where they spent nine months, and then to Quito, where an additional six months were spent in exploration and collecting. Then they left Quito and made their way slowly down the Andes until they reached Lima. Again there was no Admiral Baudin, so after some weeks in Lima they then decided to make their way to Mexico.

On March 22, 1803, Humboldt and his two companions, Bonpland and Carlos Montúfar, arrived at Acapulco on the frigate *Orúe*. Making their way inland, Humboldt was met on his arrival in Mexico City by his old schoolfriend, Andreas del Rio, now director of the School of Mines, who conducted him to an audience with the viceroy, José de Iturrigaray. Humboldt was received with marked attention and offered aid and assistance for his Mexican investigations.

In 1803–1804, New Spain was at the apogee of its prosperity. As the result of an outstanding group of viceroys and administrators, there had been a reorganization of Mexico, followed by a relaxation

A typical suspension bridge in South America, from a sketch by Alexander von Humboldt.

of trade restrictions, and new capital flowed in. The government of New Spain made available to Humboldt the greatest collection of data (statistical, economic, mining, maps, geographic descriptions, and censuses) ever offered to a private individual. This information would prove to be an important factor to the United States in its purchase of Louisiana.

Humboldt set up an apartment and office at Avenida San Augustin in Mexico City, where he sat for his portrait by the artist Rafael Jiménez, posing in his paramilitary jacket as Inspector of the Royal Mines. Humboldt was enchanted with Mexico. He visited Cholula, the famous Aztec capital; he went to the silver mines of Pachuca, the same mines that had been worked by the Saxon-Germans in 1545 and which would again be worked by another group of German miners in 1825. Humboldt extended his personal survey to the mines of Guanajuato, moved on to Michoacán, and then set off to Tula, where the ruins of the Toltecs were still buried.

By October 10, 1803, Humboldt was again back in Mexico City, where he began to work on the collections of data given him by the viceroy. Putting his copyists to work, Humboldt made duplicates of all that interested him—which was almost everything. Although Humboldt visited only ten of the twenty states within Mexico, he supplemented his lack of personal observation with a continuous correspondence and, of course, the immense amount of statistics at his disposal. He first began a small study called *Statistique du Mexique*, which would be enlarged in 1811 to the formidable *Essai politique sur le Royaume de la Nouvelle Espagne*, published in two thick volumes with a huge folio atlas of maps.

Humboldt would follow this book with a huge folio, *Vues des Cordillères et Monuments des Peuples Indigènes de l'Amérique,* on American archaeology, his thesis being that archaeological remains were fragments of history. Without Humboldt's masterful assemblage of material, American archaeology would have been set adrift in the nineteenth century, with its whirlpool of scientific speculations over presumed Old World origins. As it is, Humboldt gave the American historian William H. Prescott, a base upon which to ground his theories.

The Mexicans, as well as the Spaniards, were flattered by this beautiful folio, with its wealth of hand-colored lithographs and engravings. At last a qualified European savant confirmed what had long been averred in Mexico but dismissed elsewhere as typical Spanish hyperbole. In addition, Humboldt encouraged Mexican scholarship. His continued interest in the growth of the young republic was a source of pride and influence.

In March, 1804, Humboldt and his friends took the old colonial road from Mexico City to Jalapa and on down to Veracruz, from whence they sailed to Cuba. Cuba had been the depository for Humboldt's herbarium, collected in the Americas during the last five years, as well as a depot for notes, journals, and other materials. Humboldt had the time to supplement his personal observations on Cuba, which, added to the official statistics he gathered, resulted in his *Essai politique sur l'île de Cuba*, one of the best economic and geographical studies on Cuba until recent times.

It was in Havana, in April, 1804, that an alert American consul, Vincent Gray, met Humboldt. It was Gray's belief that the United

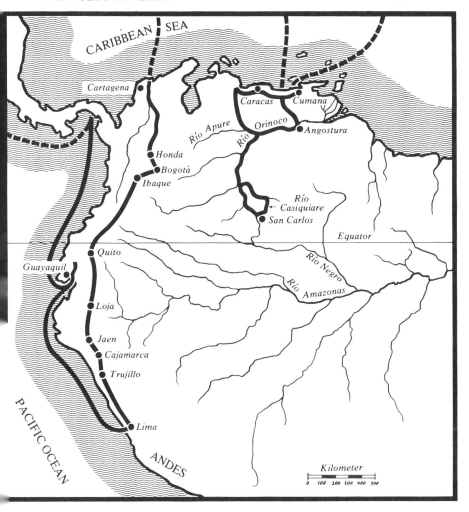

The journeys of Humboldt, 1799–1804.

States should take advantage of his presence to meet the president. He communicated with James Madison, then Secretary of State: "Baron Humboldt . . . in the Service of His Prussian Majesty and Member of the Royal Academy of Sciences at Berlin, traveling for the purpose of advancing the progress of Natural History, being on his return from South America and New Spain, to the Dominions of His Prussian Majesty . . . I take leave to recommend him to your particular friendship. . . ."

An invitation was quickly extended to Humboldt and his two companions. They embarked on the Spanish commercial ship *Concepcion* on April 29, sailing to Philadelphia. On the 24th of May, *Poulson's American Daily Advertiser* noted the ship's arrival, carrying "molasses, sugar and logwood"—and Alexander von Humboldt.

In Philadelphia the members of the American Philosophical Society received the news of Humboldt's arrival with consuming interest. Founded in 1734 by Benjamin Franklin and modeled on the Royal Society in London, it was then, and is still, very influential. Many of the names on its roster in 1804 were men of distinction. At the Society Humboldt met Benjamin Rush, Caspar Wistar, then professor of anatomy at the University of Pennsylvania, William Bartram, the botanist, and John Bachman, who was to aid in the publication of Audubon's book of North American animals.

Humboldt then left to meet President Thomas Jefferson, taking the post road to Washington. Wistar wrote ahead to announce their arrival:

I beg leave to present to you two very respectable travellers who are on their way to the Seat of Government for the purpose of offering their respects to you. It is most probable that you are already well acquainted with the name & great merits of each. . . . The Baron Humboldt has just returned from an expedition to South America & to Mexico where he had spent five or six years passing the heights of Chimborasso & Phinchinka to the bottom of Mines, navigating the Oranoka & the River of the Amazon, traversing forests of the Chincona or Peruvian Barc Tree & investigating the history & antiquities of the ancient Mexicans. These Gentlemen will recommend themselves much more than it is in my power to do.

Charles Willson Peale, the artist who painted Humboldt's portrait and who accompanied them, kept an account of their journey in his

Alexander von Humboldt (1769–1859) explored the South Ameri-
can continent in extensive travels. His thirty-six-volume description
is the largest private report of an exploratory journey in history.

daybook: "May 29th, 1804. I began a journey into Maryland, in company with . . . Baron Humboldt, and his two companions that travelled with him into South America. We took the Mail Stage . . . and left Philada. at 10 minutes before 8 o'clock." In a letter Peale told how while traveling

Humboldt . . . kept up a constant flow of talk: altho two of our company could not speak a word of English, nevertheless it amused them. The Baron spoke English very well, in the German dialect [that is, with an accent]. Here I shall take notice that he possessed fluency of Speach & it was amusing to hear him speak English, French, and Spanish Language, mixing them together in rapid Speach. He is very communicative and possesses a surprising fund of knowledge . . . with a liberal Education, he has been collecting information from learned men of allmost all quarters of the world; for he has been traveling ever since he was 11 years of age and never lived in any one place more than 6 months together, as he informed us. . . .

Their arrival in Washington, D.C., was noted in *United States Gazette*: "Yesterday [May 30] there arrived from Philadelphia, the celebrated . . . Baron Humboldt." Washington had then a population of no more than forty-five hundred people and eight hundred buildings. There were a few hostels, such as Stellas Hotel and the City Tavern, and there was the Navy Yard. The White House then was a small structure.

Humboldt arrived in Washington at a dramatic moment in the history of the United States. On Thomas Jefferson's initiative, Louisiana had just been purchased from France.[1] Napoleon had been planning to reopen this vast region to sugar and cotton plantations under French control. This worried Jefferson, who felt that the United States must purchase from France at least the mouth of the Mississippi in order to control its river commerce. Then Napoleon changed his mind about new overseas development and instructed Talleyrand, his foreign minister, to broach the sale of Louisiana to the American ambassador. On April 11, Talleyrand asked Livingston: "What would you give for the whole of Louisiana?" An offer of $15 million was made, and the United States purchased it in November,

---

[1]In the Treaty of Paris (1763), France had ceded all of the territory east to the Mississippi River and the city of New Orleans to Spain. In 1800, Spain agreed to transfer Louisiana to France for European dominions.

1803. At the time of Humboldt's arrival in 1804, Thomas Jefferson was being attacked in the press. He believed he would have trouble seeking congressional approval for the Louisiana Purchase and it would also affect his reelection in 1804.

The meeting between Thomas Jefferson and Humboldt was described by Margret Bayard Smith in her commonplace book:

June 4th. Around the walls [of Jefferson's house] were maps, globes, charts, books &c., in the window recesses were stands for the flowers & plants which it was his delight to attend . . . and the cage of his favorite mocking bird which he cherished with peculiar fondness. . . . Humboldt found Mr. Jefferson seated on the floor, surrounded [by] half a dozen of his little grandchildren so eagerly & noisily engaged in a game of romps, that for some moments his [Humboldt's] entrance was not perceived—when his presence was discovered Mr. Jefferson rose up & shaking hands with him said "You have found me playing the fool, Baron, but I am sure to you I need no apology."

On June 5, Jefferson introduced Humboldt to James Madison, William Thornton, and Albert Gallatin. Gallatin, who had been born in Switzerland and was a cousin of Madame de Staël, was then Secretary of the Treasury. After the meeting Gallatin wrote: "I have received an exquisite treat from Baron Humboldt, the Prussian traveller, who is on his return from Peru and Mexico, where he travelled five years, and from which he has brought a mass of natural, philosophical, and political information which will render geography, productions, and statistics of that country better known than those of most European countries. We all consider him as a very extraordinary man."

The meeting between Jefferson and Humboldt was memorable, for each man, in his own way, was the supreme representative of his age. Humanists and scientists both, they were equally interested in the curiosities of the world, and they found an immediate sphere of interest in South America. Of the eight weeks that Humboldt spent in the United States, three were spent at Monticello. There Thomas Jefferson communicated to Humboldt his ideas about the future division of the continent into three great republics, into which were to be incorporated the Spanish possessions of Mexico and South America. Humboldt made available to Jefferson all the material he

The volcanoes of Turbaco, an Indian village in Colombia, from a sketch by Humboldt.

had collected to date. "Thomas Jefferson asks leave," the master of Monticello wrote, "to observe to Baron von Humboldt that the question of limits of Louisiana between Spain and U.S. is this: they claim to hold to the river Mexicana or Sabine & from the head of that Northwardly along the heads of the waters of the Mississippi to the head of the Red river & so on. We claim to the North river from its mouth to the source either of its Eastern or Western branch, thence to the head of Red river & so on. Can the Baron inform me what population may be between those lines of white, red, or black people? and what mines are within them?"

The immediate result was that Thomas Jefferson was supplied with technical information on Louisiana which made it easier for him to have its purchase confirmed by Congress. After that Humboldt and Jefferson became close friends and their correspondence extended over fifteen years until the time of Jefferson's death.

In July, 1804, after visits to Washington, Monticello, Baltimore, and Philadelphia, Humboldt sailed down the Delaware on the frigate *Favorita* bound for France by way of Cuba. James Madison gave him carte blanche: ". . . we require the Commanders of all armed vessels to the United States, public and private to suffer them to pass without hindrance, and in case of need to give them all necessary aid and succour in their Voyage."

The mere statistics of Humboldt's output are terrifying. He traveled by mule or boat forty thousand miles throughout the Americas (Brazil, Venezuela, Colombia, the Amazon, Ecuador, Peru, Cuba, and Mexico). He returned with thirty immense cases of material: fifteen hundred measurements used in his *Recueil d'Observations*

View of Christmas Harbor, main base of many expeditions of that time.

Astronomiques; sixty thousand plant specimens, of which more than six thousand were new to science. Botany is generously sprinkled with plants bearing the initials HBK—Humboldt, Bonpland, and Kunth. He wrote and published thirty volumes on the scientific results of his five years' voyage: botany, physics, zoology, archaeology, cartography, geography, and history. His thirty volumes—twenty folio and ten quarto, *Voyage aux régions équinoxiales du Nouveau Continent* being his "personal narrative"—consisted of over 150,000 pages and 426 illustrations and maps. The engravings alone cost him 600,000 gold francs, the paper 840,000 francs, the printing 2,753 Prussian thalers. The task of seeing these works through the presses in Paris took him seventeen years. He also was to have been his own bookseller, for he records that twenty folio volumes were priced at Ł500, twice the sum that John James Audubon asked for his folios on American birds.

The Second American Revolution   XIV

After the Battle of Waterloo (1815) the second American Revolution ceased to be a local affair. Henceforth the war would be internationalized, with contingents of German, British, and Irish condottieri ranged on the side of Simón Bolívar. Between 1807 and 1818 it had been a war waged between native Americans and Spain, but in May, 1815, on a battlefield in Venezuela, the Spanish general Pablo Morillo found "among the dead . . . more than forty officers of which ten are in English service . . . and Germans."

Where had they come from and why?

There had been uprisings in the Spanish colonies for many years, but when Napoleon invaded Spain, threw out King Ferdinand VII, and replaced him with his brother Joseph, revolts burst out in various parts of Latin America. It was, in effect, a revolt against the usurpation of Napoleon, but the authorities in Spanish America made no such distinction: revolt was revolt. Carlos Montúfar, the same who had been a companion to Humboldt, had observed the democratic institutions of the United States, and in Paris he had inhaled Humboldt's liberalism. Carlos Montúfar was one of the first to die, in the abortive uprising in Quito in 1809.

Argentina also became one of the areas of organized resistance to Spanish rule and this eventuated in the leadership of José de San Martín, who crossed the Andes and laid siege to Chile.

In Venezuela, Francisco de Miranda led a less organized revolt against the Spaniards. After many stormy years of intrigue, he was shot, which brought to the fore the real genius of embattled liberties—Simón Bolívar.

Bolívar had been born in Caracas, on July 24, 1783, scion of one of the illustrious families of Venezuela. Caracas was then a city of between thirty-five and forty-five thousand inhabitants, including twelve

Simón Bolívar (1783–1830), descended from a prominent creole family, became the liberator of South America from Spanish rule. He remained a life-long friend of Humboldt.

thousand whites and twenty-seven thousand colored freemen. According to Humboldt, Caracas enjoyed a perennial spring. "What more delight than a temperature which . . . favors the cultivation of the banana, orange, coffee, apple, apricot, and wheat?" In comparison with the several kingdoms of the Indies, Humboldt found "a marked tendency to deep study of sciences in Mexico and Santa Fe de Bogotá; more taste for letters. . . ." Humboldt continued: "I found in many families of Caracas a zest for education, a knowledge of the masterpieces of French and Italian literature, a pronounced fondness for music, which is successfully cultivated and as is always the case with the fine arts, brings together all the several classes of society."

Simón Bolívar was an aristocrat in his own right, of a family whose roots had been in Venezuela since the sixteenth century. When Bolívar was only three, his father died. Henceforth he was educated and cared for by his mother and grandmother. While Humboldt was exploring his country in 1799 and staying in one of their country homes, Simón Bolívar was being educated in Madrid. At fourteen he was a cadet; by 1798 he was a subaltern; and in 1802, when not quite nineteen, he married Maria Teresa de Toro. They left for Venezuela and within a year he was a widower.

The next year (1804) he was in France witnessing the coronation of Napoleon. And there he met Humboldt. Bolívar admired Humboldt and deliberatedly set about to meet him. According to one of his biographers, Bolívar asked him whether, in his view, the Spanish colonies would be able to govern themselves. Humboldt thought that "they had already reached their political maturity, yet he knew no one calculated to lead their emancipation."

Humboldt's position vis-à-vis Spain is well known. "Throughout the world," he wrote to his brother in 1801, "there is perhaps no land where one could live with more enjoyment and in greater peace and security than in the Spanish colonies where I have now been traveling for the last fifteen months." Humboldt repeatedly recorded the generosity with which the Spanish government fostered scientific studies, both on the European mainland and in its colonies.

Still, he listened to Bolívar, although he knew that the social problems of the New World were complex. His attitude toward an immediate solution was restrained. Humboldt disliked any form of woolly thinking, and at first made light of Bolívar. Later, as Bolívar began to succeed, Humboldt admitted that he had then been unable to fathom his qualities. In spite of this, Simón Bolívar insisted that Alexander von Humboldt had inspired the revolt.

As early as 1797 the British had organized a base for the invasion of the South American mainland. Even while Napoleon and the Directory were preparing to invade Egypt, the British, at the behest of Miranda, sent an armada of sixty-nine ships under Admiral Harvey with 6,750 soldiers and invaded the island of Trinidad off the coast of

Venezuela. In this operation were seventeen hundred Germans attached to the British army.

Five years after Waterloo, when England suffered from unemployment, the British began active intervention. It was then that General Morillo found German and British officers dead on one of the battlefields of Venezuela. Spain openly wondered how its ally, Britain, with whom they had fought in Spain and to whose General Wellington they had given an estate in Grenada and the title of grandee, could now openly allow men to be recruited to fight against Spain.

Toward the close of 1817 an expedition of five ships, over the vehement protest of the Spanish ambassador at Whitehall, sailed with a complement of officers, men, and equipment. An American writer sought to explain this particular political dichotomy:

[The British] have so long been accustomed to look at the world through their commercial and manufacturing eyes that they can see nothing . . . except huge granaries with which to replenish their coffers. China is a great tea warehouse; Jamaica, Demerara, Ceylon, Brazil, Java, Mocha, and "Araby the blest" are coffee plantations; American southern states are his cotton fields. Australia is a sheep pasture. Virginia is his tobacco farm, Carolina sends him his rice . . . Hudson's Bay his furs, Mexico, Peru, and Potosí his silver.

Then, of course, there was the unemployment of British soldiers. Since Britain had saved the world from Napoleon, it was only right that her soldiers be allowed to find employment elsewhere. The *London Chronicle*, on January 1, 1817, confirmed: "The commencement of the year 1817 finds this country in a very difficult situation. . . . Thousands of officers and men have been engaged in military work for so long that they are unfitted for civilian pursuits and suddenly thrown out of employment, are looking elsewhere." Officially, the policy of the prime minister was opposed to the recruiting of troops for Simón Bolívar, but the law was so lax that by the end of 1817 an expedition of five ships was ready to sail. The liberties that England had denied to her own North American colonies in 1776 she was now willing to give to others—in return, of course, for a strong foothold in its commerce.

By this time, German veterans of the Napoleonic wars were also being accepted for the "British Legion." Heinrich von Lutzöw, was

On July 19, 1816, a congress in Tucumán declared the independence of the United Provinces of the Rio de la Plata after Belgrano had ousted the Spanish troops from Argentina and San Martín had liberated Chile.

actively recruiting in Hamburg. However, at the request of the Spanish minister, the Senate of the city of Hamburg arrested a number of Germans who had enrolled. Others, however, managed to escape.

Once in South America, death by disease rather than battle claimed many a German and British legionnaire. The small engagements fought throughout Venezuela were only distinguishable by the manner of death and the number of participants. Many Germans found long-lost friends in this "Foreign Legion." An anonymous publication of a Hanoverian officer speaks of his meeting Colonel Friedrich von Eben (later a general) who had seen service with him in Portugal; and there was Count Lückner, who had left his native Holstein to look into the struggle.

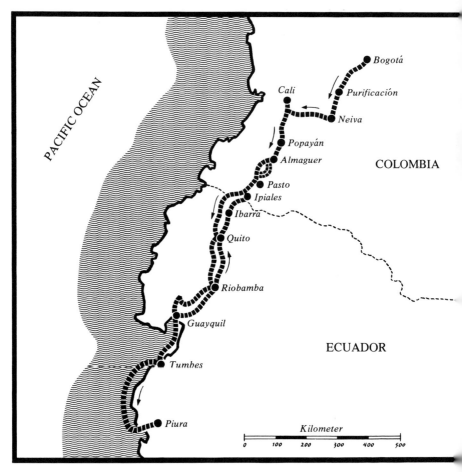

The route of Bolívar in the years 1822 and 1823.

The leading figure among them was Uslar. Baron Johannes von Uslar-Gleichen, commander of the Hanoverians, was typical of this period where war service knew no national boundaries. He was born in Lockum, sent to England, studied at the Royal College, joined the King's German Legion, saw service in the Peninsular Campaign, and fought at Waterloo. He remained in England, reaching the rank of major in one of its exclusive regiments. Then, in 1818, cooperating with López-Mendez, Bolívar's agent in London, he raised a Hanoverian legion of three hundred German veterans. They were sent on the ships *Gambler* and *Plutus* to Venezuela. Once in Venezuela, Uslar reorganized his legions, which numbered over a thousand soldiers, and took part in many of its important engagements.

Uslar's legionnaires were, by agreement, merged with those of the British regiment, and in so doing their place in South American history became a mere asterisk—just as the decisive participation of Field Marshal Blücher's German armies were mostly forgotten in the Battle of Waterloo. How English the regiment was can be seen by the names of some of its members preserved in the official documents: Wilhelm Franklin, Johannes Meyers, Moritz Rietzen, August Zinkennagle, Wilhelm Schzacks, Karl Minnecke. The commander of the Boyacá battalion was a Colonel Flegel, whose adjutant went by the name of Gregor Schneider. Two German captains from Hamburg, Heinrich Meyer and Otto Joithan, took part in the battles of Venezuela and at one of Bolívar's first victories at Carabobo. Thomas Reber was a first lieutenant in the 6th Battalion of militia; a Colonel Elsam also served in the British regiment. Such a list of German participation could be extended indefinitely. But whatever their nationality, all legionnaires were classified generically as English. "Everybody," wrote General Morillo in 1819, "was thinking English." So Spain's war minister decreed that every captured foreign legionnaire would be summarily shot.

There was reason for this anxiety. The legionnaires were providing Bolívar's depleted armies with military backbone, advanced training, and battle discipline—not to mention resplendent uniforms. Since the Spanish offered them death if captured, the legionnaires turned the motto *Morir o vencer*—Death or victory—into song. Some rhymester supplied verses to the English country air "Ye Gentlemen of England":

Behold with pride yon hallow'd isle
Where freedom's root has driven,
Your march is sanction'd by her smile,
And cheer'd by that of Heaven.
To plant the tree
Of Liberty
Is ever hail'd on high:
Then falter none,
But sally on
To conquer or to die.

Whether or not their march was "sanction'd by her smile," the German and British legionnaires, with a sprinkling of Irish, a few Belgians, and a Swede here and there, took part in the victory of Boyacá, in Colombia.

This broke the Spanish resistance. On August 10, 1819, Bolívar, at the head of his army and the British regiment, marched in triumph into Bogotá. Although history seems to have forgotten the Germans who took part in the victory, the official archives at Bogotá have given many of them a formal tribute. Few then recalled that Bogotá had been founded with the aid of Nikolaus Federmann in 1535 when he was searching for El Dorado.

By 1820 the war for liberation had reached the stage where Spanish resistance had been compressed into the colonial territories of Quito and Peru. In the south the patriots had won those territories after San Martín had made a terrible march over the Andes to crush the royalists in Chile.

José de San Martín was born in Yapeyú, Argentina, in 1778. He was schooled in Madrid, fought with the Spanish-British forces in the Peninsular War, returned to Argentina, took part in the revolution, and, as general of the armies, had liberated Chile. With an army that numbered several Germans—Friedrich Brandson was notable, Clemente Althaus another ("brave, intelligent, a gentleman in every sense, and well conducted in danger")—General San Martín finally took Lima on July 28, 1821. It was not, however, a complete victory, since the Spanish army retired intact to the high cordilleras.

Simón Bolívar, in an immense pincer movement, now moved into Ecuador. Many Germans were given official posts: Baron Friedrich

José de San Martín (1778–1850), next to Bolívar, was the most important figure in South American wars of independence.

von Eben was raised to general's rank; Karl Richard was promoted to major and put on the staff of General Sucre; Colonel von Reinholdt was to command the Jägers; Karl Wilhelm was made aide-de-camp to General Santander; Colonel Friedrich Rasch left the Hussars to take over a regiment of foot soldiers; Thomas Boysen of Hanover commanded a ship in the insurgent fleet, along with Captain Otto Tritten of Hamburg.

On May 24, 1822, the armies of Gran Colombia under General Antonio José de Sucre won the battle of Pichincha, which thereby liberated Quito. Celebrations and decorations for the victors went on for many days.

In 1822 José San Martín and Simón Bolívar were aware that one of them must emerge as the leader of South America. Each man had a different concept of what political form South America should have after the final victory. San Martín was a soldier, a martinet without heroics, and, for these times, an enigma. He was without personal ambition. Tall, erect, and reserved, he was a handsome man with a large aquiline nose and sweeping sideburns. His military knowledge and leadership were outstanding.

On July 26–27, 1822, the two men met at Guayaquil, the port of Ecuador. Bolívar was gay and offhand. San Martín was tired. At the age of forty-four he was worn out, perhaps from an excess of sleeping drugs containing morphine. He had been unable to defeat the Spaniards, who continued to hold Peru. The meeting was only between these two; no one else attended. No notes were taken. The only thing known was the result: San Martín resigned and withdrew in favor of Bolívar, who marched into Peru with his triumphant army with the object of finally defeating Spain.

On August 6, 1824, Bolívar was reviewing his troops on the top of the world. He had brought nine thousand troops up from the coast; they were now assembled at Junín. At a height of twelve thousand feet, soldiers who were unaccustomed to it suffered from mountain sickness, which prostrated them in rapid movement. The Spanish commanders, José de la Serna and José Canterac, aware of their presence, made the fatal mistake of dividing their army and sending columns on each side of an immense, glacial lake. La Serna and Canterac sent the cavalry into action; it was coolly met by Sucre's lancers. Bolívar, from his vantage place, strained his eyes into the mist and thought he had been defeated. But Sergeant Major Philip Braun had led a counterattack, and the Spaniards were routed. Later Braun was raised to a colonel for leading his cavalry to victory at Junín.

Bolívar then returned to Lima to assume the government, turning active command of the army over to General Sucre. By this time San Martín's veterans had joined those of Gran Colombia, so that many

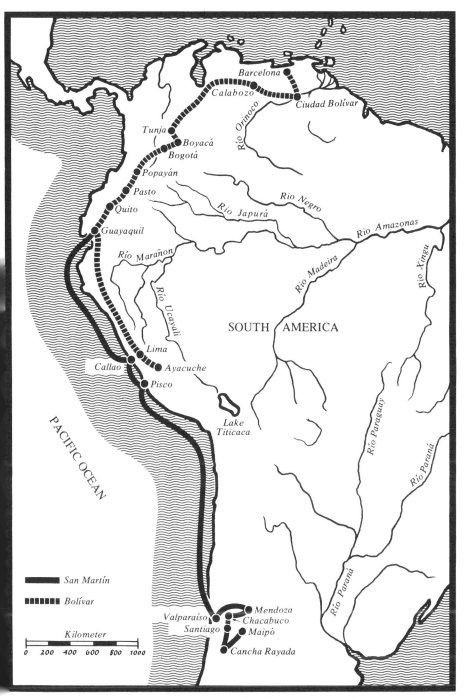

The routes of the expeditions of San Martín and Bolívar.

who had seen the first battles were there to enjoy the final victory. Among them was Clemente Althaus. As chief of the Engineer Corps, he was making a survey of roads and possible battlefields when he was captured by the royalists. He was taken as a prisoner in the van of the Spanish army, and on December 9, 1824, he was allowed to watch the battle of Ayacucho from the heights overlooking the field.

Within an hour of first combat, the battle was over. It was one of those decisive historical engagements, for the last of the Imperial Spanish armies in South America was defeated.

By the summer of 1826 all of the battles had been won. However, while honors poured onto Bolívar from all sides, he found that peace did not bring order. Gran Colombia was coming apart at its political seams, forcing Bolívar to leave Peru and return to Colombia.

In the chaotic political atmosphere, many of the foreign legionnaires drifted off. Some went back to their homelands; others remained in the army, such as General von Reinholdt who, in 1824, became a naturalized citizen of Colombia.

The nation was bankrupt, the treasury empty. Colombia was besieged by creditors. Commerce was at a standstill. The plantations which had flowered under Spanish rule had declined as a natural consequence of war. Roads, once maintained by the Crown, now were quagmires. Old soldiers were everywhere, diseased, miserable, and penniless. Bolívar threw himself into the economic battle to relieve the strain. He occupied himself with custom duties, agriculture, education, hospitals, slavery, and soldiers' welfare, while behind his back opponents talked revolt.

It was at this time that the scientific mission arrived from Paris. Bolívar had forgotten that he had written Alexander von Humboldt in 1821 after the capture of Bogotá. The scientific institutions, which Humboldt had so highly praised, Bolívar found in ruins, and he had asked Humboldt to send a group of young scientists to reestablish these institutions in Colombia. This mission was to have a considerable impact on the scientific history of South America. It was to give us, among other things, the fascinating memoirs of Jean Baptiste Boussingault, who carried Humboldt's letter. Dated Paris, July 29, 1822, it was addressed "To His Excellency General Bolívar, President of the Republic of Colombia."

"The friendship," the letter began, "with which General Bolívar was kind enough to honor me after my return from Mexico, at a time when he hoped for the independence and liberty of the new continent. . . . I flatter myself that the amiableness of the character of M. Boussingault will make him worthy of the same kind of hospitality of which I received such touching testimonies during my stay in Caracas, Santa Fe, and Quito.

"The explorations of the mines, ores, and the reopening of the Pamplona mines near Santa Fe and of the southern part of Quito, the special researches on platinum the new metal, the leveling of ground to build the Isthmus of Panama Canal, are matters worthy of the efforts of this scientist and bound to be of interest to all aspects of industry and trade of your country. . . ."

The letter and the scientific mission was more than a footnote to history, since Boussingault was to become one of the first scientific agronomists, demonstrating that plants absorb nitrogen from the soil and that carbon is assimilated by plants from the carbon dioxide of the atmosphere. He would write countless scientific papers and would one day be president of the Academy of Sciences. Boussingault was also an eyewitness to the disintegration of Colombia (1822–30), as told in his witty, informative, and little-known memoirs.

Boussingault stayed in Colombia until Simón Bolívar resigned the presidency. He was one of the party who rode out with him in May, 1830, when Bolívar was taking the road to Cartagena and, shortly thereafter, death on December 17, 1830.

Venezuela broke into open revolt. Colombia did not regain political normalcy until 1840. Ecuador was in constant revolution. The conditions in Peru were such that immigration was closed for decades. Chile went through a long period of misery. Argentina was in the throes of "becoming."

The South America of 1830 was not the South America Humboldt had visited in 1799. Freedom had come, but it also had brought chaos. Dictators reigned; wild and unmanageable *cimarrones* roamed the pampas. The states that had won their freedom by fighting together now fought each other. Anarchy was everywhere.

Latin America Lifts the Portcullis

When the Germans reappeared, Brazil had not yet been swept by revolution. It was, however, not unscathed, for when Napoleon invaded Portugal in the hope of gaining its vast overseas colonies, the Portuguese made a rapid decision. The royal house of Braganza, its municipal council, its leading officers, its clergy, generals, and most of the nobility (along with a treasury of two hundred million cruzados) crossed the Atlantic under the protection of the British fleet. There King João (John) IV became Emperor of Brazil.

When the Brazilian revolution did come, it was, like the Brazilians themselves, casual, legal, and nonviolent. Though unready for self-government, they demanded complete independence from Portugal. João IV returned to Portugal after the expulsion of Napoleon and declared Brazil an independent empire under the rule of his son, Don Pedro I of Brazil, who believed he would have a better chance to rule Brazil without so many prejudices attached to his person because he was a Brazilian.

The Germans now reappeared in Brazil after an absence of two hundred sixty years. The reason was simple enough. The Austrian archduchess Leopoldina had married the Crown Prince of Brazil, who became Don Pedro I, Emperor of Brazil. Because Maximilian Joseph of Bavaria thus had kinship with Leopoldina of Brazil, it was arranged that German naturalists would form part of her suite when she made her entrance into Brazil.

Even before this time, it will be remembered, Germans had arrived in Brazil. Baron von Langsdorff, as physician-naturalist aboard the vessel that made the first Russian circumnavigation of the world, was, in 1810, "der kaiserlich russische General-Konsul in Brasilien." He had traveled widely in Portugal (where he learned the language) while physician to the German troops of Prince Christian of Waldeck,

Brazil was the only country in South America which achieved in-
dependence without wars. Pedro I, son of the last Portuguese regent
in Brazil and married to Leopoldina von Hapsburg, the daughter of
the Austrian emperor, was crowned emperor of Brazil in 1822. The
illustration depicts his arrival in Pernambuco.

serving in the Peninsular campaign under Wellington. It was there
that he met two other Germans, Varnhagen and Eschwege, who,
like himself, would later gravitate to Brazil. His first voyage to Brazil
acquainted him with the natural wonders of that land, so that by 1810,
when he was posted as the Russian consul-general in Rio de Janeiro,
he was already familiar with the country. In addition to aiding the
German naturalists, he financed the first voyages of the artist Johann
Moritz Rugendas. Langsdorff also organized the first German immigration to Brazil in 1818, a movement which, in one hundred fifty
years, would send over two million Germanic peoples to the land
under the Southern Cross.

Baron Ludwig von Eschwege had been born in Nieder-Hessen and
had studied geology under the famed Johann Friedrich Blumenbach

at Göttingen. He later found employment as manager of an iron foundry in Portugal, and when the French invaded Portugal he was gazetted as a captain in the Portuguese army. When events forced the royal family to move to Brazil, Eschwege was included in the trek. Some of the Eschwege family had already had a taste of the Americas, three of them having served with the Hessians in the first American Revolution, but Baron von Eschwege's interests were mineralogical. Within two years of his arrival in Brazil he moved into Minas Gerais province, the large mining center in the interior of Brazil. There, with several German technicians, he set up an iron foundry where he made the first iron castings in Brazil. Later appointed lieutenant colonel of the Royal Portuguese Engineer Corps, he assumed the general management of all the gold mines, which resulted in his publication of the first geological map of Brazil. His *Journal von Brasilien* (1818) is a pioneer work, and he is acknowledged by the Brazilians themselves as the father of geology and mining in Brazil.

Consequently, there were many well-placed Germans on hand to welcome Prince Maximilian of Wied when he arrived at Rio de Janeiro on July 16, 1815. Destined to become one of the pioneer ethnographers in both South and North America, Prince Maximilian was born (1782) near Coblenz. He had also studied under Professor Blumenbach at Göttengen and, while reading Humboldt, was inspired to make science his career. War, however, interrupted his studies. At twenty he took part in the Battle of Jena and in the rout of the Prussian army was captured and personally interrogated by Napoleon, who granted him release from captivity in order to return to his studies. In 1813, Prince Maximilian was again called back to arms, this time as a major in the Brandenburg Hussar regiment. He saw action at Chalons and Chateau Thierry, was awarded the Iron Cross, and marched into Paris. At war's end, he boarded a ship in London and set off for Brazil. "The late war," as he explained in the preface of his book, "opposed . . . any attempt . . . to travel in foreign regions; but once peace was restored I went. . . ."

Prince Maximilian found on his arrival in Brazil that his "letters of introduction procured me the kindest reception . . . at Rio . . . with the Russian Consul von Langsdorff. . . . My countryman, Engineer Major Feldner . . . [helped me to] form several agreeable traveling parties." Joined by two other German residents, Sellow and Freyreiss,

Prince Maximilian, an excellent naturalist, published his travel experiences and research results in Trip to Brazil in the Years 1815–17, *illustrated by Karl Bodmer.*

along with passports, interpreters, pack mules, and hounds imported from Germany, the expedition set off to explore the east coast. Between the years 1815–17 they managed to travel and collect widely.

After Napoleon had been sent to his last exile at St. Helena, the revolutionary wars in South America remained in full course, but through it all Prince Maximilian kept to his writing desk. In 1820 the

REIZE
NAAR BRAZILIË,

in de jaren 1815 tot 1817,

DOOR

MAXIMILIAAN,

PRINS VAN WIED-NEUWIED.

Uit het Hoogduitsch.

MET PLATEN.

EERSTE DEEL.

Bl. 25.

Te GRONINGEN, bij
W. VAN BOEKEREN
MDCCCXXII.

The title page of Maximilian's book.

A painting of an Indian from the Wied collection.

first volume of his *Reise* was issued in Frankfurt, followed by the second in 1821. They were immediately translated into French and English the same year. In 1830, Maximilian left for the wilds of North America.

No sooner had Prince Maximilian left Brazil in 1817 than the second contingent of German explorers arrived. Spix and Martius, were, through their exploration in Brazil, destined to have a great impact on the botanical and zoological sciences.

Johann Baptiste von Spix (born in 1781) began his studies at Bamberg with metaphysics—that is, theology—but changed to medicine and zoology. Karl Friedrich von Martius was born in 1794, and was fortunate in that his father was connected with the Bavarian court as the royal pharmacist. He met Spix while studying botany at Erlangen,

Karl Friedrich Philipp von Martius undertook an extensive expedition to Brazil from 1817 until 1820. Later director of the Botanical Garden in Munich, he was interested primarily in the animal and plant life of the country.

and between them they planned the program for an expedition. Since now it was fashionable for princes to aid science, the Bavarian court provided thirty thousand gulden toward the costs of the expedition.

Therefore, when H.R.H. Leopoldina sailed from Trieste for Brazil, Spix and Martius were in her royal suite, as well as the other members of the expedition (Matterer, Pohl, Schott, and the botanical illustrator Johann Buchberger, Thomas Ender, and the artist Steingrubel). On arrival at Rio de Janeiro in April, 1817, the expedition began at once to collect botanical and zoological specimens over an immense area of jungle and pampas—from São Paulo to the Amazon, from the provinces of Minas Gerais, Goiás, Bahia, and Pernambuco to fatiguing river travels up the Madeira and Negro rivers. It was the most concentrated botanical survey ever made in Brazil—and exceedingly difficult. Martius, who specialized in palm trees, found the pressing and drying of the outsize leaves an enormous task. His personal narrative, *Reise nach Brasilien* (1823), is one of the basic works on New World explorations.

The expedition ended four years later. The collections were so numerous that duplicates of rare plants were distributed to the world's herbariums. Munich was especially enriched; a grateful King Joseph I of Bavaria decorated them both and granted them titles.

Martius immediately began writing his gargantuan publication on the natural history of Brazilian palms, *Nova genera et species plantarum* (1823–32). Spix, who worked on his zoological collections, was not as fortunate. The malaria that he had picked up in Brazil at last consumed him; he died in 1826. But Martius, robust and indefatigable, lived on until 1868. Mount Martius in New Zealand is named for him.

In the same year that Martius and Spix left Brazil, Baron von Langsdorff returned with Johann Moritz Rugendas. For thirty years Rugendas would travel widely from Mexico to Patagonia, recording people and places, bringing to Europeans and Americans alike, by his facile pen and brush, an illustrated history of Latin America.

When the contract between Langsdorff (who intended to write a book) and Rugendas (who was expected to illustrate it) was signed on September 18, 1821, Rugendas had barely reached his majority (he was born in Augsburg on March 29, 1802). Once in Brazil, under the aegis of Langsdorff, he traveled widely, mostly on horse with a small cavalcade of cargo mules, Negro servants, and a few soldiers. From Minas Gerais with its outstanding baroque churches, he moved on to the jungles of the Mato Grosso, and then down the coast to Bahia. "While in Rio," he wrote home in May, 1822, "I live splendidly, for I am staying . . . in the house of . . . the Imperial Austrian representative." He was there to record the arrival of Dom Pedro I, the Emperor of Brazil. Later, his portfolios bulging with five hundred sketches, he returned to Augsburg and arranged the publication of *Die Malerische Reise in Brasilien*. This immense work, published when he was only twenty-five, drew him to Humboldt's attention.

Johann Moritz Rugendas (1802–58), painter from Augsburg, accompanied the Baron von Langsdorff to Brazil in 1821 and later undertook still more journeys to South America on his own.

Humboldt had always wanted an artist to capture the majestic fullness of the American landscape. Therefore Rugendas was employed to do some engravings for Humboldt's new work on plant geography.

Rugendas then decided to travel to Mexico, but since travel is closely allied to one's cash reserve, his plans remained in abeyance until two sympathetic art collectors, Victor Aimé Huber and Count Fugger, arranged expenses. Rugendas wrote to Humboldt in Paris telling him of his program. He intended to start his trip at the

In lively drawings and oil sketches Rugendas portrayed the entire colorful splendor of the tropical landscape and the exotic beauty of its inhabitants.

Antilles and then continue on to Mexico in order to explore it in detail. The Mayan ruins at Palenque were to have his special attention. He planned later to go to South America, cross over the Cordilleras, go through the pampas as far as Buenos Aires, so as to reach Tucumán and Bolivia, then go to the Pacific and devote himself to studying Peru and Colombia. He wrote hoping that Humboldt could help in realizing his trip. Humboldt assured him of his admiration for his talents and that he was pleased about his decision to go to America. "You should go where there are palms, high ferns, cactus, snow mountains and volcanoes, i.e., the Andes . . . Quindío and Tolima on the way from Santa Fe to Popayán or Quito."

So Rugendas went. His funds, however, were scarcely sufficient for so extended a journey. Therefore he supplemented his limited capital by agreeing to collect various vocabularies of Mexican languages for Eduard Buschmann, the linguist-collaborator of Wilhelm von Humboldt, Alexander's brother.

Rugendas landed in Veracruz in the summer of 1831 and made his way immediately to Jalapa and the hacienda El Mirador, owned and operated by Karl Christian Sartorius, who had fled from Germany as a result of the political reaction to the first taste of German liberalism. He was one of those young idealists whose aim was to unite the Germanies into a single political entity. Karl Sartorius spent his long months in captivity dreaming of the ideal state which he planned to set up in the New World. When released from prison, Sartorius joined the expedition of miners going to Mexico.

Once again, as they had in the sixteenth and eighteenth centuries, German mining experts went to Mexico. But the Mexico of 1824 was far different from the Mexico Humboldt had visited in 1802. During the years that Humboldt was publishing the books which helped Mexico form a new concept of itself, the country was torn by revolution. Ferdinand VII of Spain, released from French captivity, led the reaction, and the Mexican clergy became its propagandists. A Mexican government was established, after which presidents arrived and departed with the regularity of the seasons. "In this atmosphere," writes H. B. Parkes, the British historian of Mexico,

Great Britain which had coveted for three centuries a share of the wealth of Spanish-America . . . under the façade of championing the rights of entailed nations, could make use of it to further her own commercial exploitations. Boatloads of Consuls and entrepreneurs were despatched to Republican Mexico. There Great Britain began the "loans": Three millions pounds sterling was floated on the market, only half reaching Mexico because of the excessive discount rate demanded by the bankers. . . . For several years there was a boom market in Europe for mining shares.

Mining, of course, was still synonymous with German. "British conviction that the interests of Britain were identical with those of Mexico," was quick to encourage German mining interests because of their proven ability to exploit and manage mines, believing this would have the effect of increasing world interest in England's Mexican investments. A modest German organization, growing out of the Rheinisch-Westindischen Kompagnie die Deutsch-Amerikanischen Bergwerkvereine, was formed. Thus for the third time within three hundred years German miners again came to Mexico.

Friedrich von Gerolt became one of its moving figures. Another was Wilhelm Steins; born in Kirchen and educated at Göttingen, he fought in 1814 against Napoleon. Mining was in his blood, his father having been an experienced mine overseer. Along with Karl Sartorius, who would be an important figure in the decades to follow, in 1824 they led the new group of miners into turbulent Mexico.

While they were Mexico bound, the Spanish government under Ferdinand VII, intent on the reconquest of its lost colonies, took over the fortress at Veracruz. When the ship carrying the Germans appeared, it was fired upon and then seized. It was a prelude to what they might expect during their years in Mexico.

Many of the old mines, all worked with Indians as slave labor, were reopened and new mines were exploited. The German miners had to submit to the use of peons; it was a fact of Mexican life. "In Valencia" wrote one German home, "for many years [the mine] had yielded its owners an annual profit of a million piasters. The shafts of the mine alone cost several million. There are broad paths cut through firm rock to a great depth. The ore is conveyed to the surface. . . . Upward of three thousand persons were occupied by it; about 160,000 pounds of blasting powder were used. The annual outlay amounted to a million piasters."

Added to the strange mining methods were the incessant wars. Veracruz, the principal port of entry, was constantly changing hands;

Dr. Harcort, a friend of the artist, in a tent, after a drawing by Rugendas.

needed machinery was held up and mine receipts were always subject to seizure. It is understandable that the letters the Germans wrote home were mostly full of complaints.

Karl Sartorius soon left the mining group. For a few silver pesos he purchased a huge slice of Mexican land lying in the upland tropics above Veracruz between Jalapa and Cordoba. In full view of the snow-covered volcano of Orizaba, Sartorius built his hacienda, El Mirador. There, at the age of twenty-eight, he began systematic agriculture with the large-scale cultivation of yams, manioc, and potatoes. As he grew confident, he turned to the cultivation of pineapples and then sugar cane. He set up the first modern *trapiche*, a steam-operated sugar-cane crusher; he became the first to cultivate sugar in Mexico on a systematic basis. Next he turned to coffee, planting ten thousand coffee trees to begin the first extended coffee plantations in Mexico (before that the Mexicans drank chocolate).

Sartorius was fascinated with botany. He began a herbarium and corresponded with the Smithsonian Institute in Washington, which furnished him with the instruments to make a systematic study of meterology. This he continued for forty years. His biography in the Smithsonian Institute ends: "He never once failed to record his observations even during his illness. He died January 16th, 1872, about 5 o'clock and in the evening before had entered his 9 P.M. observations with his own hands, so that it truly may be said, his devotion to science ended but with his life." His large herbarium, which he somehow maintained throughout all revolutions, he bequeathed on his death to the Smithsonian Institute.

When Johann Moritz Rugendas arrived at El Mirador, Sartorius was already building his "ideal state" and waiting for forty-five colonists to arrive. During his stay in Mexico (1831–34), Rugendas drew eighteen illustrations for Sartorius' only book, *Mexico About 1850*. After that, for three years, Rugendas undertook travels throughout Mexico, mounted on his "Lieblingspferd Babú" and usually in company with Dr. Eduard Harkort, who left a small book of their adventures.

Like most who traveled in this violent land, Rugendas fell into a political ambush. During one of the perennial uprisings he hid the fugitives Generals Morán and Santa Maria in his house. They were apprehended along with Rugendas, who was jailed for two months. After his release he was officially banished from Mexico by General Santa Anna. Leaving South America in 1834, his last sketch was the deserted, coconut-studded shores of Acapulco, where towering hotels now stand. The one thing Rugendas had not been able to accomplish in his three years in Mexico was to visit the Mayan ruins of Palenque.

Nature was lavish with Waldeck; she not only permitted him to be soldier, explorer, courtier, revolutionist, and archaeologist, but, in an outburst of prodigality, allowed him one hundred nine years of life to encompass them all. Waldeck was the first to limn the monuments of the Mayan culture or, as he said, "the first competent person who occupied himself with the ruins of Central America." Born in 1766 of a noble family, perhaps in Prague, Johann Friedrich—who

Jean Frederic de Waldeck from Prague, like Rugendas, contributed in making the wealth and the beauty of Middle and South America known in Europe. We are beholden to him for beautiful drawings of Indians. Opposite are his drawings of an Indian girl from Yucatán and a medicine man wearing the skin of his sacrifice at a ceremonial dance.

emerged later as Jean Frédéric Maximilian, Comte de Waldeck—was a descendant, he said, of the Fürsten of Waldeck-Pyrmont. This is somewhat dubious. There is only one unequivocal fact about his life, and that is the date of his death.

According to Waldeck, who recounted his rich and diverse travel experiences with Münchhausenesque virtuosity, he had, at the age of nineteen, accompanied François Lavaillant on an expedition to the African coast. Returning to Paris in 1788, he studied art under Jacques Louis David and Pierre-Paul Prud'hon. As an officer, he took part in the French campaign in Italy; in 1794 he was at the

siege of Toulon. In 1798 he went with the Napoleonic expedition to Egypt.

In 1820, at the age of fifty-two, he was sailing off the coast of South America under Lord Thomas Cochrane, who served the patriots in their wars against Spain. A visit to Guatemala in 1821 awakened his interest in the Mayan culture, and in London he met Edward King, Viscount Kingsborough, then engaged in collecting material for his *Antiquities of Mexico* (1830–48). Convinced that the drawings he had seen did not accurately depict the ruins, Waldeck left for Mexico in 1826 as an engineer for the British-operated silver mines at Tlalpujahua. In Mexico, the French consul referred to him as "a German painter," even though he was then carrying a British passport. Two German journalists who met him in Mexico disclaimed him as a "sehr geistreicher deutscher Landsmann"; he seemed to them more "valuable for enjoyment than for instruction."

From Waldeck's sketchbook, studies of a bird's head (above) and (top, right) an Indian girl in native dress. Below is one of the fantastic figures from a Mayan shrine at Palenque, which Waldeck depicted in many drawings.

In 1832, at the same time that Johann Rugendas arrived in Mexico, Waldeck went down to Chiapas and the Mayan ruins of Palenque. On May 12, 1832, at the age of sixty-six, Waldeck erected a palm-thatched lean-to at the foot of the pyramid of the Temple of the Cross at Palenque and began to draw the ruins that had disappeared from Mayan tribal memory. Then adversity descended on him. The police sequestered his drawings and ordered him from the ruins. He fled to Campeche.

In 1838, at the age of seventy-two, Waldeck published his first book, *Voyage pittoresque et archéologique dans la province d'Yucatan*, a large folio volume illustrated with hand-colored lithographs.

Alexander von Humboldt had urged Rugendas to travel the western coast of South America and there to draw the landscapes of the Andes and the jungle, "for your America does not have to be only Brazil."

But Humboldt was so unaware of the political chaos of these lands that he did not know Ecuador then was in constant revolution. He did not even know then who was head of government; his letter of introduction, dated Berlin, July 30, 1830, was addressed to: "Monsieur le Gouverneur."

Rugendas bypassed Ecuador and arrived in Peru by boat in December, 1842. He spent a year and a half there; his output of sketches, portraits, genre, and landscapes is enormous considering the distances involved. He made portraits of important political figures in Peruvian history; he painted the streets of Lima, the bridge of the Rimac, churches, and plazas. His large oil of a cross-section of Lima society emerging from church—with young women wearing the *saya y manta*, surrounded by all the castes of its society, with a leering Franciscan monk—had all the satiric bite of Jean Louis Forain.

There were then only a few scattered Germans in Peru, and apparently there were none whatever in the conquest. The Fugger contract in 1535 was aborted, and there were few, if any, Germans in Peru during the colonial period—excepting only the German mining mission under Baron von Nordenflycht. Humboldt, when he arrived, did not like the Limeños. He had been used to the enthusiasm of the young creoles in Venezuela, Colombia, and Ecuador, but he found none such in Lima, only an intellectually depressed society dominated by decadent aristocrats with heavy, burdensome titles.

Rugendas found that Humboldt's name was no talisman in Peru.

Even so, Rugendas met and made portraits of some of the resident Germans. He met Louis Albrecht, who had purchased an immense swathe of land in the north beyond Trujillo which he developed into Casa Grande. It was purchased in 1883 by the Gildemeister family of Bremen who made it into one of the largest sugar plantations in the world. Casa Grande created four generations of multimillionaires, until they disappeared when it was nationalized in 1969.

The land of Chile was more pleasing to Rugendas. It also would be more pleasing, in time, to German emigrants who, from 1835 onward, helped fill up the vacant land. After the Fugger debacle in 1535, the first German to make his appearance in Chile was Bartolomé Flores. He was no less than Bartholomäus Blume, who had translated his name into Flores. He had come down with the army of Pedro de Valdivia and, in February, 1541, had been one of the founders of Santiago de Chile.

When the Inquisition came, most Germans disappeared, except for some priests of German birth who attempted to Christianize the fearfully wild Araucanos. The wars of independence brought Clemente Althaus, who served with San Martín's army. At the end of the Spanish regime there was then in Chile only one German and one Austrian (both residing in Santiago) among thirteen known foreigners.

Once Chile returned to political stability, the climate and the wooded lands began to attract German emigrants. A book, now rare and costly, written by the traveler-naturalist Schmitmeyer, reported on people, places, and environment. It began the German interest in Chile.

Then Eduard Poeppig, a professor at Leipzig, was personally financed by the Austrian Emperor to make extensive voyages in Chile and Peru (1827–32); his published maps and observations were helpful in making Chile and Peru known to Europe. The later explorations of the brothers Phillippi were of the utmost importance in making known the Atacama Desert of Chile.

By 1838, at the time of Rugendas' arrival, there was a small but active German colony. There was a lithographic press in Santiago, and Rugendas took the opportunity of printing some lithographs of the Andes. He did drawings of the main street of Santiago de Chile and interesting sketches of the Pehuenche Indians, who had taken to the horse as readily as did the plains Indians of North America. His sketches of the streets of Santiago, Valparaíso, and Tacna are vignettes of history.

By the time he crossed the Andes into Argentina in 1844, Rugendas found most of the country wallowing in the misery of liberty. Juan Manuel de Rosas had risen from gaucho to president and then to dictator. An orgy of violence and bloodshed ushered in his regime. The strain of conspiracies provoked Rosas into a savagery that made his heraldic symbol, *mazorca* (an ear of corn), into an ironic pun, *más horca* (more gallows). Yet when his three-year rule had ended, he refused reelection and used the next years to exterminate the Indians and provide *lebensraum* for the settlers now pouring in from Europe.

Rugendas traveled up the Río de la Plata to San Isidro, Tigre, and San Fernando, moved across the pampas to Mendoza, and was able, despite war and havoc, to continue drawing. He limned the great-wheeled wagons of the pampas, gauchos sitting out in the windswept pampa or sipping maté tea out of their silver-lined *bombillas*.

In Buenos Aires, Rugendas found a small but impressive colony of Germans, Austrians, and Swiss. The Germans had come to this land as early as 1526. Hans Brunberger stayed behind as a Fugger agent. It was he who advised the Fuggers that they should attempt to colonize Patagonia with German settlers, but that project was overwhelmed. Ulrich Schmidel, as will be recalled, spent twenty years in Argentina with other German-speaking condottieri. Later, in 1577, "der deutsche Leonard" rode about the lands trading iron tools for handwoven textiles and maté. In 1604, Alexander Conrad came to Buenos Aires and set up a windmill for grinding flour. One Hermann Müller was the last foreigner allowed into Argentina until the coming of the German Jesuits.

War and the struggle for independence brought about a new peopling of Argentina. In March, 1812, Eduard von Holmberg made his appearance and was immediately appointed an officer in the patriot army. Many other Germans were in San Martín's ranks when he crossed the Andes and took Chile. English, Irish, Scotch, and Germans began to appear in Buenos Aires after the war's end. In 1822, Herr Thiesen founded the first national bank in Argentina, and a Hamburger named Johann Reissig began to construct the first of Argentina's trade ships.

The Zimmermanns arrived in 1816 and began the well-known Argentinian-German family; the Halbachs arrived in 1827 and opened up a large export house. Anton Martin Thyme, who appeared in 1828, had sufficient adventures to fill a novel. He built the first German beer hall in South America. As elsewhere in the Americas, the Germans brought music, theater, and opera; by 1845 there existed a good choir in Buenos Aires and a German orchestra.

Consequently, there were enough Germans of military age when General Rosas began his wars against Brazil that they found themselves in the army and pitted against other Germans in Brazil. Argentina would continue to receive German immigrants in 1848, 1880, 1900, 1920 and, after 1937, many German Jews. Still more poured in after World War II. Argentina now has the second largest German population in South America.

Uruguay, which lies across the La Plata Estuary from Argentina, had a similar history, except that when Uruguay had won its autonomy and independence it found itself a buffer state between Argentina and Brazil. Uruguay became a virtual battlefield. Baron von Holmberg was there after 1814, presumably fighting with San Martín. In 1820, Wilhelm Düssenberg came from Lübeck, and later his nephew, G. Behrens, arrived as agent for the firm of Bunge & Bornefeld.

The times being what they were, there was little appetite for German immigration to these lands. A naturalized Uruguayan, Colonel Spikermann, did bring a few settlers at this time to the Department of Canelones, but before the 1848 revolution there were only seventy-three Germans in the whole of Uruguay.

German immigrants were sent out to Chile by a Stuttgart society, and there was also a colonization scheme for southern Brazil. A Prussian consul reported on the advantages of Guatemala, and this brought the first German coffee planters. German shipping merchants stressed the advantages of Nicaragua. A Prussian prince was interested in promoting a German colony on the Mosquito Coast of Honduras and Nicaragua. Dom Pedro of Brazil promised a friendly reception to all Germans who would settle in his country. But no one recommended Paraguay. Even Rugendas bypassed Paraguay, then a no-man's land.

An exception to the aversion of Paraguay in this period was a German-Swiss, Dr. J. R. Rengger. In 1818 Rengger became friendly with Aimé Bonpland, the botanist-companion of Humboldt, who continued to collect until the dictator killed his helpers and held him captive. Rengger followed Bonpland into Paraguay and saw all of the devastation from the civil wars and witnessed the complete anarchy throughout the Banda Oriental. Paraguay had of course felt the German presence since the time of Ulrich Schmidel in 1530, and many of Paraguay's missions and baroque churches were designed by German Jesuit architects, but by 1840 these were mouldering in the jungle.

In the middle of the nineteenth century Paraguay attracted few German settlers. Groups of Mennonites came later as colonists to settle in the raw lands, since plantations had virtually to be cut out of the jungle. Despite the primitive conditions, the religious fervor of the Mennonites gradually overcame the obdurate land. Paraguay was empty of people. Its wars had reduced the population to some twenty-eight thousand men and slightly over two hundred thousand women. Because the Mennonites were apolitical and hard working, they were invited to organize colonies within Paraguay.

Of these Nueva Germania was typical. Lying northeast of San Pedro on the Jejui-guazú River, New Germany was founded by Bernhard Förster of Berlin. He had drunk deep in racial notions and wanted to found a colony of "pure" Germans, so he married Elisabeth Nietzsche, the only sister of the philosopher. Friedrich Nietzsche loathed Förster, the leader of a German anti-Semitic movement. When he heard of the marriage he wrote his sister, "I will not conceal that I consider this marriage to Förster as an insult or a stupidity." Elisabeth Nietzsche ignored his warning, however, and went out to Paraguay with her husband to form Nueva Germania.

The 135 German settlers of Nueva Germania came out complete with printing press and a newspaper, the *Anti-Semitic Correspondence*, in which parts of *Also sprach Zarathustra* were printed. Nueva Germania, like many other planned colonies, collapsed, and Förster committed suicide. Elisabeth Förster-Nietzsche returned to Germany to become, unfortunately for philosophy, Friedrich Nietzsche's editor.

Yet more and more Germans came to Paraguay. Today the German element is upward of 250,000. The present President-Dictator, General Alfredo Stroessner, was born in Bavaria of Paraguayan-German parentage.

When Johann Mortiz Rugendas returned to Brazil in 1846, he was greeted with considerable acclaim. He had traveled far and wide since the time he had first come to Brazil as a young man. No artist had traveled so widely in the Americas, and none had portrayed Latin America in all its moods with so great a fidelity. Those who knew of his publication, *Voyage Pittoresque au Brésil* (there also was a German edition) with its hundreds of lithographs, liked the manner in which he depicted the people, the coastal cities, the slave markets, the Indians of the interior, and the elegance of the well-placed and well-dressed. All were pleased with the manner in which Rugendas displayed Brazil to the world, so Dom Pedro II, King of Brazil, whom he knew personally, awarded him both a title and a decoration.

While Rugendas was there, Prince Adalbert of Prussia arrived in Brazil. A Hohenzollern, he was received with marked attention. "All the ministers and the Court," the Prince wrote, "came to meet me at the door of the carriage, and conducted me through several apartments to the Emperor, who stood waiting in the middle of the Audience chamber. . . . I handed to his Minister . . . the insignia of the Order of the Black Eagle. The Emperor accepted the Order with evident pleasure, and expressed his thanks. . . . His Majesty then . . . was pleased to create me a Knight of the most honourable Order of the Southern Cross."

An extended journey up the Amazon into one of its larger tributaries, the Xingu River, was then very difficult, but the Prince seemed to take the hardships well. Later he turned author; the book, in two volumes, was surprisingly well written, with statistical information on peoples and places. It was of such worth that Sir Robert Schomburgk did not hesitate to translate it into English.

Prince Adalbert had noted the number of mushrooming German colonies and was surprised to see them so widely scattered in the interior of Brazil in so short a space of time. For the Germans, it was certainly not an idyll. A Prussian physician, Dr. Johann Rennow, had married a Brazilian and, by 1829, settled fifty-one German families on the Rio Negro. Other colonies began to arrive in Rio Grande do Sul, the wooded, hilly, fertile area bordering Uruguay and Paraguay with a climate similar to the country they had left behind.

Still, it was no paradise. They immediately became involved in its wars and revolutions. For example, Franz Joseph von Hagen, having

South America's charm also attracted Heinrich Wilhelm Adalbert, Prince of Prussia. In 1842 he explored Brazil and wrote a two-volume work about his adventurous trip. He was later to become supreme commander and admiral of the Prussian Navy.

studied the new mechanics of electricity, was sent out to Brazil ostensibly to become chief of its telegraphic service. He soon left it to found the Kolonie Bluenare. He married, sired two sons and a daughter, and soon found himself fighting in wars not of his immediate concern. He lost his life, along with that of his son, in what was called the Rosas War, a heritage of the uncertain borders between Spain and Portugal in South America.

Brazil was involved in constant border disputes in all sectors. General Juan Manuel de Rosas, an expansionist, moved his troops into Uruguay. He claimed Rio Grande do Sul in Brazil at the precise place where thousands of Germans had settled. Because the German soul, through centuries of warfare contains the necessary chromosomes for soldiering, those who had left Germany after the revolutions of 1830 and 1848 seeking peace, land, and the opportunity to escape military service soon found themselves fighting in considerable numbers in the 1851 war. As before in North America, German officers took charge of companies which were entirely staffed with Germans. Each German colony furnished men and officers to the Brazilian army.

The dead—and there were many—had one positive effect on the living: the government noted that since Germans were willing to fight and die for their new land, great strides were made in making them full Brazilian citizens. For a century the immigration continued. In 1950, out of the population of 2,148,949 in Rio Grande do Sul, more than 160,000 were of German origin.

It was also Brazil's troubled borders with the Guianas that brought the first two German explorers into this area. Guiana had been a gift to England, its first overseas colony, from Sir Walter Raleigh. Germans had migrated to Surinam, the capital state of Dutch Guiana, as early as 1799. Among the settlers, mainly Dutch, there were French, Flemings, and a sprinkling of Germans—enough at least for an early traveler, Johann Friedrich Ludwig, to prepare and publish a German handbook for travelers and settlers, complete with a "Karte der Colonie Surinam mit allen Wohnplätzen. . . ." In 1805, Albert von Sack, a botanist, traveled in Surinam and published his impressions, as well as some finely engraved botanical plates, as *A Narrative of a Voyage to Surinam* (1810).

But it was the Schomburgks who really made the riches of the Guianas known. Robert Schomburgk's beginnings were humble. He was born in 1804 in Freiburg, where he received only the rudiments of an education. Yet, while working in a Leipzig business firm, Schomburgk was fervently reading natural history. He read Humboldt, as most aspiring naturalists then did, never dreaming that one day the great man would write an introduction to a work of his own.

Schomburgk had not the means to emulate Humboldt. He began with the lowly job of shepherd, bringing a boatload of sheep to North America. At that time, in 1825, North America was no paradise for the penniless. Schomburgk wandered about until, in 1830, he settled

Sir Robert Hermann Schomburgk explored British Guiana and the Orinoco region with his brother Richard.

in the Antilles. In the Danish-held Virgin Islands he became a trader-merchant and turned his hand to the sciences, in time becoming a surveyor.

After he had surveyed the island of Anegada in the British-held Virgins, the Admiralty called Schomburgk to the attention of the Foreign Office. Noting the accuracy of his surveys, they commissioned him to explore the boundaries of British Guiana, which was bordered by Brazil, Venezuela, and Dutch Guiana, and then to chart a map defining precisely the British territory. This was the origin of the Schomburgk Line.

The first Guiana explorations, between the years 1835 and 1840, were made in collaboration with his brother, Richard (born 1811), of whom he wrote: "I am deeply indebted to my brother, and owe it to him if my labours should prove to be successful." Leaving Georgetown, the capital of British Guiana, they explored the Essequibo River, poled up it by Indians, to the granite mountains of the Pacaraima range. Here Mt. Roraima, bordering British Guiana, Brazil, and Venezuela, thrusts itself upward, lush with tropical vegetation, to 8,620 feet. Schomburgk's exploration of it and his description of its flora was the inspiration for Conan Doyle's novel *Lost World*, as well as the setting for W. H. Hudson's *Green Mansions*.

The exploration resulted in Robert Schomburgk's being knighted. Of course it did him no harm, either, when he called his discovery of the gigantic waterlily, the largest in the world, *Victoria Regina* after the Queen.

Richard Schomburgk expanded his explorations in the areas they had previously traveled. He went up the Orinoco, observing the customs and habits of Indians and animals. In the interior of Guiana he collected plants and ethnological artifacts, so that by the end of four years his mountainous collections had well repaid the Kaiser for his financial aid in sending him to Guiana. His book *Travels in British Guiana* (1840–44) was typical of the times, wherein the author painfully took the reader from his starting place in Thuringia, near the ruined castle of Rothenberg, and returned him to it. Schomburgk tried to discourage German immigration to Guiana, however, claiming that the land was unsuitable. The slaves had been emancipated in Guiana, therefore cotton grown there could no longer compete with that grown in the United States. Yet by 1842, Richard Schomburgk counted 20,071 immigrants. "The poor Germans, mostly Rhinelanders and Württembergers, enticed here by emigration agents, had the best will to work, but almost all succumbed to the awful climate."

The Coming of the Dreissigers XVI

The year 1830 began as an unruly one for the young United States. General Andrew Jackson had been elected president on the promise of broadening the franchise of citizenship, and he had pledged himself to a "just and liberal policy" toward the Indians. In practice what he did was to sign the Indian Removal Act by which all of the tribes east of the Mississippi were forcibly pushed from their territory. The frontier thus advanced caused a great westward movement in which the Germanic peoples, after the revolution of 1830, were to play a significant part.

For those who witnessed President Andrew Jackson's boisterous inaugural reception at the White House in 1829, where hard-drinking Western frontiersmen mingled with Washington society, it was obvious that the common people had arrived in their quest for political equality. This, however, was *generally* not true in the Europe of 1830, and it was *specifically* not true in the Germanies. There had been the *Hungerjahre* of 1817, the Rhine floods of 1824, and the hard winter of 1828. Through all these natural catastrophes the German liberal movement, which had begun after the cessation of the Napoleonic wars, began to show its political power. Those who had believed that they had fought against the privileges of the old ruling class now demanded a participation in government and that political guarantees be put into a written constitution. It also meant the unification of all the Germanies into one strong, centralized government.

Friedrich Ludwig Jahn—"Turnvater Jahn"—was convinced that there could be no rebirth of Germany unless the youth became strong through a program of physical training by "turn-ing." At the same time, these *Turnvereins* would foster patriotic ideals and love of country through discipline. This, Jahn believed, would make Germany liberal, free, and, above all, united. It was this movement, among

"The father of German gymnastics," Friedrich Ludwig Jahn was a prominent victim of the persecutions by demagogues which caused a large wave of immigration to North and South America.

others, and the political reaction to it that was the beginning of the great German migration to the Americas in the nineteenth century.

Jahn had learned sports in his village of Lanz, where he was born in 1778. After studying at Halle, he, like many of his generation, joined the movement against Napoleon, but upon witnessing Field Marshal Blücher's defeat near Lübeck he voiced a new spirit in his book published in 1810. One year later, after forming the first Turnverein near Berlin, he joined Ludwig von Lützow's Freicorps to fight against Napoleon. When this had been accomplished, he published in 1816 the fundamental book on physical training.

Jahn's principal aim was the rebirth of Germany. Liberal societies, *Burschenschaften*, were formed with the slogan "Freedom, Honor, Fatherland" and a flag whose colors were the black, red, and gold used by Lützow's Freicorps. The popular playwright, August von Kotzebue, then holding the post of Russian Counselor of State at Mannheim, struck out at this in his reactionary *Literary Weekly*. This in turn aroused Karl Sands, who believed that the only way to wage political war was by revolt, violence, and murder. Sands stabbed Kotzebue to death. The official reaction was immediate: Sands was jailed, tried, and hung; "Turnvater" Jahn was imprisoned for five years in Spandau; Karl Sartorius, later to appear in Mexico, was jailed; Karl Follen, who would teach German at Harvard University, was also arrested. Prince Metternich, who did not want a united Germany, used his power to crush the liberal movements; intellectuals and students were punished with marked asperity.

When the revolution of July, 1830, broke out in France, its ideas spread through much of Europe and caused political unrest in Germany. In Hesse-Cassel the people refused to pay taxes; the Duke of Brunswick had to flee to England to escape the mobs; and there was a people's movement along the central Rhine. Bavaria offered a constitution regarded as an example for other German states. Again Prince Metternich led the reaction. He would have crushed the July revolution in France had he had the means; but not having them he reacted by placing the participants in the liberal movement in Germany and Austria under strict surveillance. The result: thousands fled to the Americas.

They called themselves the Dreissigers (the "1830ers"), the political refugees of the thirties. They differed from the earlier German emigrants, who were mostly of peasant and artisan stock and apolitical. The Dreissigers, on the contrary, were worldly, educated, and politically sophisticated. Many had been students in the great German universities; others were journalists, professors, and writers. Karl Follen, one of the leaders, became a professor at Harvard; Francis Lieber, who had fought against Napoleon and was also a volunteer in the Greek war of liberation, went to Boston and introduced the Jahn system of physical education there. Later he became a distinguished American scholar, editing the first edition of the *Encyclopaedia Americana* (1829–33).

Friedrich Wislicenus, who was educated as a physician, set out from St. Louis in 1835 with an expedition to collect botanical specimens. Later he founded the St. Louis Academy and became president of its Medical Society. Franz-Joseph Grund, a Bohemian, as well as Franz W. Gräter were given posts at Harvard; Robert Wilhelm Wesselhöft became a distinguished physician in Philadelphia. Gustav Körner, who spent four months in jail for disorders which his *Burschenschaft* caused, fled to the United States and settled in Belleville, Illinois, as one of the "Latin Farmers." He rose to be a judge in the Illinois Supreme Court and later became a law partner of Abraham Lincoln.

Friedrich Münch, the poet-philosopher, settled in Missouri as a farmer; George Bunsen moved into Belleville, Illinois, across from St. Louis, opened a model school, and became superintendent of the Illinois educational system in 1856. His brother, Gustav, moved to Texas and was killed in its revolution, while his step-son, Ferdinand Lindheimer, became a pioneer botanical collector in the Texas territory. Herman von Ehrenberg practiced his profession as a topographical engineer; Ferdinand Hassler, who had known Thomas Jefferson, was put in charge of a coastal survey and figured prominently in the 1840's in securing draftsmen for army exploratory groups in the Far West. Among the Dreissigers, too, was the impetuous and optimistic Friedrich List. A Swabian born in Reutlingen in 1789, he fled to America to escape imprisonment for sedition, became a naturalized American and while he sought some gainful employment wrote his important book, *The National System of Political Economy*. His plans in this book was a forecast for the entire German railway system which was one day to radiate all over

Germany. Yet the whole of the idea was born in America. Of it List later wrote: "In the midst of the Blue Mountains of Virginia I dreamt of a German Railway System." So he returned to Europe after 1831 and built the second German railway, in 1839, between Leipzig and Dresden and despite the King's comment "I see no great pleasure in reaching Potsdam from Berlin an hour earlier or later" List's plan for a great German railway system prevailed.

Wherever Germans had settled earlier, the Dreissigers gravitated toward them. In Philadelphia the number of German churches, newspapers, bookshops, rifle clubs, and singing societies were increased. The same phenomena occurred in St. Louis, New Orleans, and Chicago. Cincinnati blossomed under the cultural impact of new German arrivals. Friedrich Ekstein founded the Academy of Fine Arts, and there was a sprouting of beergardens, bookshops and Turn-vereins. In Milwaukee the first all-German brewery was opened in 1841, and three years later the city had its first German-language paper, *Der Wiskonsin Banner*. German fire-fighting and paramilitary companies were active in the early 1840's. The first German elementary school was opened in Milwaukee in 1844, where Schiller's *Kabale und Liebe* was presented by amateurs. A German string quartet was organized in 1843 and was later transformed into the Beethoven Society near where Ludwig's Garden dispensed beer, dancing, and free concerts.

The Dreissigers carried over their political romanticism from Europe. Their ideal was Cincinnatus, leaving his plow and hurrying to the Forum to save the Roman Republic from invaders. This appealed to their imagination, and those who went to the raw lands were called "Latin Farmers" because they knew more about Latin, music, and literature than farming. "They had wielded the pen, but had never handled the hoe; they had stood in the pulpit but never behind the plow; they had lectured from the cathedra and pleaded in court, but had never driven an ox-team. They were little prepared for the hardships."

Many settled in Belleville, Illinois, which became known as Little Germany. One "Latin Farmer" milked the cows in his only dress suit; another made a soil analysis before he dug fence posts. Meanwhile hundreds of other German emigrants crossed the Mississippi and attempted to set up "ideal" communities. Hermann, Missouri, was one such. Settled in 1837 by colonists from the German Settlement Society of Philadelphia, by 1839 it had a population of four hundred fifty, a German military company, a band, and a singing society. Its settlers turned mainly to grape cultivation (the town is still famous for its wine). Its streets were named Schiller, Gutenberg, Goethe, and Mozart. A theater guild presented German plays there on Sundays from 1848 to 1866, and a German rationalist society existed there from 1852 to 1902. The "Continental Sunday" flourished there, and occasionally Germans from St. Louis made excursions to Little Germany.

Not all of the Dreissigers were intellectuals; many of the immigrants were peasants and artisans who came to America primarily because of economic reasons. The German peasant-farmers were shrewd when settling on land. They preferred wooded areas when selecting farming lands, with an immediate interest in ready markets. Traditionally conservative, they generally kept away from land speculation, and for that reason German peasant-farmers were considered a valuable asset to any state: they paid attention to their farms and never became burdens on the community. In 1833 one German farmer bought a 150-acre farm in Missouri, with thirty cleared acres, a crop of corn, wheat, oats, potatoes, and pumpkins standing in the field, and one horse, ten cows, eleven sheep, about fifty hogs, plus chickens, bees, plows, harness, and implements—all for $1,000. He added: "I have just finished a house which cost me $45.00." In the process of settling much of the Mississippi Valley, the German farmer introduced alfalfa to the plowed areas, along with asparagus and the cauliflower. One agriculture student concluded that the German farmer in the United States developed over 672,000 farms with a total area of one hundred million acres.

Once the immigrant frontiersman passed the wide Missouri, the land became new and unfamiliar. The Great Plains with its tall grasslands gave way, farther west, to short grass. Then came the sagebrush and creosote bush areas. It was only when the Rocky Mountains were approached that there were again evergreen forests. The Great Plains supported a variety of animal life. Buffalos, which had been driven from the Atlantic coast to beyond the Missouri, provided the sustenance of life for the Plains Indians. That meat which could not be

Camp of Prince Maximilian von Wied zu Neuwied and his travel escort on the Missouri River, after a drawing by Karl Bodmer.

eaten fresh was sun-dried in thin strips, called "jerky." The buffalo gave the Indians skin for clothing, tipis, and boats. Even their fuel was sun-dried buffalo dung.

St. Louis, Missouri, perched on the high west bank of the Mississippi, was the entrance to the plains. It had been founded in 1764 by Pierre Laclède and was then under jurisdiction of the Spanish, who controlled the immense shadowy area of Louisiana. Meriwether Lewis and William Clark set out from St. Louis in 1804 with specific orders from Thomas Jefferson to explore the farthest of the narrow corners of the Louisiana Purchase. The "Astorians," John Jacob Astor's trappers, made their bid for hunting in the Oregon territory by setting out from St. Louis on an overland march in 1811 to make contact with the "Astorians" who went to Oregon by way of the Cape Horn. Even earlier (1805–7), Lieutenant Zebulon Pike and his twenty-three men set out from here to cross the plains and reach Colorado.

But it was not until General William Ashley placed an advertisement in the *St. Louis Gazette* that the western plains began to swarm

with Mountain Men. "Enterprising . . . Young Men," the advertisement read, "wanted . . . to ascend the Missouri [River] to its source,
there to be employed for one, two, or three years."

In 1822, Paul Wilhelm, Duke of Württemberg, arrived in St. Louis.
A serious student of zoology, the Duke had sailed from Hamburg in
October, 1822, landed at New Orleans, explored the tributaries of the
upper Mississippi, and arrived at St. Louis to begin the first of four
voyages. His travels were extensive.[1]

In 1833 the party of Prince Maximilian of Wied, whom we last
encountered in Brazil, steamed or were paddled up two thousand
miles of rivers to reach Fort Union. This was Blackfoot country and
an outpost for the American Fur Company. The notes kept by the
stocky, bespectacled prince show that he was a careful, observant
ethnographer. Even more important was his description (as well as
the illustrations of Carl Bodmer) of the Mandan Indians, who were
wiped out one year later.

Bodmer was by far the most talented artist to paint the new frontier.
When *Travels in the Interior of North America* (1839–41) was pub-
lished, accompanied by a large folio of his illustrations, it was by far
one of the most impressive records Europe had ever seen of American
Indians. It confirmed the observations of the American artist George
Catlin, who had preceded him by three years.

Other German-born or German-descended artists were among the
first to depict the new frontier. As trappers and trading parties set
out, artists accompanied them and left pictorial records. One of the
first was John Neagle of Pennsylvania, followed by Peter Rindisbacher.

Rindisbacher had come to the Canadian Red River colony, formed
by Lord Shelkirk out of discharged foreign mercenaries. Into this
colony, which contained forty-five Germans and German-Swiss, came
Peter Rindisbacher, who had not yet reached fifteen years of age
(he was born in Berne in 1806). A self-taught artist, he was already a
competent draftsman when he arrived. Rindisbacher drew pictures of
Indians, settlers, and the milieu of the West. He then followed the
trappers down to St. Louis, where he settled and painted accurate

[1]Paul Wilhelm, Duke of Württemberg, *Travels in North America*, trans. by W.
Robert Nitske, ed. by Savoie Lottinville, illustrated with eight paintings from Duke
Paul's own collection (Norman, University of Oklahoma Press, 1974).

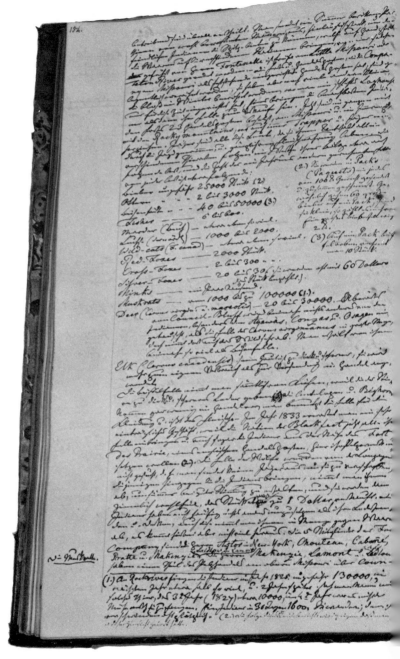

Indian pictographs on a steer hide, from Prince Maximilian's account.

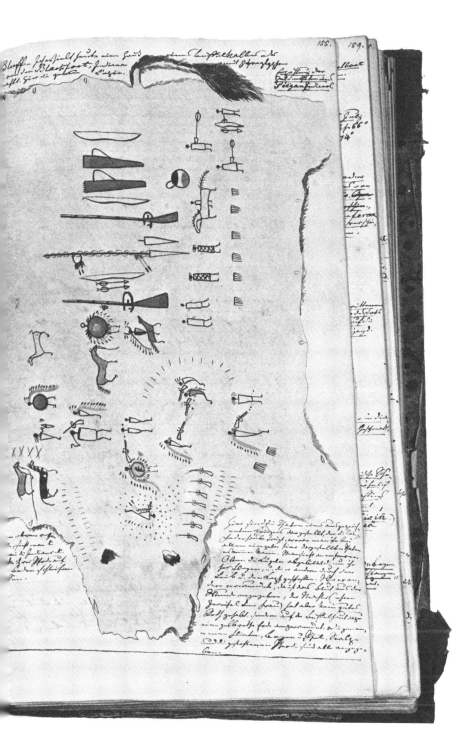

The German-Swiss painter Karl Bodmer accompanied Prince Maximilian on his trips to the New World and brought home an abundance of drawings and paintings. One of his finest paintings is of Mato-tope, chief of the Mandan tribe (opposite).

portraits of white settlers and Indians. There he died at the age of twenty-two.

Alfred Jacob Miller, born in Baltimore of German immigrant parents, was the second artist to paint the Rocky Mountains. He was employed in 1837 by Sir William Drummond Stewart to document his adventures on the plains. Miller had been a student of the great J. M. W. Turner and Thomas Sully and had drunk deep of the romantic agony; consequently his Indians are mostly "noble savages" and his natives, figures in a misty landscape. Yet his drawings of the "Mountain Men trappers who lived in raw nature, partook of raw nature, are pictured vivid and real. . . ." Another German said of them, "They looked like bears."

After 1830 the settlement of the trans-Mississippi frontier began in earnest. The Germans, along with other frontiersmen, began to push into the vacant lands—vacant, of course, except for the Indians, who in time would be pushed aside. Roy Allen Billington in his *Westward Expansion* has given us the setting:

During the first half of the nineteenth century, while ax-swinging pioneers stripped away the virgin forests of the Lake Plains and transformed piney woodlands along the Gulf into fields of snowy cotton, more adventurous Americans pressed beyond the Mississippi to begin the conquest of a new frontier. There, in a gargantuan land of rolling prairies, grass-blanketed plains, towering mountains, and parched deserts, they found what they sought: fertile farming country, lush-green pastures, glittering pockets of precious metals, and a king's fortune in shining beaver peltry. News of this wealth set other frontiersmen marching westward in an ever-growing migration that continued until the director of the census could announce, in 1890, that the unbroken frontier line was a thing of the past.

Into this frontier came people conveyed by the Conestoga wagon, the product of Pennsylvania Germans. Their other great contribution to the opening of the West, the Kentucky rifle, had long since been replaced by superior weapons, but the Conestoga wagon and the "[Cone] stogie" cigar, the long dark cheroot smoked by the drivers, were two of their contributions in winning the West. In every important military or civil survey for the next thirty years, Germans took an important part as artists, cartographers, botanists, topographers, geologists, soldiers, and settlers. By the time the German pioneers

This drawing by young Peter Rindisbacher, whose parents had immigrated to North America in 1821, is called "Indians in the Tent." The talented self-taught artist died at the age of twenty-two.

reached Texas, however, they found that Germans were already there.

Texas lay within the Spanish frontier. It had been Spanish since the first part of the sixteenth century. Many tribes of Indians had been placed in *reducciónes*, organized communities about the Catholic missions. German Jesuits had long before penetrated most of

On the way to the Wild West German immigrants take a short break in a camp.

the remote parts of Texas, Arizona, New Mexico, California. For three centuries Spain had had no political competition in this area; hence whatever commerce there was was held as a monopoly by the Jesuits. In time, with the young United States emerging as a political power, this idyll would change.

Mexico was fully aware of its indefensible frontier. They watched uneasily as the settlers from the valleys of Tennessee trekked into Texas singing the seventy verses of "Green Grow the Rushes, O!" Mexico was acutely aware that there was no way to prevent Texas being occupied. Spain had failed to follow its dictum of conquer and populate. As early as 1777 the German-Saxon miners, under the *Ordenazas de mínera*, had penetrated the northern lands of Spanish America and had made geological surveys of Texas and New Mexico with analyses of the possibilities of mineral exploitation. This was repeated in 1824 by a second group of German miners, who reorgan-

ized the mines for the Republic of Mexico. As a result of these surveys, German emigrants became aware—from information sent to
them by their kin—of the land possibilities in Texas.

Because Mexico could not match the flow of American settlers
into Texas, they formed a colonization scheme, enacted in 1824,
and set up the plan for *empresarios*. "An *empresario* must agree to
establish one hundred families on the land, receiving in return a
bonus of five leagues of grazing land and five *labors* of farming land.
Contracts were to run for six years and were void . . . if the required
one hundred families were not settled within that period."

Joseph Vehlein, a German living in Mexico City, was one of the
first *empresarios*. He was granted a huge strip of land inland from
Galveston Bay (then called Anahuac). Soon afterward Mexico offered
to sell Texas to Prussia, but the offer was not taken up. In 1843 even
the territory of California was offered to Prussia for the sum of $6
million, an offer which Prussia refused, to the chagrin of her ministers in Washington through whom the negotiations had been carried out.

Since the early 1820's, Stephen F. Austin had a contract with the
Republic of Mexico to fulfill his obligations as an *empresario*, thereby
gaining immense grants of land. By 1834 there were about thirty
thousand Anglo-Americans, including Germans, settled in Texas.
The language barrier, customs, religion, mores, the concept of common law, and Mexican unacquaintance with the legal procedures of
trial by jury—all made friction between the newly arrived and the
long-settled Mexican inevitable. Since Texas was, *de jure*, Mexican,
General Antonio López de Santa Anna (called "El Cojo" because he
limped on a wooden leg) made an attempt in 1835 to seize the sources
of administration and power in Texas. The settlers reacted by clearing out all Mexican officials. Santa Anna responded by invading
Texas with an army and besieging, between February 23 and March
6, 1836, the two Texas fortresses at San Antonio and Goliad. The
fort at San Antonio, the Alamo, refused to surrender and was overwhelmed. There were no prisoners. Goliad surrendered and had the
same fate: most of the defenders were massacred by their conquerors.
Many Germans who had survived the 1830 debacle in Germany perished in Texas. Herman Ehrenberg, the radical German-Jewish agi-
tator of 1830 who later became a topographical engineer, fought for

Texan independence at Goliad, somehow survived and wrote about it. J. V. Hecke's *Texas* (1821) aroused many a German. A group of titled European entrepreneurs ("Adelsverein") privately financed a mass movement of German settlers to Texas. Baron von Bastrop located his settlement in the lands about the Colorado River, using Galveston as his base. Baron von Meusebach founded Fredericksburg in the rich farmland on the Pedernales River, naming it after Prince Friedrich of Prussia. He concluded a treaty with the Comanche Indians on March 1, 1847, as a result of which a vast territory of over three million acres was opened to cultivation and the lands rendered safe for settlement. Meusebach founded the settlement of Castell; the "communistic" colony of Bettina was also independently founded on the Llano River near Castell in the same year.

The settlements organized by the Adelsverein were set up in some of the richest and best-watered woodlands of the whole state. The idea of a "German Texas" was talked about as early as 1820 and was finally set in motion by 1842. In May, 1841, Prince Karl von Solms-Braunfels came out with his colony of one hundred fifty families. He bought a large tract of land on the Guadalupe River, about thirty-two miles northeast of San Antonio, and laid out the village now called New Braunfels.

In this romantic period many sought for a utopia. The Germans, like the French and English idealists, thought that such could be founded, maintained, and expanded in America. Texas, they hoped, could be made into a German state, politically, culturally, economically. "New Braunfels, the chief village established under the auspices of the Society for the Protection of German Immigrants in Texas, in 1844 began to accelerate a German immigration already well under way. Continued predominance of the Germans in this and other communities in which they originally settled resulted partly from their strong attachment to the soil, a quality not possessed by numbers of Americans, who, in migrating westward, changed locations as many as three or four times."

The German settlers mostly abjured slavery, and to their eventual discomfort abjured it too loudly. They fell to cultivating their lands with their own hands; wheat, rye, and oats were raised in the 1840's without the aid of slave labor. At first the German immigrants, or the American-born, first-generation Germans, turned to tobacco.

Friedrich Ernest, who laid out a town called Industry, led his neigh-
bors into such diversified crops as silk culture and rice paddies; even
indigo culture was attempted.

The idea of founding a New Germany in the United States was
dismissed by many prominent Germans. Carl Schurz warned, "Let
us never forget that we as Germans are not called upon to form a
separate German nationality." Then there were the strictures of
Friedrich Kapp: "The well-being of the Germans does not lie in the
separation from the American educational interests, nor in fantastic
dreams of founding a German State in America." Still, by 1843,
the German element was sufficiently numerous that the Texas legislature ordered its laws to be published in both English and German.
In 1842 a charter was granted to Hermann University, the act of
incorporation stating that "no person could be appointed to any pro-
fessorship unless he understood both the English and the German
languages."

Texas had attracted a number of Dreissigers. They settled in such
communities as New Braunfels, Boerne (named after Ludwig Börne,
the German patriot), and Blum (after Robert Blum, one of the
martyrs in the Revolution of 1848). Eduard Degner, son of a Brunswick banker and member of the Frankfurt Parliament, settled at New
Braunfels; Julius Dresel, a Rhinelander, went to a farm near New
Braunfels; Lieutenant Leopold Biesel, a veteran of the revolution,
built a blockhouse on his farm, so by the time the traveler Julius
Fröbel arrived in Texas he could observe: "I have met former German farmers, officers, and professors following the oxen and the
plow, and I have found them unwilling to exchange this for their
former positions." He concluded that despite—or perhaps because
of—incredible hardships, they had grown in moral stature. He found
the Germans living on ten-acre enclosures, cultivating a diversity
of crops, and raising cotton with free labor. He was impressed with
the wide main street of New Braunfels, lined with cottages, stores,
and workshops, stuccoed or painted, many with verandas and gardens. He found an excellent inn with stenciled panels and prints on
the walls. Above all, he encountered educated and cultivated people
in the "Latin farming" districts of Texas. "You are welcomed by a
figure in a blue flannel shirt and pendant beard, quoting Tacitus,
having in one hand a long pipe, in the other a butcher's knife; Ma-

donnas upon log walls; coffee in tin cups upon Dresden saucers; barrels for seats, to hear a Beethoven symphony on the grand piano; . . . a bookcase half filled with classics, half with sweet potatoes."

But whatever hopes the German colonists had about making Texas a German republic disappeared on May 11, 1846. On that day, before a joint assembly of House and Senate, President Polk said: "Mexico has . . . shed American blood upon the American soil."

Mexico had given notice that once the Republic of Texas was annexed into the Union, it would be considered an act of war. General Mariano Arista sent in a force of sixteen hundred mounted troops against the forces of General Zachary Taylor on the disputed frontier. When Captain Seth Thornton was sent to confirm Arista's presence, he was attacked and eleven of his troopers were killed. General Taylor informed the President that "hostilities may now be considered as commenced."

The Mexican conflict, which would add Texas, Arizona, New Mexico, and California to the burgeoning United States, was not a popular war. The Republic of Texas had secretly agreed to be annexed to the United States on March 28, 1845, and in anticipation of the expected reaction by Mexico the United States had placed an army corps in readiness at Fort Jesup, Louisiana. Still, the official records confirm that the war was neither planned nor sought. In many quarters Polk's policy was given scathing criticism. It was regarded as "Mr. Polk's War" and everything about it, except the gallantry of the soldiers and the glory of the commanders, was suspect. The war was variously characterized as an "Executive war" in its origin, "unprovoked, mercenary, and base" in its purposes, and "iniquitous" in its intent.

The Mexican army, thirty-two thousand strong, was highly mobile but poorly commanded. The American army, composed of regulars and volunteers, was well officered; most of those who would be generals in the Civil War, such as Grant, Lee, Sherman, Heintzleman, Jackson, Beauregard, and Bragg, were to cut their martial teeth in Mexico. Yet the North American forces lacked good communications and transport, and there was personal friction among the generals.

On May 8, 1846, the U.S. forces advanced to the Rio Grande. Major Samuel Ringgold (whose name had originally been Rheingold) sent in his battery of "flying artillery" and with other regiments fought the Battle of Palo Alto. Ringgold was one of the first officers to die.

As the standing army of the United States was small, with no system of reservists, many Germans, along with recently arrived Irish, came forward as volunteers. Mostly from paramilitary companies or Turnvereins, the Germans came into the army from Cincinnati, St. Louis (a battalion was raised there in thirty-six hours), Milwaukee, and New York. From Maryland, Germans formed military companies out of its Turnvereins, and with the southern volunteers went Lieutenant Louis Armstead (originally Armstädt), whose ancestors had come from Hesse-Darmstadt. It was his father, Colonel George Armstead, who had defended Fort McHenry in Baltimore when "The Star Spangled Banner" was written.

In Philadelphia the Germans formed a whole brigade of artillery, infantry, and rifle corps, which was trained and ready for service in Mexico. In Charleston the Palmetto Riflemen volunteered en masse and marched with German seriousness under a flag depicting Arminius, the hero of the Teutoburg Forest against the Roman legions (9 A.D.), imposed upon the revolutionary colors of red, black, and gold, while on the other side of the flag was the star-spangled banner. Several in this company were German Jews. Jacob Valentine, the youngest in the army, would be wounded at Churubusco and be the recipient of two combat medals. In all, fifty-five German Jews served in combat.

The U.S. Army under Zachary Taylor won the battle of Matamoros and then marched over the Rio Grande to lay siege to Monterey. In September, meanwhile, Friedrich Wislicenus, one of the most distinguished of the Dreissigers based in St. Louis, set out with the 1st Regiment of Missouri Mounted Volunteers from Fort Leavenworth to Santa Fe, where, in October, they joined Colonel Alexander Doniphan. His mounted troops rode through three thousand miles of deserted, waterless lands to make an encircling movement and fall on the rear of the Mexican Army. Wislicenus was attached to it as army surgeon. Educated at Jena, Göttingen, and Tübingen, with a doctorate in medicine from Zürich, he had, in addition to his medical practice in St. Louis, traveled in the Far West with a fur-trading expedition. He was ordered by the government to attach himself to Colonel

Doniphan's group and prepare an official report for Congress. Wislicenus was by then inured to hardship. They crossed in midwinter, riding through wild country where there was not a waterhole for ninety miles. In the high, elevated, treeless mountains they went through piercing winds. "No food, no fire, no sleep. Very cold," read Dr. Wislicenus' journal. By December 27, 1846, the troops bivouacked in the small plaza of the village of El Paso.

The war was reaching the Mexican heartland. General Winfield Scott's army worked its way up from Veracruz toward Mexico City, taking the old conquest route of Hernando Cortes. The struggle fell particularly hard on the German citizens of Mexico, many of whom held positions of trust. One was a general in the army (Adrian Wohl), and since many had military experience they had to decide if they would order Mexican troops to fire on American troops containing so many of their own blood, some of whom they had fought side by side with on the barricades of the liberal revolution. Again, it was a problem of divided loyalty.

The Germans who had come to Mexico had made an undeniable contribution to its history. Heinrich Köhler reported on the prospect of German settlers in Tamaulipas in northern Mexico; Eduard Ludeus gave a description of the Mexican land in turmoil and a vivid picture of living conditions on the Mexican-American border. Karl Koppe, who traveled widely while seated on a mule's back, published letters reflecting his travels throughout Mexico. Affluent travelers, either aristocratic or scientific, moved about in the political chaos of Mexico with considerable ease, if not comfort. Heinrich von Saden wrote about the Spanish in Mexico. The geographer, Baron Ferdinand von Richthofen, made the first systematic geological explorations in Mexico and California; a peak in the Rockies is named after him. His brother, Karl Heinrich von Richthofen, who was the Royal Prussian minister in Mexico, did a magisterial study on the social history of Mexico. Baron von Gerolt, who first came to Mexico with a mining organization, wrote an important study on the principal mining districts in Mexico. This same Baron von Gerolt would eventually be Prussian minister in Mexico and later hold the same office in the United States. The linguist Eduard Buschmann, who labored with Wilhelm von Humboldt, pioneered the first philological studies of the many Mexican languages. Joseph Burkart, who resided in Mexico for ten years during the turbulent times of the German miners, gave his countrymen a picture of events that served as a guide to future colonization. Eduard Mulenpfordt left his native city of Hanover in 1824 and came to Mexico with the mining groups as a *Maschinen-Direktor*. This gave him the opportunity, during the years 1827–35, to travel widely in Mexico. His encyclopedic book on the geography, statistics, and ethnography of Mexico was for its time (1844) a tremendous contribution toward the knowledge of Mexican lands.

Carl Nebel, the architect-artist who was in Mexico at the time of Rugendas, went in search of Mexican archaeology. His work was of such merit that Alexander von Humboldt wrote a preface for it. This search for Mexican monuments was further enhanced by Baron Johann von Braunschweig, who traveled in Mexico during the same period.

Karl Sartorius, then writing his book on Mexico, suffered most. His hacienda, El Mirador, lay just off the path of General Scott's force coming up from Veracruz through Jalapa. His hacienda was overrun by both armies.

On April 19, the American forces stretched out for miles marching into Jalapa, "the most beautiful spot any of us ever saw," said one of the invaders. From a nearby vantage point Karl Sartorius wrote:

In the war with North America . . . there was no talk of a popular rising, for the Indians remained wholly indifferent. . . . If the people had risen in defense of their country, Scott's army would have been annihilated. . . . General Scott penetrated from Veracruz into the interior by the only high road, across a difficult terrain, with numerous narrow passes and across a chain of mountains rising from ten to twelve thousand feet above the sea, some seventy leagues distant from his reserves and supplies. He could have been cut off from the coast; an insignificant guerrilla party could have intercepted his communications. He would have been lost if . . . they had united to attack him, or had refused to supply his wants. . . . The laurels which General Scott gained were owing less to his tactics and bravery than to the weakness and indolence of his opponent.

One by one the citadels fell: Churubusco, Molino del Rey, Chapultepec, and finally Mexico City. On September 13, 1847, Brigadier General John A. Quitman, the son of a German immigrant who had become a cotton planter in Mississippi, was the first to lead his men into the "halls of Montezuma."

Even before the end of the Mexican War there had begun a call for "Manifest Destiny." The editor of *The United States Magazine and Democratic Review*, John L. O'Sullivan, wrote, "We are a nation of human process—and who will, what can set limits to our onward march?" In ten years the Americans had received, in bewildering succession, the telegraph, the daguerreotype, and steam-powered engines; then began the trek of the Mormons across the plains, the absorption of Texas into the Union, the Mexican War, California, and Oregon. And at the end of the rainbow an unbelievable climax: the discovery of gold.

The Eighteen Forty-eighters   XVII

At the same time that the liberal revolution of 1848 was convulsing Europe, the discovery of gold on the land of John Augustus Sutter in California was convulsing America. In their curious ways, these two unrelated events were to unleash a new flood of German emigrants on the Americas.

The opening of the Far West at first proceeded slowly. It was not until after 1806, when the Lewis and Clark expedition returned from their first journey to the frontiers of the Louisiana Purchase, that John Jacob Astor's fur traders followed. Then came the Mountain Men, the trappers virtually enslaved by the fur companies, who began to open up the West for the white man's encroachment. When Rudolph Kurz first saw the Mountain Men, they seemed as remote as the Cro-Magnon: "They stared at us as though we were bears."

Rudolph Friedrich Kurz, born in Berne in 1818, recalled in the journal of his American travels that "from my earliest youth primeval forest and Indians had an indescribable charm for me." He determined to devote his talents to the "portrayal of the aboriginal forests, the wild animals and the Indians." He had read of Prince Maximilian's travels and had consulted the artist Carl Bodmer. He was advised to study in Paris in order to learn how to depict Indians and trappers "with a few swift strokes of pen or pencils," which he did. Then in 1846 he started off for Mexico to paint the Yaquis, but war intervened. So he turned to New Orleans and then moved up to St. Louis, the mecca of those who were westward bound. He ascended the upper Missouri River on the packet *Saint Ange*, and at Fort Union, he found a position as a clerk. Fort Union, the key fortress of the American Fur Company, attracted a wide variety of Indian tribes. But a smallpox epidemic fell on them after Bodmer had painted their likenesses, so now the Indians regarded portraiture as "bad medicine." Kurz was forced to turn his pen to the activities of the trappers, and as a result American history has inherited a vast number of Kurz's genre drawings of life as it was lived on the plains in mid-nineteenth century. Rudolph Kurz returned to Berne six years later with hundreds of small pencil and pen-and-ink drawings in his sketchbook. "These deftly drawn, realistic studies," writes an art historian, "comprise a unique and well-documented pictorial record of life among the traders and their Indian customers on the upper Missouri. . . ."

The artists who followed the trappers or the military topographical engineers as they explored the West were, in effect, historians who recorded the culture of the Plains Indians before it was totally erased. It was in this capacity that George Catlin accompanied the unfortunate expedition of Colonel Henry Dodge's dragoons. He was one of the first artists to paint the Plains Indians—three years before the appearance of Carl Bodmer. Catlin and Colonel Dodge, with some five hundred men, made contact with the dreaded Comanches, who had an encampment of eight hundred tipis near Wichita, Kansas. There Catlin became ill with "fever and ague." He was fortunate to survive; one hundred others did not.

Georg Karl Ludwig Preuss (known in America as Charles Preuss) came to North America on the spinoff of the 1830 revolution. By 1840 exploration in the American West had entered a new phase, concerning itself with the problems of settlement. The United States government began to assume a major responsibility in launching expeditions into the Far West, designed for the development of the vast unpopulated regions. It was in this project that Preuss was to play a major role.

John C. Frémont, a handsome, intelligent man, believed "to have been born of an uncertain liaison," was widely admired and just as widely condemned. One American scholar believes that Frémont's reputation lay not primarily in exploration, but rather "in the field of high political strategy." It was his thoroughness that gave Frémont's explorations their great importance—especially Preuss' maps, which Frémont unhesitatingly acknowledged: "To his extraordinary skill . . . I am indebted for the continuous topographical sketches of the region through which we passed."

Charles Preuss was born in Waldeck in 1803. Through his study of geodesy he became a surveyor for the Prussian government and developed into a superb cartographer. It was Preuss who completed the first maps of the territory between the Mississippi River and the Pacific Ocean, based on modern principles of geodesy and cartography. On February 27, 1847, the United States Senate commissioned Preuss to construct a "map of Oregon [and] Upper California." He himself wrote the *Geographical Memoir* accompanying the map, one of the topographical milestones in American history. Frémont remembered his first meeting with Preuss: "One stormy evening near Christmas, when we were quietly enjoying the warm glow of firelight . . . there came a strange figure—a shock of light curly hair standing up thickly . . . and a red face. . . . I found that he was a German, a skilled topographer, who came to me with this letter from Mr. Hassler, requesting employment."

In 1842, Frémont was commissioned to explore the plains between the upper Missouri River and the Rocky Mountains to find a pass and open a road for emigrants, the famous Oregon Trail. It was, naturally, a trip of much hardship, and Preuss, in the diary which he kept for his wife, was annoyed about almost everything: "June 26th, Low wet prairie. Legions of mosquitoes. . . . June 30th, ate buffalo meat first time." Indians followed them: "These people trade their females like the Americans trade their slaves. One of our men purchased a woman yesterday for one horse and one mule. She doesn't have a bad face."

The first expedition ended in failure. But as Frémont had married the daughter of Thomas Hart Benton, the famed senator from Missouri, he was given a second expedition and set out in 1843 with Kit Carson as scout. Other Germans came along, including the botanist Lüders, who eventually reached the state of Washington only to be massacred by the Indians. Frémont insisted on bringing along a twelve-pound brass cannon and put Louis Zindel in charge of it. Zindel had served many years in the Prussian army; Preuss called him a "Berliner Schlaukopf."

In January the expedition became snowbound in the Rockies on the way to California. While Kit Carson led four men in a breakthrough, those left behind were soon reduced to eating their animals. Preuss' mule was the first to go. He confided to his diary: "I am lying in the kitchen hole on my buffalo hide near the fire to prevent things from burning. On the fire are two pots and a tea kettle. In one pot are peas and pieces of the meat of my mule Jack; in the smaller pot is half of our dog." On March 6, 1844, with the first thaw, they broke out of their snowbound position and walked into Sutter's Fort, called New Helvetia, in the Sacramento Valley.

Sutter was a large, expansive man, open-handed toward all emigrants coming across the Sierra Nevada. He had arrived in California in 1839 and presented himself to the Mexican governor, Juan Alvarado, who alloted him fifty thousand acres of land with permission to build a fort on the Sacramento River (now the site of Sacramento, California). Although Sutter had been born in Kandern in Baden in 1803, his parents were Swiss and he was officially recognized as a Swiss citizen. He attended the Berne Military Academy and saw service with the Swiss army. Faced with bankruptcy, he sailed to New York in 1834 and by slow degrees made his way to California. Preuss noted that among Sutter's staff at New Helvetia were three Germans: "Huber from Paderborn, Cordua from somewhere out of Mecklenburg, and Flugge." Henry Huber managed the agriculture; Charles Flugge was Sutter's legal adviser, and Theodor Cordua had been the first German settler on the American River at the trading post of Marysville.

Sutter laid out vineyards and taught the Indians how to sow and reap wheat; his warehouses bulged with grain. He set up iron forges and had craftsmen carve leather for saddles. Preuss remarked that there were so many cattle on his ranges that "one can kill a fat ox without asking permission; all one had to do was to give him the hide and the tallow." Sutter was a feudal frontier baron, dispensing justice and maintaining good relations with the Indians. "At a dance," Preuss wrote, "where the Indians entertained us, one had painted his penis with the Prussian colors. . . ."

Heinrich Lienhard, who followed the Frémont party, had come out of the Glarus canton in Switzerland. He made his way to St. Louis, where he stayed at Frau Werdemeister's Swiss boardinghouse. There he met and joined the "five German boys" (Heinrich Lienhard, Heinrich Thomen, Jacob Ripstein, all German-Swiss, George Zins from Alsace, Valentine Diehl from Darmstadt). The five were able to join the wagon train of Daniel Lyburz. Later they transferred to the wagons of Jacob Hoppe, a German settler from Virginia who was bound for California. They went through Indians, coyotes, buffaloes, wolves, elk, deer, and all the other phenomena of the plains, crossing

*John Augustus Sutter tried to realize his new revolutionary ideas
with "New Helvetia" in California and failed.*

Sutter's "autonomous" colony had its own laws for communal living. Everything appeared to go well until gold was found at Sutter's Mill.

the Sierra Nevada on September 30, 1848. On arriving at the safety of Sutter's Fort, Colonel Frémont offered them "$25 monthly for duty as foot soldiers." So the five Germans participated in the last phase of the war for California. Captain Sutter was so impressed with Heinrich Lienhard that he proposed sending him back east to bring out Sutter's wife and children.

The Donner party consisted of twenty wagons—high-wheeled, canvas-covered Conestogas modified into prairie schooners. George Donner, a German immigrant, first settled in North Carolina and then left an Illinois farm to move to California. At sixty-two, Donner had fathered fifteen children by three wives; his bearded face gave him the air of a biblical patriarch. The party of eighty-seven people—of whom thirty-nine were children, seventeen of them under six—were divided into Irish, English, and German nationalities. All had one object: to cross the Sierra Nevada and reach the promised land of California.

The wagon train was behind schedule. They did not cross the great salt desert until September, and by the time they reached a tarn (now Donner Lake), north of Lake Tahoe, the party was already wracked by dissensions and ill feelings. By October, 1846, they slept under the first snow; by November the snow was eight feet deep and they could go neither forward nor backward. When their plight became overwhelmingly obvious, a party was organized to seek aid. Those who remained behind built log shelters, collected wood, and killed some of the oxen. The relief party took thirty-three days to reach Sutter's Fort; of the fifteen who set out only seven arrived. While a rescue party was being organized in the Sacramento Valley, the dance of death began in earnest. Food disappeared. After the cattle, they ate horses, dogs, and boiled ox-skins. Then they began to eat each other. One survivor, Keseberg of Westphalen, considered very learned as he spoke four languages, was found partly crazed, still living among scattered human bones. In a large pan beside him were human hearts and a liver freshly taken from a human body. A dead child, partially opened up, was hanging from the wall. The surviving members of the Donner party, less than half the original eighty-seven, had been driven to cannibalism.

On January 24, 1848, while students and liberals were fighting behind barricades in Europe, James Wilson Marshall, a young carpenter working in one of Sutter's sawmills at Coloma, discovered flakes of gold in the millrace. Marshall brought them to Sutter, and although the two men pledged each other to secrecy, others working at the mill spread the news. The greatest gold rush in history began. A tidal wave of people from all over the world arrived. Some came across the prairies, others by way of Cape Horn. On they came: gold-grubbers, merchants, gamblers, harlots, thieves—and a sprinkling of honest men. Even Lola Montez, whose friendship with King Ludwig I of Bavaria was one of the causes of the 1848 German revolution, came to the gold fields, as did Heinrich Schliemann, then aged twenty-eight, long before he set out to discover the city of Troy.

The Gold Rush was the undoing of New Helvetia and finally of Sutter himself. Operations ceased at the mills; fields of ripened wheat stood unharvested; half-finished leather spoiled in the vats of the tannery; thousands of cattle were stolen. The distressed Captain Sutter wrote: "The same thing was in every branch of business which I carried on at the time. I had not an idea that people could be so mean-spirited." Soon his whole property was a sea of squatters' tents. His land titles were disputed, his cattle driven off and eaten, his wheat fields trampled, and the Indians he had befriended were forced to work in the gold fields.

Among the thousands who streamed into California were the brothers Nahl. As other Germans had been the art historians of the plains, they were destined to be the chroniclers of the Gold Rush. They designed the famous California "bear flag," the state emblem, and the great seal of California. It had been expected at birth that both would become artists. Great-grandfather Nahl was considered the foremost artist of the German rococo period; their father, Georg Valentin Nahl, had been a well-known etcher and engraver. The Nahl brothers were born in Cassel, and both studied under Vernet in Paris until the revolution. They lived briefly in New York, and then left for California by way of the Río Chagres in Panama. Once in San Francisco, both brothers, Charles and Hugo, left for the gold fields.

But they soon found that there was more gold to be gleaned from their art than the rivers of California. They sketched Indians working

Gold fever enticed many immigrants to California. This scene from the year 1856 shows gold prospectors at work.

the gold fields, Chinese carrying in supplies, affluent travelers pushing a stagecoach up the hill. San Francisco grew up before their eyes, and their drawings left a record of it. They illustrated books on early San Francisco; Charles Nahl became known as the "Cruikshank of California." "Charles Nahl's first-hand knowledge of mining camp life," says one art historian, "his technical skill, his passion for accuracy in portraying miners . . . made him the leading pictorial interpreter of the gold rush."

While immigrants streamed across the plains to reach California, the topographers of the U.S. Army Corps of Engineers kept to their surveys in an attempt to determine the most direct route for a railway to reach the Pacific coast.

In the Northwest, Captain John W. Gunnison, who had already made a survey of Great Salt Lake in Utah, was ordered in 1853 to lead a survey following the 38th parallel. Assigned to his expedition were many veterans of Frémont's group, among them Richard Kern, a descendant of German-Swiss pioneers and famed as an artist-topographer, Friedrich Creuzefeldt, and Jacob Schiel, a graduate of Heidelberg who would write a fine book on the West. A German artist-topographer, F. W. von Egloffstein, also would play an important part in these surveys. Captain Gunnison split his group into two sections, assigning the less dangerous missions to his second in command. He proceeded to the crucial phase, a survey of the Cochetopa Pass in southern Colorado, constantly being menaced by hostile Indians. In a letter to his wife he wrote: "There is a war between the Mormon settlers and the Indians and parties of less than a dozen do not dare to travel. We did not know what a risk we have lately been running until coming here. . . ."

It was his last letter. In the early morning of October 26, 1853, their cook was preparing a sparse breakfast when the Indians struck. Creuzefeldt, riddled with arrows, fell face forward into the fire; Captain Gunnison was pierced by arrows until his body looked like a porcupine; Richard Kern was scalped. Only four escaped alive. It was days before the other group was aware of what had happened. As Schiel, the first to find out about the massacre, explained:

The party was split in two sections. The smaller section under Captain Gunnison's own command went toward the lake to locate it accurately and place it on the map. . . . We had hardly left the camp, however, when we encountered the corporal and the escort which Gunnison had taken along. Breathless, pale, swaying on his naked horse, he could tell us only in broken sentences after being brought into camp that their little band had been attacked at daybreak. . . . He believed that all of them had been slaughtered with the exception of himself.

Command of the survey now fell on young Lieutenant E. G. Beckwith. His survey proved to be remarkably successful in finding passes through the Rockies into the Humboldt River Valley, which he acknowledged was largely due to the presence of von Egloffstein, the topographer, and Jacob Schiel, the geologist. Schiel, whose role in the opening of the West has largely been forgotten, came from Prussia and studied at Heidelberg. His book reveals a cultivated, urbane man, calm, detached, and accurate, with a profound insight into the cultural and natural forces that were then shaping the American destiny. He gave the first description of the Mormons, who then were taking possession of Utah, and of their polygamous society. Among them he met three Germans. "The principal of these three worthies was a penniless student, who from necessity had translated the Book of Mormon into German and then followed the missionary for whom he had done this work from Hamburg to Utah. He was the city engineer in Provo, the second city in size, and was waiting impatiently for the Holy Ghost to reveal to him the theorem of congruent and analogous triangles. . . ." The second German was a barber, and the third was a "very ordinary man" from Hamburg. As Schiel rode over the land, he observed:

> Future generations will know the buffalo only from seeing it in the museum and the descriptions of natural historians, and the buffalo hunt only from the portrayals of travelers. It can be predicted with considerable probability that in fifty or sixty years the species will have completely disappeared if treated as at present. The buffalo region is not very wide. . . . It is regarded by the Indians as neutral ground, and in summer the tribes camp on the eastern and western boundaries of the region to hunt. . . . The destruction of the buffalo is for the Indian synonymous with suicide.

In 1853, Congress authorized Secretary of War Jefferson Davis to determine a route for the transcontinental railway. The most challenging of the possible routes was northward to Puget Sound. The project fell to the command of Isaac I. Stevens, and his expedition was staffed with engineers, botanists, and topographers, among whom was a black-haired, hazel-eyed German immigrant, Gustav Sohon. Age twenty-seven, a private in Company K, 4th Infantry, Sohon was signed on as artist-interpreter, his task being to "talk" Major Stevens into Oregon. Born in Tilsit, Gustav Sohon had received a good education. He left for America in 1825 at seventeen to escape, he said, serving in the Prussian army. Upon his arrival in America he immediately enlisted in the U.S. army for service in the West.

The Stevens party left St. Paul and moved to Fort Union, high on the Missouri River, where an advance party was detached to move ahead and establish a depot among the Flathead Indians in Bitterroot Valley, west of the Continental Divide. Sohon, with fourteen enlisted men, erected log cabins among the Flatheads, learned their dialect, and became not only official interpreter to the army, but its illustrator as well. His sketches of landscapes, Indian villages, and topographical

"Crossing of the Hellgate River on May 5, 1854," is a drawing by Gustav Sohon, an immigrant from Tilsit. He belonged to Major Stevens' troops who explored the terrain for the railway connection from the Mississippi to the Pacific.

highlights are all clearly delineated, as illustrated in his official reports published by Congress. During the summer of 1854, Sohon, when his other duties allowed, executed portraits of the chiefs of the Flatheads. In May, 1855, the governor of the newly created territory of Washington held one of the largest gatherings of Indian tribes "at the place where the trees have no lower limbs," near Walla Walla. There Sohon sketched the powwow of five hundred Indians and assisted in adding, through his interpretations, another thirty-five thousand square miles to American real estate.

On December 30, 1853, James Gadsden was named to negotiate a treaty with Mexico determining the boundaries of a strip of territory in the Mesilla Valley south of the Gila River. The region, which includes the southern part of present-day Arizona and New Mexico, was regarded as a desirable route for a southern railroad to the Pacific.

Explorer and travel writer Balduin Möllhausen, the "German Cooper," who depicted American life in his 178 books. Opposite is Möllhausen's drawing of Walapai Indians at Diamond Creek.

With those assigned to work on the commission were several botanists, among them the Germans Ferdinand Lindheimer, who had collected previously in Texas, Augustus Fendler, and Arthur Schott. The latter was also an artist who saw the comic side of Indian life. No one attempted to change the drollery of his drawings, which appeared in the official reports.

Heinrich Balduin Möllhausen was the next to arrive. He became for the German-speaking world what James Fenimore Cooper had been for the English, creating out of his experiences in America an interest in Indian lore. During the 1848 revolution Möllhausen had been assigned to guard Humboldt's house against attack. There Möllhausen met Carolina Alexandra Seifert, the daughter of Hum-

boldt's manservant. Humboldt's interest in Möllhausen grew out of
this contact. Möllhausen had studied geography and had even made
a short trip to the lower Mississippi in 1849. When Möllhausen
returned to the United States in 1851 he had a personal letter from
Alexander von Humboldt addressed to Jefferson Davis, requesting
that he be allowed to join the Pacific railroad survey.

Lieutenant A. W. Whipple was directed to make the survey, whose
function was to explore a route for the Pacific railway. They set out
from Fort Smith, Arkansas, in 1853. Their goal: a survey of New
Mexico through to California. Among the group of specialists was
Möllhausen, who was listed as topographer and artist.

After four months of travel the Whipple party reached Albuquer-
que, New Mexico. All, including Möllhausen, were mentioned in
one of New Mexico's first newspapers, *Amigo del Pais*. Meanwhile,

Möllhausen wrote detailed reports of the expedition. He related that when he reached Laguna there were so many Germans already living there that "we imagined ourselves in the Fatherland."

When not making topographical maps, Möllhausen was illustrating details of the Far West. He was the first to copy Inscription Rock at El Morro, on which are carved the signatures of early Spanish explorers and American settlers, the oldest dating from April 16, 1606. He also furnished illustrations for the Report of Exploration, of which Secretary of War Davis said: "The Exploration of the route by Lieutenant Whipple, and his report thereon, are entitled to the highest commendation. . . ." Möllhausen later published his *Diary of a Journey from the Mississippi to the Coasts of the Pacific with a United States Government Expedition*, for which the now seriously ill von Humboldt wrote an introduction.

From this modest beginning Möllhausen went on to write forty-five books, one hundred and fifty-seven volumes, eighty of them novels—all the outgrowth of his experiences in the Far West with the Whipple party.

In 1859 another German artist, Albert Bierstadt, arrived in the Rockies. Although there were many before him and many after him, none achieved such widespread popularity as Bierstadt. Born in Solingen in 1830, Albert Bierstadt was brought to Massachusetts in 1831. He returned to Düsseldorf in 1853 to study at the famous international art center. He sketched the Alps, went to Italy, and then returned to America to join an official engineering expedition to the West. "I found," Bierstadt said, ". . . the figures of the Indians so enticing. . . . The manners and customs of the Indians are still as they were hundreds of years ago, and now is the time to paint them, for they are rapidly passing away. . . ." Eventually Bierstadt would achieve an international reputation as the foremost painter of America's western mountains.

As turbulent as the action was in North America's western lands, Europe in the same period was more turbulent still, and it was this unrest, both political and social, that caused the migration of thousands of German people in 1848 and 1854, culminating in a mountainous wave of 229,522 emigrants. It also marked the beginning of the first migration of German Jews.

In 1848 the European revolution began in Paris as a revolt against autocratic authority. The revival of radicalism and the emergence of "utopian" socialism were enough to cause a popular uprising. In the melee Louis Philippe was dethroned. In Belgium a new electoral law doubled the number of voters, which kept Belgium almost alone among the Continental powers in escaping revolution. In Austria the rioting of Viennese students forced Prince Metternich to loosen his grip on the helm of reaction, and he was forced to flee to England under the sobriquet of "Mr. Smith."

The Bavarian revolution of 1848, oddly enough, was set off by a romance between the aging Ludwig I of Bavaria and Lola Montez. An Irish dancer born in Limerick, Lola Montez had kept Munich in constant excitement by her extravagant whims and political machinations. Upon being elevated to Countess von Landsfeld, she used her position to foster liberalism—that is, said one, if she could distinguish between liberalism and libertinism. She so upset the burghers and patricians of Munich that they moved into reaction.

The year 1848 shook the whole continent. Its echoes were heard in Russia; the Hungarians became restless; Italy moved into Risorgimento; there was an emergence of Czech national consciousness which touched the Germanies closely; and Paris passed through its "June Days." There had been street fighting in many places. In Berlin the masses demanded reforms from their king. Friedrich Wilhelm IV, having little stomach for bloodshed, held back his troops, saluted the Republican dead, and rode in the funeral procession wearing the new national colors of black, red, and gold.

Even then, Germany, as it had been for centuries, was only a geographical expression, at best a weak union of states. Friedrich Bassermann, a bookseller of Mannheim, called for German unity and a political confederation patterned after the United States. Copies of the American Declaration of Independence and the United States Constitution were distributed as examples for political reform. Friedrich Hecker (who would play his part in North America in the Civil War) demanded, at the Frankfurt Parliament, a popular revolutionary administration, the overthrow of aristocratic dynasties, and a complete reorganization of state and church. The historian Veit Valentin said that "[when] in March, 1848, the liberals to their great surprise found

Immigrants at Bremerhaven—on account of political events in the German states many were compelled to seek their fortune in the New World.

themselves, owing to the sudden weakness of rulers, . . . in charge of all the governments of Germany, nothing was more natural than that they should graft bourgeois constitutionalism on to the existing monarchial structure." The movement spread. The liberals demanded an end to censorship and the unity of all the Germanies (except Austria). They offered not kingship, but hereditary headship (*Reichsoberhaupt*) to King Friedrich Wilhelm. Despite much persuasion, he refused. "It would be," he declared, "a dog-collar fastened round my neck by the sovereign German people."

But then Austria forced its liberals to give in to the army, and one by one the cities fell—Vienna, Cracow, Prague. Prussia being the only organized state in the Germanies, their army was sent out to undo the revolutionary juntas. Troops marched, parliaments were dissolved, and political opponents were jailed, discredited, or shot. To add to the social unrest, a potato blight appeared in Germany and hunger was added to the political unrest. "The revolution of 1848," wrote Valentin, "was the first revolt to come from the depths of the people since Martin Luther. It failed despite all its high ideals and humanism because a humane revolution is necessarily a semi-revolution." Its one positive effect is that it opened the floodgates of migration of the German peoples to the Americas.

In New York, and everywhere else Germans had settled, there were Revolution Fests to proclaim the new unity of Germany. And when it failed, requiem masses were sung for the Germans, Austrians, Hungarians, and French who had died at the barricades. When the first political émigrés arrived in New York in October, 1848, resident Germans massed about City Hall to give welcome. There came the abovementioned Friedrich Hecker, who in the Civil War would raise the 24th Illinois Infantry regiment, the so-called "Hecker Regiment." Also Franz Sigel who would settle in Missouri, first as a schoolteacher and then as a Union soldier, rising to Major General in the army. Friedrich Hassaurek, from Vienna, would go to Chicago and help to elect Lincoln, becoming the first American minister to the Republic of Ecuador. (He thanked Lincoln for giving him the "highest post" in his power "since Quito was 9,400 feet altitude.") He would write *Four Years in South America*, one of the best books ever written on Ecuador.

Carl Schurz was another refugee from Germany. A lawyer, he would, in time, campaign for Lincoln, become a major general in the army, a senator from Missouri, a Secretary of the Interior, edit the New York *Evening Post*, and write a two-volume biography of Henry Clay. There was also Gustav Struve, who would edit *Die Sociale Republik* in New York and serve in the Union army. And Heinrich Hilgard, who changed his name to Henry Villard and was active in establishing rail transportation to the Pacific Northwest; in 1890 he merged several smaller companies to found the Edison General Electric Company, later the General Electric Company. Another refugee was Rudolph Eickemeyer, a Bavarian engineer who one day would design the first electric railway for New York City and give another latter-day refugee, C. P. Steinmetz, his first job.

Friedrich Hecker (1811–81) had to flee to North America after an abortive rebellion in 1848. He fought as a colonel in the Civil War.

On they came—journalists, lawyers, university professors, carpenters, tanners, foundrymen, millers, coopers, blacksmiths, weavers, bankers, cigarmakers, butchers, brewers, and doctors. Many immigrants remained in New York state. By the close of the 1850's, the German population of New York City was estimated at one hundred thousand, with twenty churches, fifty schools, ten bookstores, five printing establishments, and a German theater. It was the beginning of the migrant flood to America. Shiploads of Germans arrived in all the leading ports—Boston, New York, Baltimore, and New Orleans, from where they spread throughout the Mississippi Valley. In the century before 1914, their numbers would swell to 5,300,000, and if one were to add to this sum all the Germanic peoples, the total exceeds seven million.

Yet for many who arrived, America was not an Arcadia. Many who had degrees in philosophy, law, or theology were unable to find positions; many perished from hunger. Some supported themselves as bootblacks, others as cigarmakers, and still others as servants. One, Colonel Leopold von Gilsa, an ex-Prussian army officer, played the piano for his living in a Bowery saloon.

As political as the 1848–54 migration was, it also had economic roots. For many an immigrant the dominant motif was land hunger. Many German artisans, trained in the discipline of the old guild apprentice system, found a ready market for their services. Friedrich Kapp, a lawyer and one of the most articulate of the refugees, estimated that the German migration to North America alone, between 1819 and 1871, stood at 2,358,709, and that they represented an actual enrichment, through the importation of money and services, to an amount of a half billion dollars and a potential productive capacity of over $1,375,000,000.

A large portion of immigrants went west. By the middle of the 1840's Ohio was in full German bloom; Cincinnati had been a German settlement from its first beginnings; Indiana had a strong representation; Illinois before 1860 had a German community of 130,000. Chicago was an early cultural center, becoming so populous that in 1969 the London *Times* called it "America's German miracle . . . and that is the main reason for the sublime power and disciplined logic of its commercial buildings. . . ."

Engineers, rigidly trained in the German system, began to build immediately upon arrival. Clemens Herschel invented the Venturi tube; Gustav Lindenthal, who was educated in Dresden, built the Hellgate steel-arch bridge over the East River in New York City; Lewis Wernwag built a 340-foot bridge across the Schuylkill River; Albert Fink engineered the first bridge across the Monongahela River in 1852, the longest iron-truss span of its time. Ottmar Mer-

Ottmar Mergenthaler (1854–99) immigrated to North America in 1872, where he invented the Linotype typesetting machine.

genthaler, a German Jew from Hachtel, came to Baltimore at the age of eighteen and revolutionized the printing industry with his invention of the Linotype machine that still bears his name. Herman Haupt was the chief engineer of the Pennsylvania Railroad, and was in charge of constructing the Hoosac Tunnel in Massachusetts, a job that took twenty-four years to complete. John Roebling, born in Mühlhausen in 1806, made the first wire rope in 1841 and built the suspension bridge over Niagara Falls and another over the Ohio River near Cincinnati. His plans for the Brooklyn Bridge were approved the year of his death (1869) and the construction was carried through by his son. This is why Carl Wittke of the University of Pennsylvania, who minutely went into the lives and contributions

John Augustus Roebling (1806–69) made the preliminary plans for the Brooklyn Bridge.

of emigrants to the United States, entitled his book *We Who Built America*.

There were also surprising numbers of revolutionary refugees in the medical profession. Dr. Johann Menninger, a physician from Hesse, practiced in New York and was the ancestor of the founders of the Menninger Clinic. Dr. Alfred von Behr, who came from Anhalt, practiced in Missouri, as did Dr. Louis Bauer, who went from the Prussian legislature to St. Louis and became the founder of the College of Physicians and Surgeons. Dr. Gustav Bruhle, working in Cincinnati, became one of America's first throat specialists. Karl Hermann Berendt came to Nicaragua in 1851 and went on to Mexico, Yucatán, and Guatemala. In 1866 he made a survey for the Smithsonian Institute, and in 1869 the American Ethnological Society published his *Analytical Alphabet of the Mexican and Central American Languages.*

By 1854 one third of the physicians in New York state were Germans. Dr. Abraham Jacobi was one name in the long list of German-Jewish physicians of this period. Of poor parents, he took his medical degree in Bonn, was jailed for two years, and when released set up practice in New York City. In 1860 he established the first children's clinic in this country and began to teach that children's diseases often differ from adults'. In 1870 he became Professor of Pediatrics in the New York College of Physicians and Surgeons, a post he held until his retirement in 1902. From the predominantly Jewish villages of the Steyermark came Dr. Ernest Krackowitzer. He had studied medicine in Vienna and taken part in the October uprising, later becoming a leading surgeon in New York and a well-known student of art and literature. Dr. Simon Pollak came out of Bohemia, took his degree in Prague, settled in St. Louis, and was on active duty in the Union army during the entire Civil War. On the Confederate side was Dr. Simon Baruch, father of the famous financier, Bernard Baruch. After the war Dr. Baruch practiced in Camden, South Carolina, moving to New York in 1881. It was there, in 1888, that he performed the first appendicitis operation in America.

The German Jews who migrated to America did so for the same economic reasons as other German emigrants. There is general agreement that the cause of the first German-Jewish exodus in the 1830's was not so much persecution as the prevailing depression that weighed upon Jew and Gentile alike.

At first the Jewish community in America grew slowly. In 1790 it numbered no more than fifteen hundred. It increased in 1830 to eight thousand, but with the events of 1848 the German Jews expanded to a population of fifty thousand. The original congregations were Sephardic descendants of Spanish and Portuguese Jews, but those that arrived after 1830 were, for the most part, Ashkenazim. One such was Frederick Warburg, scion of an old-established Hamburg clan, who arrived in the United States in 1821. Wilhelm Krauss arrived in New York from Bavaria, purchased a horse and buggy, and peddled small merchandise until he went into clothing

Wall Street in New York in the mid-19th century.

manufacture on a large scale in Cincinnati. Julius Brooks (né Bach) came from Silesia in 1846, peddled throughout New England, and then turned to mining and real estate. David Teller came out of Bavaria and after 1842 acquired vast real estate acreage in Colorado.

August Belmont, from the Rhenish Palatinate, represented the House of Rothschild in Rome, sailed to Cuba in 1836, and the following year moved on to the United States. He emerged as one of its greatest bankers and eventually as a social arbiter. One of the earliest incipient millionaires to arrive was Joseph Seligman, from Baiersdorf, Bavaria. He came to the U.S. in 1837 and by 1864 his banking house had branches in San Francisco, New Orleans, London, Paris, and Frankfurt. He supported the Union cause during the Civil War, exposed the Tweed Ring in New York, and later became chairman of that city's Rapid Transit Commission. The Lehmans first appeared in the South. Meyer Lehman arrived in 1844 and later, as cotton broker, offered his services to the South. During the war Jefferson Davis said, "He was one of the best southern patriots."

The Guggenheims came from Switzerland and moved into mining; eventually they dominated the copper industry and controlled the American Smelting and Refining Company. Joseph Sachs, of the famous New York banking firm, began as a saddlemaker in Würzburg. In 1848 he landed at Baltimore, the semi-official port of entry for Germans. The Loebs, who were to evolve into the prestigious firm of Kuhn, Loeb & Co., came from Worms. They set up themselves in Philadelphia where there were many German Jews. It was this family that produced James Loeb, a scholar, who, after his retirement from business in 1901, devoted himself to literature. He founded the famed Loeb Classical Library (red cover for Latin, green for Greek), parallel translations of the classics.

Jews moved in the same cultural milieu with Germans in the United States throughout most of the nineteenth century. They belonged to the German Turnvereins and several Jews were prominent leaders of these gymnastic societies, vigorously advocating their radical programs. Jews belonged to German-American literary clubs and generously supported the German theater. Yet many learned and cultural Jews came without employment. One refugee was encountered on the streets of New York asking for a bite of bread in German, French, English, and Italian. Scholars able to quote Homer had to work with pick and shovel as day laborers on canals and railroads; accomplished musicians became piano tuners; philosophers worked as porters and house painters; mathematicians painted signs. German dancing teachers masqueraded as French in order to attract a more fashionable clientele.

Friedrich Knefler, a German Jew who fought with Kossuth, the Hungarian leader, would rise through the ranks to become a brigadier general in the Civil War; Vaish Levy became a sailor in the Union navy; and Jacob Zeitlin was the first Marine officer to become a brigadier general. Julius Bien, born in Cassel where he was trained as a map engraver, was put to work by Jefferson Davis. From 1826 to 1908 there was seldom a major geological publication issued by the government which did not state "Engraved by Julius Bien." Julius Ochs arrived in Frankfort, Kentucky, in 1845 and carried on his trade as a bookbinder as he had in Bavaria. He served in the Mexican War, became an abolitionist, and joined an Ohio company as captain. One of his three sons, Adolph, went on to head the *New York Times*.

The impact of 230,000 Germans pouring into new lands in a space of only a few years became culturally unnerving for many native Americans. The German Turnverein movement, which brought physical education into so many cities, had an influence that cannot be overemphasized. The Froebel kindergarten system, which first appeared in Germany in 1836, had a lasting influence. In many states the German language had equal status with English. The labor movement felt the impetus; the immigrants gave a new life to the movement whose members were, in the beginning, largely German.

Music had come with the colonial Germans. Bethlehem, Pennsylvania, with its Bach cult, was an early music center. To organ concerts, the Germans introduced a larger orchestra, with viola and French horn. Haydn's *Creation* and *The Seasons* had their American premieres there. With the advent of the 1848ers, a whole new range of musical experience descended on America. The Puritan tradition did not have a very high standard of musical appreciation, and the Quakers held all music suspect except psalm-singing and the like. There was such a naïve approach to harmony that when a Virginia physician heard a German quartet playing he said: "You Germans are a queer people. You don't make music as we Americans do. If several of us play simultaneously, we at least play the same melody, but the four of you have each played a different piece."

Many of the Forty-eighters arrived with their baggage filled with musical scores. The German-Czech Wehle family from Prague arrived with two grand pianos among their impedimenta. Männerchor and Liederkranz groups sprang up; there were *Sängerfeste* wherever there was a musical quorum. The Germania Orchestra, which later became the New York Philharmonic, was organized in New York by twenty-three émigrés. They offered the first American presentation of Wagner's *Tannhäuser*. In Boston, Chicago, St. Louis, Cincinnati, and Philadelphia, wherever there were Germans there were orchestras and chorales. The large German settlement in New Orleans helped to establish grand opera before the Civil War, and from the union of Creole *joie de vivre* and German *gemütlichkeit* came the music of Louis Gottschalk. Born in New Orleans of German immigrant parents, is considered by some the first true American-born composer.

Music schools and conservatories were, in the main, German.

August Waldhauer came to St. Louis in 1844 and founded the Beethoven conservatory; Schlesinger of Hamburg gave piano lessons in
New York; Julius Eichberg of Düsseldorf began the Boston Conservatory of Music. Dr. Florenz Ziegfeld of Oldenburg, whose son
would one day glorify the American girl in his Ziegfeld Follies,
developed the musical conservatory in Chicago. "Finally," wrote
Professor Wittke, "the number of makers of musical instruments in
the United States who were Germans is remarkable." Heinrich Stein-
weg, founder of the firm of Steinwey & Sons, was born in Wolfhagen.
He and his several sons worked with different American piano manufacturers in order to learn American methods. They then began to
make Steinway pianos. The names of other well-known American
piano manufacturers testify to their German origin: Knabe, Weber,
Lindemann, Stultz and Butter, Kranich and Bach, and Wurlitzer.

The Germans also gave the Americans many of their Christmas
traditions. Puritans did not celebrate Christmas; an early traveler in
America remembered that Christmas was acknowledged by "mischief
and drunken uproariousness. Effigies were erected in the streets,
much after the manner of Hallowe'en." The Germans brought the
Christmas tree. There were lighted Christmas trees as early as 1833,
long before the legendary Pastor Schwan used a Christmas tree in a
church service in 1851. Christmas cakes and Christmas songs—such
as the immortal *Stille Nacht, Heilige Nacht*—became in time part of
America's musical heritage. Even the Christmas card was introduced
to America by Louis Prang in 1875.

These cultural contributions were not immediately recognized or
accepted. "We opened our doors wide to the emigrant," a well-known
American complained, ". . . but it is becoming a traffic inundation."
Philip Hone, the witty diarist of early New York, complained that
"All Europe is coming across the ocean. They increase our taxes,
eat our bread, encumber our streets." The native American (hence
the term "nativist") denounced the immigrants "as the outcast, the
offal of society." It was the clash of the German Sunday with the
Puritan Sunday which aggravated the distaste. Sunday for the native
American was a day of utter resignation; after church, Sunday for the
German, whether Protestant or Catholic, was for singing, picnics,
and shooting-fests (*Schützenvereine*) followed by beer-drinking. The

German immigrants observed many customs of their homeland in the New World. Annually the Germans in New Jersey celebrated a Low German national festival with a great procession in historical costumes.

Puritans complained that the Germans were "bringing upon us the wretched immoralities of European society."

The Germans were often overbearing and aggressive in forcing their customs on reluctant Americans. "Let the Germans respect our customs if they want us to respect theirs," the nativists said. *The New York Times* lectured the Germans about wanting to convert the Sabbath "into a Saturnalia." German leaders, such as Gustav Körner, who settled in Illinois in 1830 and became one of Lincoln's law partners, blamed this ill will on his fellow Germans: "Instead of recognizing the flexibility of American life and becoming attuned to this 'Paradise of the poor man' where there was complete freedom and a minimum of government, too many German intellectuals talked only of becoming 'the yeast of the fermenting process of the modern age; the oxygen in the process of combustion of national and religious prejudices.'" Körner specifically attributed the emergence of nativism "to the arrogance, imperious, and domineering conduct of the refugees."

Friedrich Kapp, then a lawyer in New York, told the Germans that it was not necessary to transplant Germany onto American soil. "America will become the fatherland of those born here . . . the grandchildren of immigrants will completely forget the languages of their forebears." A concerned German intellectual wrote: "There is no American people, it is fashioned from those who came from all corners of the earth. The only unity exists in the principle of civil, religious, and political liberty."

The clash between nativist and immigrant was inevitable. In 1844 outbreaks of violence between nativists and the recently arrived were widespread. There were deaths, burnings, stonings, destruction, and riots in Cincinnati, Columbus, and Louisville. In New Orleans the nativists set fire to the German theater; in Columbus, Germans on their way home from a typical day's outing were fired upon. Police raided German homes without warrants. Negroes joined the nativists, urging "kill the damned Dutch."

The nativists formed a political party known as the Know Nothings and tried to force legislation to curb the rights of the recently arrived. They often succeeded. Foreign militia companies were disbanded; the Irish were dismissed from hotels and fire departments; advertisements for male and female help read, "Irish need not apply." During local elections, ruffians in Baltimore delighted in striking Irish and German residents with large carpenters' awls, the symbol of their nativism. German picnics were fired on by sling shots and revolvers, and the Turnvereins formed paramilitary companies in self-defense.

Because of these disturbances, immigration declined noticeably in 1855. In the 1830's the German author Gottfried Duden had painted the American West in roseate colors as a prospective center for German culture. Now Ferdinand Kurnberger described the prairie near Pittsburg as a place where the air burned as in a blast furnace. There was not a bird or butterfly visible, and no sound of an animal, not even the hum of an insect. "Everything that was not a salamander seemed to be dead." Even Heinrich Heine distrusted America.

But by 1860 much of this was in the background. A new crisis had settled over the land.

The Lessons of the Battlefield   XVIII

The year 1856 opened with a chorus of recrimination and hatred. There were no longer any doubts about the political drift of things: the argument over the extension of slavery to new territories had brought about "bleeding Kansas," where many an immigrant would lose his life. To that issue was now added that of the preservation of the union.

German opposition to slavery was unequivocal. Slavery and its economics were the issues. Gustav Körner recorded in his diary that "Negro slavery is the only rope by which the devil holds the American people." Carl Schurz referred to the South's peculiar institution as the "one shrill discord" in American democracy, while Friedrich Kapp concluded that the Americans and Germans were destined, after a separation of fifteen hundred years, "to reunite in the common struggle to extend the frontiers of human liberty." The slavery controversy drew many political refugees of 1848 into a field of political activity that was to quicken their Americanization.

Despite the fact that most Germans were openly opposed to slavery, not all Germans shared this view. A large number of Germans had settled in the South. Virginia and the Carolinas were peopled with Germans as early as the North had been. Since 1750 the Shenandoah Valley had been the main avenue for their advance into Virginia, Tennessee, and Kentucky, and many would serve under Confederate General Stonewall Jackson. Even today, in the remote Carolina mountains, descendants of prisoners who served with Burgoyne are called "Hessians." Virginia had rifle companies, Turnvereins, a Schiller Society, and a newspaper, *Die Virginische Zeitung*, for their seven thousand Germans. Kentucky had a sufficient number of Germans to read the *Louisville Anzeiger*, and Tennessee had settlements at Wartburg and Hohenwald. Alabama listed its Germans in *Der*

Alabama Pionier. Charleston had a German colony dating back to 1680. By the time of the Civil War there were twelve hundred settled there with the usual volunteer fire company, a literary society, and the well-known Palmetto Regiment which had marched off *en bloc* to the Mexican War.

Louisiana contained one fifth of all the Germans in the South, so many that both sides of the Mississippi above New Orleans were called the "Côte des Allemands." Over ten thousand would serve in the Confederacy, not a few reaching command rank. The Confederate Secretary of the Treasury would be Christopher Gustavus Memminger, who had been brought over as a child from Württemberg. One of the high commissioners in Europe attempting to gain political recognition for the South would be Harald Holz, a German-Swiss. And Captain Henry Wirz, a German-Swiss immigrant who served as the hapless commander of the notorious Andersonville prison, would be the only man tried and hanged for war crimes. Even the assassination of Abraham Lincoln would involve three Germans.

Once more the leitmotif of German-against-German was heard across a troubled land. The Sängerfest of 1859 had an overtone of disunion, and the annual Turnverein contests were clouded with North-South contention. The national meeting of the Turnvereins wanted to draft an antislavery resolution, which caused the Southern groups to withdraw with a warning that all this agitation would bring civil war. They were right. New Braunfels, Texas, a stronghold of liberal culture in the South, would not give a single vote to Lincoln in the 1860 elections.

The death of Alexander von Humboldt in May, 1859, gave the northern and southern Germans one last opportunity to cooperate before war splintered their relationships. Throughout the country there were obsequies and memorial services for Humboldt. "The German population in America," read one of the many resolutions, "expresses the most sincere sympathy of the Germans in the Western Hemisphere with those of the Eastern world." The New York *Herald Tribune*, on June 24, 1859, took the occasion of one ceremony (much to the annoyance of the Southern Germans) to editorialize: "*Humboldt on American Slavery.* He looks upon the attempts in the United States to take Slavery to the Pacific through the free Western prairies and across the Rocky Mountains, with an utter abhorrence. To

The First Kindergarten in the U.S.A.
Watertown, Wisconsin

Carl Schurz

Margarethe Schurz

On the postcard (above) Carl Schurz (1829–1906) and his wife Margarethe are credited with founding the first American kindergarten. Schurz assisted in Lincoln's election and held influential offices. Shown below in his Civil War uniform of brigadier-general, this "greatest German in America" also served as Secretary of the Interior.

Schurz (at the piano) was a welcome guest of the President of the United States.

attempt to introduce Slavery where it does not now exist, Humboldt regards as a crime."

The trustees of the John Jacob Astor Library had been left the unprecedented sum of four hundred thousand dollars in 1848 to form a free library, and they decided to use the money to purchase Humboldt's library. In a codicil to his will, written in 1853, Humboldt bequeathed to Seifert, his manservant, "All the goods that are in my house . . . medals, clocks, chronometers, books. . . ." *Books!!!* It was his entire private library of 11,164 volumes, many of which were presentation copies with biographical or critical marginalia, and included a collection of four thousand separate scientific treatises plus copies of Humboldt's *Kosmos* with enough new notes and marginalia to have made a revised edition.

Seifert sold Humboldt's library to a Hamburg bookseller, who in turn offered it to various societies in Germany. All declined, perhaps for a reason. A year after Humboldt's death his friend, Varnhagen von Ense, allowed Humboldt's letters to be published. "Hundreds of influential people," said a reviewer, "some of them belonging to the highest ranks of society, will be stung to the quick by these revelations." Immediately a cold chill descended in monied circles over Humboldt's memory. "My friend Humboldt," was one person's comment, "had the most affectionate heart and the most slanderous tongue of anyone I ever knew." Unable to be sold in Germany, the library was shipped to London, where Joseph Cogswell, a trustee of the Astor Library, "expressed a strong wish to add it to that other library in America which owed its origin to a German," and arranged to purchase it in its entirety. The outbreak of the Civil War and the chance of losing the books by sea made the Astor Library hesitate; they allowed their option to lapse. Henry Stevens, an American bookseller in London, offered it up for auction at Sotheby's. The sale of the great library had scarcely reached the third day when, in June, 1865, the auction rooms took fire. Humboldt's library was totally destroyed.

May 16, 1860, was the prelude to war. The Republican convention met in Chicago to nominate a presidential candidate. Present were forty-two German-born delegates who formed part of the Republican "Dutch" plank to elect Lincoln. After he was nominated, the Republican appeal for German votes was spearheaded by a galaxy of orators speaking interchangeably in German and English.

Abraham Lincoln carried eighteen states in the election. Where the German population predominated, he was elected by wide margins. In the South the Germans gave him not a single vote. The result of the campaign is well-known: Lincoln received 1,866,452 popular votes, Douglas 1,376,957 (electoral votes, 180 to 12). It has been shown that if one vote in twenty changed, Douglas would have won over Lincoln. The German vote was so important that many agree it was decisive in electing Lincoln. At least Lincoln thought so, for he set about at once to distribute among the German leadership a major part of the political spoils.

Victory, yes, but also, as the Texas Germans predicted, war. As soon as Lincoln's election was known, the state of South Carolina, on December 20, 1860, seceded from the Union. Within two months, six more southern states—Mississippi, Florida, Alabama, Georgia, Louisiana, and Texas—followed South Carolina into secession.

By that time "union," as much as "slavery," had become the issue. The Southern states had a one-crop economy, cotton, which had saddled the South with a labor system that most considered not only outdated, but uneconomical. Lincoln stressed "union" because he was aware that southern-grown cotton fed the mills of England. It stood to reason that the British would be economically inconvenienced by an American civil war. The South believed that if England and France could not obtain cotton, they would intervene and underwrite the Confederacy's independence in order to ensure their future supply. On April 12, 1861, the Southerners opened fire on Fort Sumter in Charleston harbor.

The Civil War had begun.

"The essential nature of the thing," wrote one German author, "remains the physical, the primitive struggle, and no matter how intellectualized the man, it is the duty of a man to remain a man. If he is not willing to give his arm, his leg, his life for the ideal that he professes, then he is not worthy of it." The Germans were to give many arms, legs, and lives for their ideals. In Lincoln's first call for volunteers, six thousand Germans enlisted from New York, four thousand from Pennsylvania. Ohio furnished eleven infantry regiments, artillery batteries, and cavalry. Within six months there was a good-sized army of six thousand from Illinois. In Baltimore, although Maryland was a neutral state, its Turnverein society enlisted *en bloc*. When the first shot was fired, Franz Sigel was teaching school in St. Louis, Missouri. Educated at the Military Academy in Karlsruhe, Sigel had led four thousand men in the revolution of 1848 and commanded additional troops in 1849. He was considered a resourceful military leader. In May, 1861, he organized a regiment of Missouri volunteers which, although beset by controversies, served throughout as "a symbol of the German participation in the war."

Missouri put more than eight thousand men into the Union army, four of whom rose to be major generals. Wisconsin, heavily larded with Germans, put in an equal number. The Ninth Wisconsin Regi-

General Franz Sigel at the Battle of Pea Ridge. The German immigrant participated in the Civil War with a Union Army volunteer unit from Missouri.

ment had a large band with special uniforms; it even published its own paper in the battlefield, *Der deutsche Kreiger*. The XI Corps of the Army of the Potomac consisted of twenty-six regiments, of which fifteen were entirely German. The 5th and 11th New York Regiments were composed almost exclusively of German members of the Liederkranz and Teutonia Männerchor, "whose musical directors," said one, "laid down their batons to become army buglers." Of the total number of 2,018,000 Union soldiers, 289,080 were German—one tenth of the entire fighting force of the North. Of these, five hundred had officers who were born in Germany.

Missouri's four volunteer regiments, commanded by Franz Sigel, were recruited in two days. Friedrich Hecker put aside his plow in Illinois to raise a regiment (he was severely wounded at the Battle of Chancellorsville). Adolph Engelmann, who had done geological surveys for the army topographical corps and was a veteran of the war with Mexico, became a general; Karl Eberhard Salomon of Saxony became a colonel, while his brother rose to the rank of general; Alexander Schimmelpfennig, trained in a Prussian military school, was a colonel in the Army of the Potomac; Max Weber, a veteran of the revolutions in Germany, commanded a German Turnverein regiment and was killed at Antietam. Peter Osterhaus, veteran of the Prussian army who settled in St. Louis in 1851, entered the army as a private and was mustered out a major general. He took part in no less than thirty-four engagements, including Vicksburg and Sherman's march from Atlanta to the sea, and was regarded by many military experts as the best of the German officers.

Gustav Struve enlisted as a private in 1861 and then obtained a captaincy in Blenker's Regiment. Bernard Domschke closed his desk as editor of a Milwaukee newspaper and served in the Sigel Regiment; he was captured and spent two years in the notorious Libby prison. Captain Ernest Hoffmann, who seemed to have fought everywhere—in the revolution in Germany, with the British in the Crimea, and as a staff officer in Italy under Garibaldi—commanded an artillery battery in Missouri and Arkansas. Karl Knodere was killed while serving as a colonel; John Albert Dettweiler, a European veteran who fled Germany with Carl Schurz in 1848, served as an artillery officer. Julius Stahel, who fought at Bull Run, became a major general. August Willich, a former Prussian officer, a strict disciplinarian, and a bold fighter, took part in a number of engagements. He was severely wounded and left the army with the rank of brigadier general. Colonel Eugene von Kielmansegg, an ancestor of the former NATO commander, left the sanctuary of Maryland to enter the Union army.

Colonel Gottfried Becker lost a leg at Gettysburg; Colonel Adolf Dengler, a "Latin Farmer" from Belleville, Illinois, died at the siege of Vicksburg; Ernest Fähtz, an Austrian who fought in the 1848 revolution, became a colonel in a Maryland regiment. Emil Haas was a regimental surgeon; Wilhelm Peter Heine, one of several Germans who had been with Commodore Perry in the Far East, entered the engineer corps; Konrad Krez, a New York lawyer, became a major general.

"The Germans like everybody else," as Professor Wittke points out, "wanted commissions, gold braid, and the prestige of military titles, and the Civil War had its quota of political generals and un-

The Germans in America formed volunteer battalions from their gymnastic organizations during the Civil War.

principled adventurers." "The first theater of war for most of the German colonels," Karl Heinzen wrote in 1861, "was the beer house," and Otto von Corvin agreed. This veteran of the 1848 revolution reported on the Civil War as the correspondent for the *Augsburger Allgemeine Zeitung.* He discovered many an ex-German officer who had left the Fatherland because of financial troubles or for adventure.

There were, of course, the "professionals," mostly from West Point. Major General Henry Halleck, for a while chief of staff for the Union army, was a Californian of German descent. Brigadier General Samuel P. Heintzelman, who possessed a stern, buttoned-up appearance, was from Manheim, Pennsylvania. He had fought in Mexico and was one of the more prominent officers in the Union army, as was August von Kautz, who commanded the first Negro troops. William S. Rosecrans, who was born Rosenkranz but called "Old Rosy" by his men, was a descendant of Catholic Germans from Ohio (his brother was the Bishop of Cincinnati). A genial West Pointer, he commanded the Army of the Cumberland. Lieutenant George Custer, who rose to be a general and "came down from the Point," was a descendant of a German Hessian named Köster who surrendered after the Battle of Saratoga.

Those German Jews who lived in the South were generally sympathetic to the Confederacy; over one thousand German Jews served in the Confederate army. Louisiana, with the largest amount of German elements, had 233 Jewish combatants on its rolls. There were many in the Macon, Georgia, artillery, and in Mississippi, where Dr. Simon Baruch served as physician-general, the large enlistment included five Jonas brothers from one family. In North Carolina, where hundreds served, six Cohen brothers enlisted in the same regiment, and four Oppenheimers were found in a Texas volunteer company. In all, twenty-four German Jews would hold commands in the Confederacy.

Simon Wolf, a leading attorney in Washington, had been born in Bavaria. He came to America in 1848 to study law, and resided in Washington. It was Wolf who was largely responsible for persuading Lincoln to rescind General Grant's order of 1862 expelling all Jewish civilians from the Department of Tennessee "for trading with the enemy." After the war he read an article which began: "I served in the field about eighteen months before being permanently disabled in action, and was quite familiar with several regiments; was then transferred to two different recruiting stations, but I cannot remember meeting one Jew in uniform, or hearing of any Jewish soldier." Simon Wolf searched the records and wrote a book on the services of the German Jews on both sides of the conflict. He showed that over six thousand served in the Union army (twenty-four reaching staff-officer rank). Colonel Edward Salomon served in Hecker's Regiment. Colonel Newman was fatally wounded in the first battle and President Lincoln brought his brevet rank of brigadier general to his deathbed. Colonel Leopold Blumenberg of Baltimore was severely wounded at the battle of Antietam; Colonel Spiegel was shot at Vicksburg; Leo Karpeles was awarded a Congressional Medal; August Bruckner was killed at the Battle of Bull Run; Colonel H. A. Seligson led a Vermont regiment; Frederick Kenffler, a resident of Indianapolis, commanded the 79th Indians and attained the rank of major general.

If the Germans complained that their massive contribution was largely overlooked during and after the war, it was not the fault of their press. There were over three hundred German-language newspapers and their participation was heavily reported. There was even a German edition of *Leslie's Illustrated Weekly* published throughout the war. Frank Leslie's illustrated papers employed many special artists who worked under fire. The editor of *Harper's Weekly* called them "a noble army of artists." They had portrayed it with pencil and sketch pad in the fields, he said, "with freezing or fevered fingers, making their sketches in ambulances and field hospitals, in trenches and on decks. . . . They had shared the fighting men's months of idleness and his moments of danger. . . ."

Among the small army of reporters were many Germans or German-descended artists. The Schell brothers, Frank and Frederick, were born in Pennsylvania; one was with General Grant at the siege of Vicksburg; another reported Sherman's advance before Atlanta.

Henty Lovie, né Löwe, from Alsace-Lorraine, of the firm of Bauerie, Bruen, and Lovie in Cincinnati, was in Missouri where he sketched the death of General Nathaniel Lyon at the Battle of Wilson' Creek. John G. Keyser became "regimental artist to a company of New Jersey Volunteers." Another artist, known only as "Kaiser," did art reportage on the Union armies operating in Virginia. Carl von Iwonski was born in Silesia and came to the United States with Prinz Solms-Braunfels, who established New Braunfels, Texas. There he studied art and limned the battles of Texas. John Omenhauser served with the Virginians and illustrated the horrible life in prisons when he himself was captured.

The best known of the German-born artists was Thomas Nast. Born in Landau, the son of a trombone player in the 9th Bavarian Regiment, he was brought as a child to New York, studied art, and in the summer of 1862 joined *Harper's Weekly*. His drawings of recruits for Union posters caused Lincoln to call him "our best recruiting sergeant." His later crusade against the Tweed Ring in New York made him the most powerful cartoonist of his time.

Adalbert Volck tried to emulate Nast for the Southern press. The son of Andreas von Volzsch, a prominent landowner in Nürnberg, he entered the University of Munich and specialized in chemistry. He marched with the liberals of 1848 and then fled to America, where he changed his name to Volck. He tried gold mining, then turned to dentistry, and in Baltimore he built up a lucrative practice. Also an artist under the *nom de plume* of "Blada," Volck acidly caricatured Lincoln and other Union leaders. He was eventually such a *bête noire* to the North that he was jailed in Fort McHenry. He made the death mask of Stonewall Jackson and the portrait of Jefferson Davis that was engraved on the ten-cent stamps of the Confederacy. He also painted a portrait of General Robert E. Lee.

The divided state of Maryland dramatically illustrated the division among the German elements. While it could produce a Dr. Volck, it also produced Barbara Fritchie, the daughter of the immigrant Caspar Fritchie. According to legend, Barbara fearlessly hung out the Union flag in the face of the Confederates in the town of Frederick.

The Battle of Antietam was fought in Maryland with a terrible loss of soldiers. When President Theodore Roosevelt stood before the memorial windows of the Lutheran Church at Antietam, he saw "the names of the German dead who belonged to the Maryland regiment recruited largely from that region for the Civil War and mainly composed of men of German extraction." He was made aware of their massive contribution: "It would be difficult to paint in too strong colours . . . the attitude of the American citizens of German birth . . . toward the cause of the Union. . . ."

The Union armies, less well officered than the Southern, lost battle after battle. The Confederates took parts of Maryland and came within miles of Washington. So certain were they of victory that the British, who at first declared themselves neutral, were on the verge of granting outright recognition to the South. This would have meant loans and the open building of ships in their shipyards, which was then being done surreptitiously.

The French were leaning heavily toward a Southern victory, and Russia even sent over its fleet for a courtesy visit, with the overtone of a warning to Britain. But fifty years later, when the Russian state archives disgorged their secret papers, it was learned that the Russian fleet had only visited American ports in 1863 to protect itself from being bottled up in the Baltic should France and Britain declare war over the Tsar's suppression of Poland.

There were constant international incidents. Britain threatened war many times. Napoleon III planned a Mexican intervention to give his troops and his officer corps war training so as to sharpen them for a showdown with Prussia. Prussia knew that the *Zessionskrieg*, as they called the American Civil War, was utilizing techniques that would revolutionize modern warfare—railways, telegraphy, ironclad ships, observation balloons equipped with telegraph—and was anxious to see them in action. The General Staff sent over Captain Justus Scheibert as a military observer accredited to the Southern states.

Scheibert, a talented, amiable young officer, won the confidence of General Robert E. Lee, who often explained to him his methods of planning strategy. So much did Scheibert identify himself with the Southern cause that he was once captured in a raid by several Union officers. All of his battlefield observations, a series of long memorandums to Helmuth von Moltke, chief of the Prussian General Staff, were used in planning the Franco-Prussian War of 1870. Scheibert's book, *Der Bürgerkrieg in den nordamerikanischen Staaten*, was a detailed summary of the South at war.

There he met Major Heros von Borcke, a gigantic Guards officer whom Lee called "the German Goliath" because he weighed 250 pounds (125 kilograms) and stood sixty-two inches (1.87 meters). Von Borcke had been a lieutenant in the cuirassiers of the Royal Guard in Berlin. Prolonged arguments with his father over his debts forced him to leave the Guards, and since the Southern struggle touched his romantic feeling, he sought out Mr. Mason, the Confederate agent in Paris, and arranged to run the blockade to Virginia. He was first attached to General Lee's headquarters as a major, and after that he rode with J. E. B. Stuart. He was a favorite of the Southerners and, as his memoirs show, he remembered his exploits the rest of his life.

On May 3, 1863, during the Battle of Chancellorsville in Virginia,

Major Heros von Borcke was severely wounded. A bullet entered his collar and passed into his throat, and "for months thereafter," said the man who saved him, "he coughed up pieces of his uniform which had been carried into the wound." Thus ended von Borcke's service to the South. However, on his return to Germany, he took part in the Seven Weeks' War and was at the Battle of Sadowa (July 3, 1866) serving on the staff of Prince Friedrich Karl. He made a memorable return to Baltimore in 1884, and when he was visited in Europe by those under whom he had served, he would run up on his castle's tower the Prussian flag alongside that of the Confederacy.

Von Borcke was unusual, since most German officers preferred the North. Felix Nepomuk, Prince Salm-Salm, like von Borcke, had been a lieutenant in the *Gardekurassierregiment* in Berlin, serving in the war against Denmark. He left his regiment because of debts and entered the American Civil War, becoming chief of staff to the Blenker Division in the Army of the Potomac. That a Prussian prince should be an officer in their regiment aroused so much consternation among the liberal Germans that several officers resigned and Gustav Struve wrote a pamphlet denouncing him. But Salm-Salm was not just another Prussian officer. He would become intimately involved in the last days of the Mexican Emperor Maximilian and later a *cause célèbre* when he was killed in the Franco-Prussian War by a surplus gun that the victorious North had sold to France. It raised another furor among the German veterans of the Civil War.

Count Ferdinand von Zeppelin's position was entirely different. As a young lieutenant, he was interested in seeing the war at close range in order to observe the organization of the Union Army and, as the "Americans were inventive," to study their improvisations. The Zeppelin family had originally come from Mecklenburg in Prussia, but Count Ferdinand himself was born in what had once been a Dominican cloister fronting Lake Constance. After classical studies, young Zeppelin attended the military school at Ludwigsburg and, in accordance with his birth, was attached as a staff officer to the King of Württemberg. This sinecure not being to his liking, he secured first his father's and then the King's permission to take a leave of absence to observe the Civil War.

In April, 1863, Washington did not, he wrote in his memoirs, "make a great impression on me. The streets were dusty and un-

As a young officer Ferdinand von Zeppelin (1838–1917) (second from the left), inventor of the airship, traveled in North America. He gained valuable military experience in the Army of the Potomac during the Civil War.

paved." The main thoroughfare, Pennsylvania Avenue, conceived as a broad and imposing boulevard, was almost devoid of buildings; the wide, neglected street wore an air of desolation. In dry weather the street was thick with dust; in winter a channel of mud. Hotels in Washington were a recent development; halls were crowded, prices high, the clerks haughty, the din frightful. "One obviously did not live in Washington for pleasure. . . ."

Through Baron von Gerolt, the Prussian minister, Zeppelin was granted an interview with President Lincoln. "I remember him as a very tall, lean person with an overlarge head, uncared for beard and hair, and striking high and sharp cheek bones, but with intelligent and friendly looking eyes." Lincoln seemed to be at ease with Zeppelin; here, at least, was a visitor who did tell him how to win the war.[1]

After expressing his satisfaction that Zeppelin wished to take part as an observer with the Union army, Lincoln turned him over to the minister of war who gave Zeppelin a general pass to go anywhere he wished with whatever army he wished in the Union forces. Such a pass, he was assured, had only been given to three other personalities, all of them French.

Zeppelin was recommended to Lieutenant General Daniel Butterfield, chief of staff of the Army of the Potomac. A New Yorker, Butterfield had operated the first stagecoach service between Mississippi and California, twice weekly over twenty-eight hundred miles of plains, mountains, and deserts, a trip that took twenty-five days. With a hard-set mouth and a thatch of white hair, Butterfield had, as Zeppelin remarked, "a proven talent for organization." On his uniform collar Zeppelin pinned a star, the Prussian insignia of a first lieutenant. He soon found himself taking salutes from colonels since the star made him a brigadier general in the Union army. "I was not prepared," he said, "for so quick an advance in rank—even in America."

Colonel von Radowitz, formerly of the Prussian cavalry, supplied him with his horse and a newly adopted cavalry saddle. The modified Mexican saddle, known as the "McClellan," so impressed him that Zeppelin recommended it to the Prussian chief of staff, who used it in the Franco-Prussian War. Zeppelin journeyed to the advanced headquarters of the Army of the Potomac among the XI Corps composed of German troops. There he met Joseph "Fighting Joe" Hooker, commander of the Army of the Potomac. A tall West Pointer with blond hair, Hooker had the reputation of being excitable, indiscreet in speech, and too fond of liquor. "He welcomed me in a very friendly manner," wrote Zeppelin, "and assigned me a tent of my own and at every possibility offered me a glass of whiskey."

[1]Everyone, it seemed, had an opinion; Lincoln's mail was filled with letters from "experts." He had been receiving of late letters from London containing surprisingly mature observations signed, in a young girl's handwriting, "Respectfully yours, Tussy Marx." It was only when Lincoln read similar views in the New York *Herald Tribune* under the signature of Karl Marx that he was able to put the two together. Born in Trier, the author of the *Communist Manifesto* had arrived in London at the age of thirty-one and was living with his wife and three children in Chelsea, meanwhile trying to earn enough for his family by writing for the *Tribune*.

Count Zeppelin (with the rifle) also explored the headwaters of the Mississippi.

The Germans were everywhere. An officer who had befriended him once in Ehrenbreitstein in 1857 was now a captain in the Union army; Zeppelin found him standing on a beer cask delivering a speech in German to his troops on the State of the Union. At Fairfax Courthouse he came upon and was introduced to General Carl Schurz, division commander of the XI Corps who had asked to be relieved of his post as ambassador to Spain in order to take an active command in the Union army. As a soldier, Schurz did not impress Zeppelin: "There was something theatrical about him. He . . . was obviously anxious to give himself a military air."

Zeppelin was in the Army of the Potomac's advance across the Rapidan River into the Virginian heartland. He saw action at Fairfax Courthouse and rode with the Union cavalry general Alfred Pleasonton ("At the beginning of the war he promised not to cut his hair until the Rebs were conquered: now his hair fell far down over the collar of his military jacket"). By the terms of his pass Zeppelin was not allowed any active participation on either side. "However, I would have very much wished to go over to the Southern side to continue my observations, but it was questionable if they would not have hung me to the nearest tree, even though I never once drew my saber, and in addition carried a very cordial letter of introduction to General Lee which I had received from his charming niece whom I had met in Philadelphia."

Count Zeppelin, out of his experiences in the American Civil War, was able to reform the German army by proposing the McClellan saddle and showing how to use cavalry not as an instrument of attack, but as Jeb Stuart used it, for strategical reconnaissance. Even more important, he pointed out to the German army that parades and uniforms were not the most essential items in making a good fighting soldier.

The greatest influence of the Civil War on future European wars was the balloon. While in America, Zeppelin began to conceive the idea of a guided dirigible. Moreover, he lived to see his idea become a fact in World War I. Thaddeus Lowe, a young, enterprising aeronaut, had already perfected a balloon which was used for military observations. It was constructed of silk and inflated with hydrogen gas from portable generators. Later the balloons were linked by telegraph to the ground. Count Zeppelin was so impressed that after the war he made several ascents. Henceforth, despite his subsequent military fame, Zeppelin devoted his life to dirigible balloon experiments.

By May, 1864, Union troops were involved in the Battle of the Wilderness. Major General Sigel's divisions were dreadfully mawled; the IX Corps of the Army of the Potomac, which had lost heavily before now, was taking still further losses.

While the armies of General Grant pressed on to Virginia, General Sherman was making his infamous March to the Sea, much to the applause of Karl Marx who had already informed the North in one of his articles that such a step should be taken to destroy the war-making potential in the South. Sherman and his men were destroying more than "war-making potential"; for many he was destroying a whole way of life as well as irreplaceable collections of books and art, such as those of John Bachman. The son of a German immigrant from Württemberg, Bachman had collaborated with John Audubon on a huge work on American mammals with 155 large hand-colored lithographic plates. He had unpublished Audubon material in his library when Sherman's holocaust swept through Columbia, South Carolina. War, like death, is no respecter of persons, and Bachman's "whole library," he recalled with anguish, "and all of my collections . . . the accumulation of the labors of a long life, were burned by Sherman's vandal army."

Many a German-born soldier serving under the German generals Schimmelpfennig and Osterhaus took part in the march. The most conspicuous was Herman Haupt. Haupt had been educated at West Point and rose to be chief engineer of the Pennsylvania Railroad. When war came he was made a colonel and then a general, chief of the entire U.S. military rail transportation. His men learned to tear railways apart as well as build them, and bridges were his speciality. When President Lincoln crossed one of Haupt's bridges over Potomac Creek in April, 1863, he said: "I have witnessed the most remarkable structure that human eyes ever rested upon. That man Haupt has built a bridge across the Potomac about four hundred feet long, eighty feet high in nine days with common soldiers, over which loaded trains are running every hour, and upon my word there is nothing in it but beanpoles and cornstalks."

By December 22, 1864, General Sherman had completed his March to the Sea and the President received his dispatch: "I beg to present you as a Christmas gift the city of Savannah, Georgia." On April 9, 1865, General Lee asked for and was given the conditions of surrender. After signing, Lee wrote to his soldiers: "The Civil War being at the end . . . I believe it to be the duty of every one to unite in the restoration of the country, and the establishment of peace and harmony. . . ."

But everyone was not going to unite in the restoration of the country. General Edmund Kirby-Smith in Texas refused to give up his army and by that time he was sending matériel across the Mexican

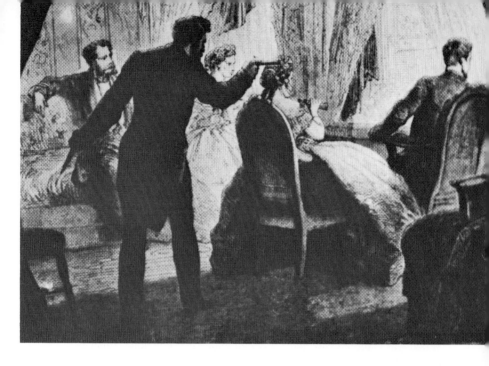

Assassination of President Abraham Lincoln, April 14, 1865, in Ford's Theater in Washington, by John Wilkes Booth. At right are shown two Germans involved in the assassination: George Atzerodt (top) and Edward Spangler.

President Lincoln and his son Tad.

border. Numerous Southern officers, in touch with the Emperor
Maximilians' agents, were planning to send two thousand Southern
families to settle in the Mexican state of Sonora. Along with twenty
thousand veterans and numerous generals, they planned to set up a
northern Mexican empire and continue the Civil War.

On April 14, 1865, Abraham Lincoln was assassinated. The gal-
vanizing figure was John Wilkes Booth, the twenty-six-year-old
romantic actor from Maryland. He was obsessed with hatred for
Lincoln and formed a band of conspirators, of which three were

Germans. One was Louis Weichmann who worked in the War Department, a large, timid, scholarly student, descendant of Pennsylvania German immigrants. His part in the proceedings vaguely had to do with the abduction of Secretary of War Stanton, but, fearful of the consequences, he disclosed the plan, which did not save him from prison. George Atzerodt, a droll, disreputable German immigrant, had been a secret ferryman feeding the underground road to the South; by profession he was a carriage maker in Maryland. His part was to kill Vice President Andrew Johnson and then aid in ferrying the kidnapped cabinet officers into Southern territory where they would be held "to ransom the South." In July, Atzerodt was hanged. Edward Spangler, a middle-aged, hard-drinking, good-natured hostler who looked after Booth's horses, was, on the night of Lincoln's murder, acting as a stagehand at Ford's Theater. He was apprehended, loaded with double iron cuffs, and thrown into the hold of the monitor *Montauk* anchored in the Navy Yard. As he had taken no active part in the murder conspiracy, Spangler was jailed on the barren rocks of the Dry Tortugas.

Those Germans who had taken an active part in the Civil War, this participation gave them a new sense of belonging. Major General Friedrich Hecker praised the "three miracles of America" in a Fourth of July speech in Stuttgart. With his own eyes he had seen these miracles: the abolition of slavery, the return of huge armies to civilian pursuits, and the decision of the victorious not to bestow medals on their generals.

The Regeneration of Mexico   XIX

When French troops landed in Mexico on December 17, 1861, the North and South were locked in battle. The North was powerless to interfere, but newspapers reflecting public opinion demanded action: "Send fifty thousand troops and drive the invaders into the sea." When rumors began to float that Archduke Maximilian of Austria would assume the "crown" of Mexico, American diplomats in France and Austria demanded some sort of action from Washington. The Secretary of State replied, "Why should we gasconade about Mexico when we are in a struggle for our life?" and President Lincoln said, "One war at a time."

France, England, and Spain viewed the financial chaos of Mexico with the frayed tempers of distraught bankers. Great Britain, who for three centuries had coveted an entrance into the Latin American market, gave encouragement to Mexican independence in order to negotiate favorable commercial treaties. Loans were floated in London with a discount rate so heavy that only half the original sums ever reached the Mexican treasury. France had also floated loans which had not been repaid. Spain continued to regard Mexico as a rebellious colony and had, as late as 1830, bombarded its principal ports.

When Benito Juárez was elected president in 1861, he inherited an empty treasury. Because Spain had intervened in Mexico's affairs, Juárez threw out their ambassador. A long mule train of silver coming from the English-controlled mines of San Luis Potosí had been hijacked and England demanded compensation. The French as well had a long list of claims. When Juárez decreed a suspension of all payments on foreign debts for two years, Spain, England, and France formed a triple alliance against Mexico. Spain and England supplied the convoys and warships, France the troops. In June, 1863, twenty thousand legionnaires, toughened by war in Algeria, marched into

Emperor Maximilian's adversary, Benito Juárez (1806–72), President of the Republic of Mexico.

Mexico City. It would be the last attempt of a European government to attempt to establish a monarchy in the Americas.

The court of Louis Napoleon (later Napoleon III) was a rendezvous for formerly high-placed but now exiled Mexicans, who asked France to intervene for the "regeneration of Mexico." It was agreed that the country should be offered to Archduke Maximilian, younger brother of Franz Joseph I of Austria. Accordingly, in October, 1862, a delegation of Mexican exiles journeyed to Miramar, a palatial mansion overlooking the Gulf of Trieste, and offered the crown to Maximilian.

"The Emperor," wrote Prince Salm-Salm, "was about six feet tall and slender. His movements were graceful and light. He had fair hair which he wore carefully parted in the middle. His beard was also fair and very long, and he nursed it with great care. He wore it parted in the middle, and his hand was very frequently occupied with its arrangement. His eyes were blue, his mouth had the unmistakable stamp of the Austrian imperial house, with the Hapsburg lip."

Maximilian disliked the snobbery of the Austrian court and the conservatism of his brother. He had a vague and romantic faith in progress and democracy. But he also had a certain competency; his political and military administration of the Lombardo-Venetian territory, then under Austria, was, by all accounts performed well enough; when he had been an admiral in the Imperial navy he had made impressive reforms. In the years 1859–60 he had conducted a scientific expedition between Mexico and Brazil on the flagship *Elisabeth*, one of the results being a splendidly illustrated botanical publication by Heinrich Wawra Ritter von Fernsee. In addition, Maximilian was also the author of *Aus meinem Leben*, published privately in seven volumes.

Though Maximilian was exceedingly vain, he was not a fool, nor did he at any time consider himself a puppet. He was, however, ambitious, and moreover he wished to escape from the domination of his emperor-brother. Brazil offered him hope first because he was affianced to Maria, daughter of Pedro I, Emperor of Brazil, but she died early of tuberculosis. Then he met Princess Carlota, aged sixteen, daughter of the King Leopold I of Belgium. Carlota adored her handsome husband and wanted him to assume a place in the world which his birth and intelligence demanded. Therefore when the Mexican exiles arrived to suggest that he come to Mexico as Emperor "to bring about its regeneration," Carlota tirelessly urged it on him.

This act was to set off a concatenation of events which would tumble France and unite Germany. Bismarck allowed the Austrian-French-Mexican folly to develop without imposing his powerful political will one way or the other. He had won his short war against Denmark and was preparing for a similar conflict with Austria. His thoughts on Austria, however, came out of the dispatches of John Motley, the American minister in Vienna. Bismarck confided in Motley, who no doubt echoed Bismarck's attitude on Maximilian. "The step is unpopular in Austria," Motley reported. "That a Prince of the House of Hapsburg should become the satrap of the Bonaparte

The unfortunate Emperor of Mexico, Maximilian von Hapsburg (1832–67).

Festive Entry of the Austrian imperial couple in Mexico in 1864.

dynasty, and should sit on an American throne which could not exist a moment but for French bayonets . . . is most galling to all classes of Austrians. . . . The matter is a very serious and menacing one to the United States."[1] In the early spring of 1864, Motley reported again: "Next Sunday . . . the Archduke Maximilian will accept the imperial crown of Mexico, and within two or three months he will have arrived in that country. Then our difficulties . . . will begin . . . when the new 'Emperor' shall notify his succession to the Washington Government, we shall perhaps be put into an embarrassing position."

On May 30, 1864, the day that the Confederate and Union armies were locked in the Battle of the Wilderness—a battle which produced thirty thousand dead in one month—on that day, Maximilian and his

---

[1] And for Austria too, as Karl Marx pointed out in a series of articles for the press in Vienna. He wrote scathingly about a Hapsburg sitting on the throne of Mexico, asking how many cannon balls would be necessary to put him there and how many to keep him there.

wife arrived at Veracruz aboard the Austrian frigate *Novara* escorted by French men-of-war. Veracruz gave the Emperor a tepid welcome. The recently built railway ran for only a short distance, and then the royal party had to transfer to horse-drawn coaches which traveled over roads in gross disrepair. Their arrival in Mexico City was ill prepared; the first night Maximilian had to sleep on a billiard table in the gaming room of the palace. In spite of that he wrote to his brother, "Our welcome has been cordial and open, without any comedy of the sort of disgusting, official servility one finds frequently at such occasions in Europe." And Carlota as well reported in her letters home: "I am entirely happy, and Max too. . . . We can see every day how this spoiled and humiliated nation is growing conscious of its dignity and future."

At first Maximilian occupied himself with promoting commerce, transit, tax, and road reform. He planned a zoological garden in the park at Chapultepec and proposed a national theater. He drew up plans to make Mexico City the Paris of the Americas; the splendid Avenida de la Reforma was one of his plans that was carried out. Education was to be reformed on the German plan of gymnasiums, and the Jahn system of physical education introduced. He proposed a navy, visualizing Mexico taking over Central America until it extended to Panama. In his eagerness Maximilian wished to "reorganize everything" in order to enable the Mexican nation "to stand by the leading peoples of the world." He wanted to set up a natural history museum and a school for the study of classical languages—in a country that was 85 per cent illiterate. He even founded an academy of science.

Maximilian sincerely wanted to be Emperor of all the Mexicans. In his naïveté he even invited the legally elected Mexican president, Benito Juárez, to discuss the political situation with him. Maximilian was bewildered by Juárez' refusal. Maximilian seemed to float on an air of unreality. His fetes were grand, with fireworks and Strauss waltzes; the Imperial household contained as many as twenty-six helpers in the kitchen, three master chefs—French, Viennese, Hungarian—as well as many pastry chefs. His royal stables had fifteen hostlers, and in addition there were ladies-in-waiting. The household cost annually 320,000 Mexican pesos to maintain.

When Maximilian turned to the internal affairs of Mexico he became convinced that the country could not fully flower without a large European immigration. At first he expected that his arrival would attract a mass migration, but it did not. He engaged Otto von Brackel-Welda to work on and publish a project for emigration. Yucatán was proposed as a likely site, and Herr von Hiller of Silesia arrived with five hundred Germans, but disease killed many. The descendants of those who remained are still found in Campeche and Mérida. For the moment, in 1865, Maximilian was allowed his dreams. The glitter of new court life, the brief revival of trade, and the abundance of money from French loans momentarily dazzled the people.

Yet the stage from Veracruz was attacked daily; guerrillas tore up the rails of the Paso del Macho Railroad and infested the roads everywhere, even to the capital. Soon after his arrival, Marshal Achille Bazaine had most of Mexico under command, except for the narrow northern corner where no one but Mexican patriots dared enter. The "empire" of Maximilian seemed to be an accomplished fact; ambassadors of Prussia, England, France, and Belgium arrived, but the most important, the United States, refused recognition.

Louis Napoleon had been led to believe that Mexico could easily be conquered. In the beginning, it is true, Bazaine had conquered much territory, but now it had to be occupied. Because Louis Napoleon believed that the Southern states would win, he created Bazaine a Marshal of France. Emperor Maximilian gave a Grand Ball to celebrate the event, and there, during a dance, Bazaine met a young Mexican girl, Maria de la Peña, seventeen years of age. The Marshal was struck by her beauty and the fact that she "reminded me of my dead wife." The courtship was short. Maximilian gave her a dowry, the huge hacienda of San Cosmé, worth over one hundred thousand dollars. It was but one more episode in the approaching fall.[2]

Upon the arrival of Maximilian, the German citizens of Mexico found themselves in a dubious position. When the French landed in 1861 there were few problems of divided loyalties; the Germans

[2]When Bazaine was forced into surrendering the French forces at Metz in 1870, he was sentenced to death, but the sentence was commuted to twenty years' imprisonment on the Ile de Ste. Marguerite near Cannes. In 1874 this same lady waited under the prison walls in a rowboat and spirited him safely to Spain.

Empress Carlota of Mexico (1840–1927), daughter of the King of Belgium, contributed greatly to Maximilian's participation in the Mexican adventure. After his execution she became mentally deranged.

wholly backed the Mexicans and many took part in the fighting. But Maximilian and his advisers were something else again, and the German citizens were concerned about their being tainted with the same hatred. In one riot the people shouted: "Death to Maximilian. Death to Carlota. Kill the French and the Belgians. Kill all foreigners." Maximilian was quick to note that many of the thousand or more German citizens held positions of trust and were generally respected as bankers, businessmen, hotelkeepers, and soldiers. Karl Sartorius, whose fame had grown with his years in Mexico, was sought out by Maximilian and offered a cabinet post. He refused, saying, "We must defend our adopted country whether it be with the saber or pen to vindicate her honor."

Many a German officer fought with the republicans, such as Colonel Karl von Gagern, an idealist and a liberal who, by conviction, sided with Benito Juárez. In 1853 he entered the Mexican army and fought through to the war's end. He reformed the Colegio Militar at Chapultepec and was made Minister of Public Works. The book he eventually published gave a complete panorama of the terrible struggles of this period. Bodo von Glümer, who had fought in the Union army with General Grant, became an officer with Juárez and was present at the execution of Emperor Maximilian.

It was obviously distasteful for a German officer to order his Mexican troops to fire on Austrians and Germans in the Imperialist ranks of Maximilian, but when Prussia and Austria went to war such punctiliousness was somewhat abrogated.

In anticipation of the withdrawal of most of the French troops, Maximilian's agents in Europe had recruited six thousand Austrian and fifteen hundred Belgian legions, mostly Uhlans, Hussars, and engineers. Many notable European names were among them. Colonel (later General) Franz, Count Thun und Hohenstein, short in stature and black-bearded, was proud, easily wounded, and arrogant. He lived by the code of honor of his caste, with strict loyalty to the Hapsburgs. Count von Khevenhüller, one of the famous names of Austria-Hungary, recruited a regiment of Hussars. Young, handsome, and elegant, he was loyal to Maximilian, but he lived as lavishly in Mexico as he had in Vienna. And there were many more names, remembered and unremembered, such as Alberto Hans, who commanded a company of artillery. When the debacle was over he remained and by 1890 was

The Austrian Volunteer Corps, which could not save the cause of Maximilian I, after its return to Vienna.

one of the oldest Germans living in Mexico. Among the Austrians was Captain Teobert Maler, who escaped the war, went down into the jungles of Chiapas and Guatemala, and became enmeshed in the mysteries of the Mayan civilization. Alone except for Indian bearers, he moved through the jungles taking photographs, making casts of Mayan monuments, and systematically measuring and studying the ruins. In Mérida, Yucatán, a monument calls him "the father of Mayan archaeology."

When Baron Fürstenwärther arrived with the last group of the Foreign Legion, war had already broken out with Prussia. The Austrian Emperor refused to allow any more Austrians to depart for

Mexico. "This," said Maximilian, "is an act of treason and disloyalty on the part of the Emperor Franz Joseph toward his brother." The United States now threatened intervention in Mexico. Matías Romero, Juárez' astute Mexican ambassador to Washington, pointed out that thousands of former Confederate troops were crossing the border and reminded Washington that the American Civil War would continue in Mexico if they did not intervene.

Commander Matthew Fontaine Maury was already there. Virginia born and bred, Maury was a scientist who commanded Confederate ships, developing underwater mines to explode on contact. He was lost to America when he migrated to Mexico and formed the Mexican navy. William C. Preston was the Confederate minister to Mexico and through him General Slaughter, ex-officer of the Confederate armies, had opened negotiations with Marshal Bazaine. They agreed that he would bring over thirty-five thousand Confederate troops with weapons, wagons, and cannons with the ostensible purpose of colonizing. In June, 1865, many Southern generals had gone over: Kirby-Smith, the last to surrender in Texas; General C. M. Wilcox of Tennessee; General "Prince" John Magruder of Virginia, famed for his dramatic flare. They and many more were planning to bring over all that could be transported. Lincoln's postmaster general, Montgomery Blair, wanted to have the Union and the Confederacy declare an armistice, and then join the two armies together to drive out the French and Maximilian, believing that a common enemy would help dispel the hatred engendered by the Civil War.

It was then that Secretary of War Stanton ordered General Philip Sheridan, with sixty thousand Union army veterans, to seal off the Mexican-American border. Sheridan was a young, scrawny, Irish cavalry officer with short legs and enormously wide shoulders; he wore a mustache with imperial beard on his reddish, coarse-featured face. He had commanded the Army of the Shenandoah and had played an important part throughout the war. Friendly with Count Zeppelin, it was he who recommended the McClellan saddle which Zeppelin was to use in the Franco-Prussian War. Sheridan later would be sent to Germany as a military observer of that war, where he shared a hill with Bismarck overlooking the Battle of Sedan.

General Sheridan had no need to give Marshal Bazaine an ultimatum. Bazaine, aware of the sixty thousand veterans poised on the

In the battle at Camerone, the Mexicans destroyed the French Zouave companies.

border, telegraphed Louis Napoleon, and by March, 1866, he began the retreat with his entire French forces to Veracruz for embarcation. Maximilian could not believe that the French would leave him without military support.

Maximilian wavered. Should he abdicate? "Never," said Carlota. She herself would go to Paris to face Louis Napoleon. Therefore Maximilian resolved not to abdicate, and Carlota went down to Veracruz—a dreadful journey performed during torrential rains amid constant danger of capture by guerrillas—listening everywhere to the scurrilous verses of "Adios Mama Carlota." In Europe she went from court to court seeking aid for Maximilian. During her final audience with the pope, Carlota suddenly passed into the twilight zone of the insane. She never again saw her Maximilian.

The Emperor put on his uniform and took over command of the

army. Basically the army was Mexican, officered by Mexicans, but stiffened by the Austrian legion, Belgians, a few Germans, and a sprinkling of Confederate soldiers. In January, 1866, when the French withdrew the last of their troops, the Imperial army had numbered an impressive 43,500, but by October only twenty-eight thousand remained.

Maximilian faced the army of Benito Juárez coming out of northern Mexico, now well armed with American rifles and equipment. Civil War veterans under the command of General Nathaniel Banks were coming over the border to aid the republicans. Maximilian himself, humane in battle and in thought, against his judgment had signed an executive order drawn up by Marshal Bazaine stating that anyone captured while fighting with the troops of Benito Juárez would be summarily executed. And with that, Maximilian signed his own death warrant.

Maximilian was now surrounded by a strange motley of advisers. His personal physician was Dr. Samuel Basch, a German Jew who had been in Mexico only a short time. On his arrival in 1866, he had been recommended to the Emperor by Maximilian's personal physician, who was retiring with the French army. Basch, cultivated and intelligent, was one of the few men about him with whom Maximilian could discuss his interests in science, philosophy, and his theory of beauty. Basch was, Prince Salm-Salm said, "a small, very intelligent, modest gentleman, an excellent physician, and was very devoted to his master." In the memoirs which Dr. Basch wrote after the event, one sees that he was genuinely sorry for Mexico and the Mexicans, although he was equally touched by the tragic figure of Maximilian, deserted by Louis Napoleon and the Emperor Franz Joseph. He remained with Maximilian to the end.

Augustin Fischer, who became "Chief of the Imperial Cabinet," organized demonstrations of enthusiasm in order to convince Maximilian that the Mexican people still wanted him. It was Fischer who told him that since Carlota had sacrificed herself for the Empire, he could do no less; and it was Fischer who constantly told him that abdication would be a blot on the honor of the Hapsburgs. With a full red face, somewhat ascetic in appearance but not in habits, he had a persuasive, almost hypnotic effect on Maximilian. He was said to have been a bastard of the royal family of Württemberg and baptized a Protestant. Before he joined Maximilian he had been a farmer in Texas, a goldminer in California, and when he was admitted to the Society of Jesus he became secretary to the Bishop of Durango until his numerous affairs and free use of church tithes caused him to be expelled. He took refuge with a friend, whose wife he seduced, and precipitated yet another scandal by removing gems from a church effigy and substituting false ones. He finally eloped with still another girl, by whom he had four or five children. He intrigued against every side and finally left the country ostensibly to find a lawyer to defend Maximilian. He did not forget to take with him many rare books from the national library, which he sold in Europe.

Prince Salm-Salm and his wife were added to Maximilian's entourage. This was the same Prussian officer whose presence in the Union army had caused so many German liberals to resign their commands in protest. His marriage to Agnes, daughter of Colonel Leclerce, had been one of the highlights of the Washington social season in 1862. Agnes was young (twenty-five) with translucent skin, high forehead, green eyes, and a fine mouth. She was valiant and generous. When her husband was killed at Gravelotte in 1870, Princess Salm-Salm organized a hospital brigade and served throughout the Franco-Prussian War.

When the Civil War ended, Salm-Salm "resolved to offer my services to the Emperor Maximilian of Mexico, for whose person and civilizing task I had always felt great sympathy. . . . With letters of recommendation . . . I embarked for Mexico from New York, February 20th, 1866, accompanied by Captain Baron von Groeben, a distant relative of mine, who had been my aide-de-camp in the U.S. wars."

The entire Imperial army corps of eight thousand men marched northward in 1867 and reached Querétaro, one hundred sixty miles northwest of Mexico City. As soon as they arrived, the republican armies of Benito Juárez moved down and surrounded the city. Eventually Maximilian's troops would be outnumbered five to one. By March 6, Querétaro was surrounded and Maximilian's supply lines were cut. Messengers sent out from the beleaguered city were caught and hung. It was proposed that a picked regiment of twelve hundred men, under the Mexican generals Marquez and Vidaurri, break out of the siege and return with supplies. Maximilian's requests

Before his execution Emperor Maximilian bids farewell to his closest confidants (after a painting by J. P. Laurens).

were as unreal as ever: they were to return with books, piano music, and a supply of burgundy. The breakout succeeded, but instead of returning to lift the siege the generals went instead in the opposite direction.

Maximilian was doomed. If news of his position reached Paris, Louis Napoleon did not reveal it. The Krupps were displaying their new cannons at the International Paris Exhibition, and the drama in Mexico was all but forgotten. Otto von Bismarck visited the Exhibition, accompanied by Helmuth von Moltke, with the object of seeing not the exhibition, but Napoleon III. The Russians also came, and Tsar Alexander asked the Emperor some embarrassing questions about Mexico.

By May, 1867, food was growing scarce in Querétaro. Soldiers were put on half rations. Maximilian could have escaped, but he was told that he would have to cut his hair and beard since his appearance was so distinctive he would have been immediately detected. He would not hear of it. Prince Salm-Salm, who shared Maximilian's last days, spoke often of his beard. In the morning he had it carefully groomed, "he nursed it with great care," and wore it parted in the middle. Each morning, to the sound of the cannonade, he would carefully study his handsome face and groom his hair and beard before appearing in the uniform of General of the Armies.

On May 14, at three o'clock in the morning, the republicans broke the siege. Colonel Lopez, an officer in charge of the fortifications and known for his disarming manners and a tendency toward treachery, had secured his own neck by guiding the republicans through the lines. By daybreak it was over. The republicans swarmed up the hills of Querétaro. Maximilian was awakened to the victors singing, to the tune of "La Paloma," the scurrilous verses of "Adios Mama Carlota."

As expected, Maximilian was court-martialed, and, just as unexpected, he was sentenced to death. Over the newly laid Atlantic cable the news spread to Europe. The American Secretary of State, who had only a few months before insulted Austria and promised war upon France if it did not withdraw her forces, now sought aid for Maximilian. He hoped "that the President of Mexico, through a spirit of clemency and also for her friendship of the United States, that Prince Maximilian may be spared his life. . . ." Queen Victoria, through her minister to the United States, asked that they intervene in his behalf. Louis Napoleon asked that intercession be made, and other courts of Europe joined. Franz Joseph let it be known that after Maximilian's release he would renounce all of his projects in Mexico and reestablish him in all his rights of succession as Archduke of Austria.

Juárez was unmoved. Through his representative in Washington he observed: "I am afraid that if he is allowed to go back to Europe he will be a constant menace to the peace of Mexico. He will keep on styling himself, to our shame, *Emperor of Mexico*; all dissatisfied

Execution of Emperor Maximilian on June 19, 1867. His Generals Mejía (left) and Miramón were shot with him.

Mexicans will keep up an active correspondence with him about his supposed popularity."

On the night of June 18, an officer read Maximilian's death sentence. He at once sat down and wrote a letter to Juárez. "I die for having tried to see whether a new institution could put an end to the war which had so long disturbed this bloody land," and he penned the last letter to Carlota, one that she would never read.

On the morning of June 19 he arose at 3 A.M., dressed carefully, combed his hair, and once again, for the last time, combed and dressed his handsome beard. At five-thirty he breakfasted. As the church bells were tolling six o'clock, the Mexican officer arrived. Maximilian refused to be blindfolded. As the soldiers raised their rifles to fire, an officer asked Maximilian if he had a final wish to convey. He had. "Please command your soldiers," he said slowly to the officer, "not to shoot at my face."

Ten days later, on June 29, while Louis Napoleon was distributing prizes beside the Sultan of Turkey, a newspaper was brought to him:

The Emperor Maximilian executed! Ferdinand Maximilian, a Hapsburg, Archduke of Austria, in league with Napoleon III to rob Mexico of its independence and institutions, usurper of its sovereignty, overthrown by the national will, and made prisoner by the republican forces in Querétaro, on the 15th of May, 1867, and judged by the law upon offenses against the independence of the nation of the 25th January, 1862, and sentenced by the respective council of war to the extreme penalty, was executed in Querétaro, on the 19th of June, 1867, at seven o'clock in the morning, together with his ex-Mexican generals, Miramon and Mejia. Peace to his ashes.

Louis Napoleon could no longer dissemble. The celebrations were canceled.

The Americas, particularly Mexico, had been the staging ground for German unity. The Prussians applied the lessons learned in the American Civil War and built railways with a particular eye to military needs. They adopted the Union army's tactic of having a trained corps of telegraphers, and Count Zeppelin brought back Southern army tactics in the use of cavalry and himself applied them in war. Many who had fought in the Civil War fought in the Franco-Prussian conflict, one of whom was Prince Salm-Salm who was killed in one of the first battles. The German-language press in America was angered that surplus American rifles had been sold to France and were killing German soldiers who had fought for the victory of the Union. The unification of Germany was taking place, and the 1848ers had to adjust themselves to it.

The Hyphen and the Hyphenated   XX

In 1871 a unified Germany finally emerged. Unification did not, of course, come on the wings of doves, but on the pinions of eagles, and this worried the German-Americans who, in earlier attempts to bring about unity by parliamentary principles, had been forced to find in other lands the political freedom denied them in their own. They had envisaged German unification along much different lines. The emergence of Bismarckian unity continued to worry those German liberals who were now respected citizens in America. "We believe," said one of them, "that the only result will be the aggrandizement of Prussia, . . . but the more of Germany it consumes, the less it will remain Prussian and the more it will become German." Another, who had fought in American wars, disliked "the servility and title sickness and the German obsequious attitude toward nobility." Yet, when Carl Schurz visited the new Germany and met Bismarck, he was impressed with his personality. "Perhaps the feudal ideas inculcated in him persist," Schurz observed, but in a modern industrial age, a "feudal reaction" in Germany would be impossible.

But Henry Villard (born Heinrich Hilgard), the liberal German owner of the New York *Evening Post*, told his readers that they must accept Bismarck, despite his faults, as "the trenchant instrument of Providence which hewed a way to German national unity, and made their fatherland more respected abroad than it had been since the reign of Charles V." This same attitude found an echo in the legal mind of Rudolf von Jhering: "Who would believe that I would write a paean of praise to Bismarck, but I cannot help myself! I leave it to my stubborn colleagues . . . to abuse him! . . . For years they have yelled and drunk themselves hoarse for German unity, and then someone comes on the scene and achieves the impossible by transferring German unity from a book of student songs into reality. . . ."

*The German lawyer Rudolf von Ihering (1818–92) symbolized the
attitude of the intellectuals toward Bismarck's unification policy.*

It was inevitable that this event would fan the flames of "German-
ism" in the souls of all those who had left their country and become
adopted citizens in the Americas. "A national pride," remarked Professor Wittke, "is one of the strongest emotions of every immigrant
people. German-Americans who had been called 'damned Dutchmen'
long enough now demanded recognition in the United States as
equals."

There was a deep emotional hurt in the souls of German citizens.
They were aware of their many contributions toward the exploration
and settlement of the Americas, whether in Argentina, Mexico, or
the United States. The attacks on them by the nativists in the 1840's
had left deep scars. Attacked physically and politically, many a German immigrant retreated into his own Germanness; many German

families, trying to overcome the feeling of inferiority which all immigrants feel upon arrival in a new country, emphasized their German origins. Eventually they turned to political activism, especially after the migrations of 1830 and 1848, so that many states published public laws in German. Maryland, for one, continued to do so until World War II.

Much of the same reaction occurred to the German Jews, who shared the same cultural and political background. Those who soared to prominence maintained all the features of German culture. They were, as they said of themselves, "more German than Jewish." German was their cultural language, spoken in the home and often in business. They made pilgrimages to Germany seeking wives of their lineage. Many were educated in Germany. Their cellars were full of German wines. They were convinced that nineteenth-century Germany embodied the finest in the arts, sciences, and technology. The music children practiced was German music. When they traveled to Europe, they sailed on the Hamburg-America Line. When a rest was needed they took the waters at German spas. When illness struck, the ailing were hurried off to German hospitals.

The Bismarck era released a tremendous national vigor that was mirrored in rapid material success. Germany doubled her population as well as her railway mileage; steamship traffic multiplied its tonnage sevenfold. Coal and iron production surpassed that of Britain, and personal incomes quadrupled. Meanwhile, peripatetic salesmen sold German-made goods from Mexico to Baghdad. "Made in Germany" was a cachet invented by the British, Robert Graves explained in his autobiography *Good-bye to All That*: "It was a label that Germany was forced to put on all German-made goods. Businessmen's sons . . . used to discuss hotly the threat, and even the necessity, of a trade war with the Reich. 'German' meant 'dirty German.' It meant cheap, shoddy goods competing with our sterling industries."

Yet much self-criticism arose within Germany itself; Germans criticized themselves for their loss of proportion, their complete lack of a sense of balance. The bickering and quarreling of dynasties and towns left its imprint on the German character and gave it a touchiness. As is natural in any country which had been a European battlefield for three centuries and now suddenly found itself on top of the pile, there was ostentation, vapid posturing, and heady talk about the superiority of German culture. "What is surprising is what passes for 'culture' in Germany . . ." wrote the philosopher Nietzsche. "Culture is above all unity of artistic style in all the manifestations of a people's life. But to have learned and to know a great deal is neither a means to culture nor a sign of it. . . ."

Yet professors on both sides of the Atlantic expounded German ideals. Kuno Francke, professor of the history of German culture at Harvard University, for example, pictured Germany as pulsing with "ardent life and intense activity in every field of national aspirations." "Healthfulness, power, orderliness meets the eye on every square mile of German soil. No visitor could fail to be impressed by these flourishing, well-kept farms and estates, thriving villages, carefully replenished forests . . . these bursting cities teeming with a well-fed and well-behaved population . . . with theatres and museums rising everywhere, admirable means of communication. . . . Over all was the magnificent Army with its discipline and high standards of professional conduct."

Germans living in the Americas naturally basked in the reflected glory of their former homeland. Everywhere the Germans became the best established of minorities. Of all other emigrants, they were the most preferred; census figures revealed that they were more prone to become naturalized. Americanization was proceeding so quickly that a large number of German-language newspapers went out of business for lack of readership. This was fully recognized by the Imperial German government, which replied in answer to a questionnaire: "There is no disposition on the part of this government to promote, or encourage emigration. On the contrary, whatever official influence is exerted is all to retain them at home, or if they must emigrate, to direct their course toward one of the German colonies, to Brazil, or to some other country than the United States, where their identity as German subjects is so soon and inevitably merged in their new allegiance."

In 1891 the *Alldeutsche Verband* (Pan-German League) was founded. Its goal was the union of all members of the German "race," wherever they resided. Posters distributed for display read: *Dem Deutschen gehört die Welt* (The world belongs to the Germans). Yet between Germany and the Americas there was an ocean, and that ocean was controlled by Great Britain. "It must not be forgotten,"

The brothers, Thomas (left) and Heinrich Mann, were among the many German intellectuals who had to seek sanctuary in the New World during the Third Reich. While Thomas Mann returned to Europe as an American citizen after the war, his brother died in exile in 1950.

Otto von Bismarck tirelessly repeated, "the most important political fact in the modern world is that British and Americans speak the same language."

On German Day, October 6, 1904, Senator Carl Schurz, making the principal address, said: "German Day in the United States is the celebration of the friendship of the German and American peoples. We German-Americans are the hyphen between Germany and America; we present the living demonstration of the fact that a large population may be transplanted from one to another country and may be devoted to the new fatherland for life and death, and yet preserve a reverent love for the old. We are the embodiment of the necessity of peace and friendship between the two nations."

When war broke out between England and Imperial Germany in 1914, those citizens of German origin living in the Americas were placed in a dilemma. What should be their position? Since it was immediately obvious that the blockade would prevent any material aid to their former country, German-Americans urged neutrality on themselves. In Latin America, knowing Imperial Germany to be powerless, many states thoughtlessly sequestered the property of Germans who had been citizens for generations. Because the United States was ostensibly neutral, until 1917 it was not a crime, as one German-language newspaper pointed out, to defend Germany's position. But it was rapidly becoming unpatriotic, and moreover, unwise. What had been freedom of speech before war was declared would soon be "high treason."

In 1914, ninety-seven German intellectuals (including Thomas Mann, the most vocal) signed a manifesto justifying the war. Albert Einstein alone refused. All of England's finest writers fell to turning out propaganda, except for George Bernard Shaw, who refused.

The outbreak of war had the same effect on the German Jews. For example, Jacob Schiff, the well-known banker who came originally from Frankfurt, found the war "deep and unsettling." This was equally true of millions of other Americans of German origin; the thought of war between their adopted country and the land of their birth was unnerving. The Anglo-American press of Baltimore published several articles on the difficult psychological situation of the German-Americans. It understood "the travail of spirit which must have been the lot of most German-born citizens and of their sons and

Nobel Prize winner Albert Einstein (left) found a new place to work in North America in 1933. Physicist Robert Oppenheimer (right), who had received his doctor's degree in Göttingen, became the father of the atomic bomb.

daughters in these terrible times. Other Americans, we are sure, will sympathize with them and stand ready to help them think their way through their difficulties." But this small voice was lost in the increasing anti-German clamor.

Americans of German origin suddenly became "Huns." Almost everywhere people joined in the "patriotic" sport of *Hunnenfressers*— "Hun-eaters." War hysteria drowned America. Everything German was attacked: music, language, frankfurters, names, speech, literature, dachshunds, schnauzers, and German shepherd dogs. The patriot found German propaganda in every Bismarck herring and in every beer mug. August Lüchow, the famous German restaurant on 14th Street in New York City, prudently dropped the umlaut, for the umlaut and the particle "von" became as dangerous to one's person as the foreskin was in Arabia.

*A new wave of immigration began after the end of World War II
with the coming of the German rocket specialists from Peenemünde.
From left to right are Eberhard Rees, American commander of the
experimental facility Medaris, Werner von Braun, Ernst Stuhlinger,
and (standing) W. A. Mrazek and Walter Häussermann, behind an
Explorer model.*

*Werner von Braun (opposite, top), born in Posen in 1912, has played
a decisive part in the successes of the American space program. In the
bottom photograph is technical director Kurt H. Debus (center),
who was on von Braun's staff at Cape Kennedy.*

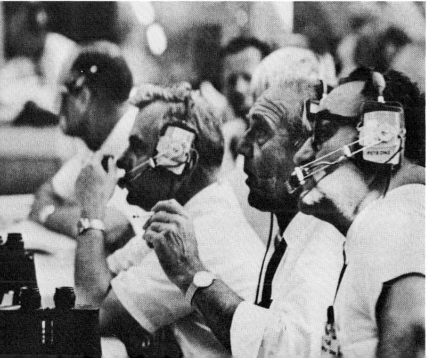

Astronaut Frank Borman (left), commander of Apollo 8, which orbited the moon on December 24, 1968, during a visit to Berlin in 1969. Borman had German ancestors. At right he stands with fellow crewmen Anders and Lovell.

Hysteria came and then, like a summer storm, disappeared. After 1918 emigrants from German lands poured out in still another flood. They went to North America and more went to Brazil, Chile, Argentina, and Mexico. Venezuela filled with vital young men who could no longer face a dreary future in Germany. In Colombia and Bolivia they built airlines; in Guatemala they returned to rebuild their huge, well-run coffee plantations.

But in Europe guilt was inextricably bound up with victory, and, since Germany had lost the war it carried the sole burden of guilt. In turn, since the Germans could not forever blame themselves alone, they blamed the Jews. These unfortunate people were now going to get, in Germany, the same treatment—the pogrom—that

President Dwight D. Eisenhower, of German ancestry.

had been given to Germans in America. As Hitler's power grew, laws were passed that would take the Jews completely out of German life. "The highly cultivated, self-conscious German Jews, the great majority of whom were completely assimilated, . . . were systematically deprived of their property, their family connections, and the opportunity to practice their professions." Soon six million would be deprived of their lives.

And so another Diaspora began. Most came to the Americas, just as they had during the religious persecutions of the seventeenth century and the liberal upheavals of 1848. A quarter of a million people, representing some of the finest talents and greatest intellects

President Lyndon B. Johnson had German ancestors, too.

in Germany, left Europe. The enrichment for the Americas was incalculable, the loss to Germany catastrophic. German Jews brought their vast talents to every profession: they were architects, physicists, physicians, engineers, artists, writers, historians, mathematicians, dramatists. The list is so long and so impressive that one is tempted to ask who was left in Germany after this intellectual diaspora.

As World War II came into focus, there were relatively few German-Americans who were willing to defend the Thousand Year Reich. Therefore, in 1940, German Day disappeared, never to be revived again. Many resident Germans, however, objected just as strenuously to Hitler's political system as did their expatriate brothers.

They believed it was their duty to remain, compelling even the best of them to support a policy that was leading Germany to disaster.

The German collapse was total. "We fought in Russia with gallant fierceness," one German soldier wrote bitterly. "Our total defeat was traumatic. The general re-education that followed the brainwashing, the reevaluation of traditional values further destroyed us. There was no heroic welcome for prisoners, decorations were not allowed to be worn, traitors were honored, heroes persecuted, 'the spinal bone of Germany was dissolved in the gastric juices of the *Fragebogen*.'"

The result of total defeat was that once again Germany was divided. Once again the migrations began. The most significant was "Operation Paper-Clip," in which the American army rushed upon the Peenemünde proving grounds to capture German rocket scientists. Each contending power, Russian and American, took its quota of experts.

Inevitably, under the tension of East-West rivalry, a new phase in relations came into operation between Germany and America. Soldiers quartered in Germany were acquiring German wives, just as before, in the war of 1776, German soldiers had acquired American wives. A continuous stream of German soldiers were being trained and educated in America, so that on return their children carried an invisible cachet, "Made in America." Chicago, which for a century had been a cultural center for Americans of German origin, now became the most populous "German" city in the world—that city which the London *Times* called "America's German miracle."

Even the stratosphere was drawing the two countries into a natural relationship. German rocket experts helped plan the moon shots. When Colonel Frank Borman, a descendant of German immigrants, glided through space and read that "God created the heaven and the earth," it was part of a dual triumph. Wernher von Braun, a veteran of Peenemünde, designed the ship that landed men on the moon for the first time, another triumph of German-American unity.

As the world moves toward the year 2000, the Americas are filled with people whose families came from Germanic lands. The great migrations seem now to have come to an end.

Or have they?

Bibliography

Adalbert, Heinrich Wilhelm. *Aus meinem Reisetagebuch 1842–1843.* Berlin, 1847.

Becker-Donner, Etta. *Guatemala und seine Volkskunst. Sonderausstellung Frühjahr 1967.* Vienna, 1967.

Beidelmann, William. *The Story of the Pennsylvania Germans.* Philadelphia, 1896.

Bonpland, Aimé. *Plantes équinoxiales receuillies en Mexique.* Paris, 1805.

Bry, Theodore de. *Americae, Pars Quinta.* Frankfurt am Main, 1595.

————. *Wunderbarliche, doch wahrhafftige Erklärung von den Begebenheiten und Sitten der Wilden in Virginia.* Frankfurt am Main, 1590.

Burgoyne, John. *Orderly Book.* E. B. O'Callaghan, ed. New York, 1860.

Burkart, Joseph. *Aufenthalt und Reisen in Mexiko 1824 bis 1834.* Stuttgart, 1836.

Closen, Ludwig Baron von. *The Revolutionary Journal.* Chapel Hill, 1958.

Codex Vindobonensis S. N. 1600. Cartas de relacíon de la conquista de la Nueva España escritas por Hernán Cortés al Emperador Carlos v., y otros documentos relativos a la conquista años de 1519–1527. Neudruck Graz, 1960.

Columbus, Christopher. *Bordbuch. Aufzeichnungen seiner ersten Entdeckungsfahrt nach Amerika 1492–1493.* Zürich and Leipzig, 1941.

————. *Eyn schön hubsch lesen von etlichen insslen . . .* Strassburg, 1497.

Croix, Teodore de. *Memorias de los virreyes que han gobernado el Péru.* Lima, 1857.

Deubel, Stefan. *Der Deutsch-Amerikaner von heute.* Cleveland, n.d.

Diaz del Castillo, Bernal. *Denkwürdigkeiten des Hauptmanns Bernal Diaz del Castillo oder Wahrhafte Geschichte der Entdeckung und Eroberung von Neu-Spanien.* Georg Adolf Narciss, ed. Stuttgart, 1965.

Dobrizhoffer, Martin. *Geschichte der Abiponier.* Vienna, 1783.

Doehla, Johann Konrad. *Tagebuch eines Bayreuther Soldaten, des Johann Conrad Doehla aus dem Nordamerikanischen Freiheitskrieg von 1777–1783.* Bayreuth, 1913.

Elking, Max von. *Leben und Wirken des herzoglich braunschweigischen General-Lieutnants Friedrich Adolph Riedesel Frhr. zu Eisenbach.* Leipzig, 1856.

Faust, Albert Bernhardt. *The German Element in the United States.* New York, 1927.

Fischer, S. G. *The Making of Pennsylvania.* Philadelphia, 1896.

Fiske, John. *The American Revolution.* Boston, 1901.

Forster, J. George. *Voyage philosophique et pittoresque en Angleterre et en France, fait en 1790.* Paris, 1795.

Frezier, Amédée François. *Relation du voyage de la mer du Sud aux côtes du Chili et du Perou.* Paris, 1716.

Friede, Juan. *Los Welser en la conquista de Venezuela. Ed. conmem. del 4. centenario de la muerte de Bortolomé Welser, jefe de la Compañia alemana de Augsburgo.* Caracas and Madrid, 1961.

Froebel, Julius. *Die Deutsche Auswanderung und ihre culturhistorische Bedeutung.* Leipzig, 1858.

Furlong, Guillermo. *Los jesuitas y la escision del reino des Indias.* Buenos Aires, 1960.

———. *S. J. Antonio Sepp y su "Gobierno temporal" (1732).* Buenos Aires, 1962.

Gicklhorn, Renée. *Die Bergexpedition des Freiherrn von Nordenflycht und die deutschen Bergleute in Peru.* Leipzig, 1963.

———. *Thaddäus Haenkes Reisen und Arbeiten in Südamerika.* Wiesbaden, 1966.

Goetzmann, William H. *Exploration and Empire. The Explorer and the Scientist in the Winning of the American West.* New York, 1966.

Haebler, Konrad. *Die deutschen Buchdrucker des xv. Jahrhunderts im Auslande.* Munich, 1924.

———. *Geschichte des spanischen Buchdrucks in Stammbäumen.* Leipzig, 1923.

Hagen, Victor Wolfgang von. *Heerstrassen des Sonnengottes.* Vienna, 1957.

———. *Die Kultur der Maya.* Hamburg and Vienna, 1960.

———. *Manuelas Jahreszeiten der Liebe.* Vienna and Hamburg, 1952.

———. *Sonnenkönigreiche.* Munich, 1963.

———. *Südamerika ruft.* Berlin, 1959.

———. "Waldeck," in *Natural History Magazine.* New York, Dec. 1964.

————. *Was this the Fate of the Library of Alexander von Humboldt? An Inquiry.* New York, 1950.

————. *Die Wüstenkönigreiche Perus.* Vienna and Hamburg, 1964.

Hall-Tharp, Louise. *The Baroness and the General.* Boston, 1967.

Hawgood, John A. *The Tragedy of German-America in the United States.* New York, 1940.

Hellwald, Ferdinand von. *Max I., Kaiser von Mexiko, sein Leben, Wirken und sein Tod.* Vienna, 1869.

Helms, Anton Zacharias. *Tagebuch einer Reise durch Peru von Buenos Aires an dem grossen Plata-Flusse, über Potosi nach Lima, der Hauptstadt des Königreichs Peru, vom Königlich Spanischen Hüttendirektor Anton Zacharias Helms.* Dresden, 1798.

Holland, Ruth. *The German Immigrants in America.* New York, 1969.

Humboldt, Alexander von. *Atlas géographique du royaume de la Nouvelle Espagne.* Paris, 1812.

————. *Essai politique sur le royaume de la Nouvelle Espagne. Avec un Atlas physique et géographique fondé sur des observations astronomiques etc. . . .* Paris, 1811.

————. *Voyages aux régions équinoxiales du Nouveau Continent.* Paris, 1805–1834.

————. *Aus dem Tagebuch vom Orinoko.* Nürnberg, 1926.

————. *Vom Orinoko zum Amazonas.* Wiesbaden, 1966.

———— and Aimé Bonpland. *Essai sur la géographie des plantes.* Paris, 1805.

Iguiniz, Juan B. *La imprenta en la Nueva Espagna.* Mexico, 1938.

Ioyfull News out of the New-found World. John Frampton Merchant, trans. London, 1596.

Kaufmann, Wilhelm. *Die Deutschen im amerikanischen Bürgerkrieg.* Munich, 1911.

Kienzl, Florian. *Bolivar, der Befreier. Ein Lebensbild.* Berlin, 1936.

Kipping, Ernest. *Die Truppen von Hessen-Kassel im amerikanischen Unabhängigkeitskrieg 1776–1783.* Darmstadt, 1965.

Kleinpaul, Johannes. *Die Fuggerzeitung 1568–1805.* Leipzig, 1921.

Kottenkamp, F. *Geschichte der Kolonisation Amerikas.* Frankfurt am Main, 1850.

Kotzebue, Otto von. *Neue Reise um die Welt in den Jahren 1823–1826.* Weimar, 1830.

Kühnel, Joseph. *Thaddaeus Haenke. Leben und Wirken eines Forschers.* Munich, 1960.

Langsdorff, Georg Heinrich von. *Bemerkungen auf einer Reise um die Welt in den Jahren 1805 bis 1807.* Frankfurt am Main, 1812.

Léry, Jean de. *Brasilianisches Tagebuch 1557. Historia navigationis in Brasiliam, quae et America dicitur. Aus dem Französischen übersetzt von Ernst Bluth.* Tübingen, 1967.

————. *Histoire d'un voyage fait en la terre du Brésil, autrement dite Amérique.* La Rochelle, 1578.

Lorant, Stefan. *The new world. The first pictures of America. Made by John White and Jacques Le Moyne and engraved by Johann Theodore de Bry. With contemporary Narratives of the French Settlements in Florida, 1562 to 1565 and the English Colonies in Virginia, 1585–1590.* New, rev. ed.; ed. and annot. New York, 1965.

Lowell, Eduard J. *The Hessians and other German Auxiliaries of Great Britain.* Port Washington, 1965.

Madariaga, Salvador de. *Bolivar.* Stuttgart, 1961.

Marius, André. "Le Baron de Nordenflicht . . . et les mineurs allemands du Peru." *Revue de l'Amerique latine,* VIII, 1924.

Marius, Georgius. *Noriberga Urbs Imperialis . . . Elegiaco Carmine celebratum.* Ulm, 1615.

Martin, P. G. *Maximilian in Mexico. The story of the French Intervention.* New York, 1914.

Martius, Karl Friedrich Philipp von. *Nova genera et species plantarum.* Munich, 1824–32.

————. *Die Pflanzen und Tiere des tropischen Amerika.* Munich, 1831.

———— and Johann Baptist Spix. *Reise in Brasilien in den Jahren 1817–1820.* Munich, 1823–24.

Möllhausen, Balduin. *Tagebuch einer Reise vom Mississippi nach den Küsten der Südsee.* 1858.

————. *Reisen in die Felsengebirge Nordamerikas bis zum Hochplateau von Neu-Mexiko.* 1861.

O'Connor, Richard. *The German-Americans.* Boston, 1968.

O'Leary, Daniel F. *Historia de la Independencia Americana. La emancipación del Perú, segun la correspondencia del General Heres con el Libertador, 1821–1830.* Madrid, 1919.

Oliviedo y Valdes, Gonzalo Fernandez de. *La historia general de las Indias.* Seville, 1535.

Panhorst, Karl. *Deutschland und Amerika.* Munich, 1928.

Parkes, H. B. *A History of Mexiko.* Boston, 1938.

Paucke, Florian: *Zwettler-Codex 420. Von Pater Florian Paucke S. J. Hin und Her, Hin süsse und vergnügt, Her bitter und betrübt.* Etta Becker-Donner, ed. Vienna, 1959.

Plattner, Felix Alfred. *Deutsche Meister des Barock in Südamerika im 17. und 18. Jahrhundert.* Basel, 1960.

Pochmann, Henry. *German Culture in America, Philosophical and Literary Influences 1600–1900.* Madison, Wisc., 1957.

Pölnitz, Götz von. *Anton Fugger.* Tübingen, 1958.

———. *Die Fugger.* Frankfurt am Main, 1960.

Poeppig, Eduard. *Im Schatten der Cordillera. Reisen in Chile.* Leipzig, 1927.

——— and Stephan Endlicher. *Nova genera ac species plantarum quas in Regno Chilensi Peruviano et in terra Amazonica, annis 1827–1832.* Leipzig, 1835–45.

Porter, K. W. *John Jacob Astor, Businessman.* Cambridge, 1931.

Ratto, Hector. *La Expedición de Malaspina.* Buenos Aires, 1945.

Ravenstein, E. G. *Martin Behaim. His Life and his Globe.* London, 1908.

Reissner, H. G. *The German-American Jews 1800–1850.* London, 1965.

Richert, Gertrud. *Johann Moritz Rugendas. Ein deutscher Maler des XIX. Jahrhunderts.* Berlin, 1959.

Riedesel, Friederike. *Die Berufsreise nach Amerika. Briefe von Friederike Riedesel, Freifrau zu Eisenbach, Geborene von Massow, und Friedrich Riedesel, Freiherr zu Eisenbach, Braunschweiger Generalleutnant 1776–1783.* Berlin, 1801.

Rights, Douglas Le Tell, and William P. Cumming. *The Discoveries of John Lederer with unpublished letters by and about Lederer to Governor John Winthorp, Jr.* Charlottesville, 1958.

Salm-Salm, Felix. *Quéretaro. Blätter aus meinem Tagebuch in Mexico.* Stuttgart, 1868–69.

Schapelle, B. F. *The German Element in Brazil.* Philadelphia, 1917.

Schedel, Hartmann. *Buch der Chroniken und Geschichten mit Figuren und pildnussen von anbeginn der welt bis auf die unsere zeit.* Nürnberg, 1493.

Schiller, Friedrich. *Kabale und Liebe. Ein bürgerliches Trauerspiel.*

Schmidel, Ulrich. *Wahrhaftige Historien einer wunderbaren Schiffahrt.* (Noribergae 1602). Neudruck Graz, 1962.

Schoepf, J. D. *Reise durch einige der mittleren und südlichen vereinigten nordamerikanischen Staaten. 1783 und 1784.* Erlangen, 1788.

Schöner, Johann. *Luculentissima quaeda terrae totius descriptio.* Noribergae, 1515.

Schomburgk, Robert Hermann. *Description of British Guiana.* London, 1840.

———. *Reisen in Guiana und am Orinoko.* Leipzig, 1841.

———. *Twelve Views in the Interior of Guaiana.* London, 1841.

Skelton, R. A. "The Cartography of Columbus' First Voyage." In L. A. Vigneras, *Journal of Christopher Columbus.* London, 1960.

Spörri, Felix. *Amerikanische Reisebeschreibung.* Zürich, 1677.

Sprengel, C. M. *Allgemeines historisches Taschenbuch der Neuen Welt oder Abriss der merkwürdigsten Begebenheiten enthaltend für 1784 die Geschichte der Revolution von Nord-America.* Berlin, 1784.

Staden, Johann von. *Wahrhaftig Historia und beschreibung eyner Landschaft der Wilden Nacketen Grimmigen Menschfresser Leuthen in der Newenwelt America gelegen vor und nach Christi Geburt im Land zu Hessen unbekannt bis uff diese nechst vergangene jahr Da sie Hans Staden von Domberg ausz Hessen durch seyn eygne erfahrung erkant und jetzo durch den truck an tag gibt.* Marburg, 1557.

Stewart, George Rippey. *Ordeal by Hunger. The Story of the Donner Party.* London, 1962.

Tschudi, J. J. von. *Peru. Reiseskizzen aus den Jahren 1838–1842.* St. Gallen, 1846.

Valton, Emilio. *Impresores Mexicanos del siglo XVI.* Mexico, 1935.

Van Doren, Carl. *Secret History of the American Revolution.* New York, 1941.

Veit, Valentin. *Knaurs deutsche Geschichte. Eingeleitet und bis zur Gegenwart fortgeführt von Albert Wuchen.* Munich and Zürich, 1960.

Waldeck, Jean Frédéric. *Voyage pittoresque et archéologique dans la Province de Yucatan pendant les années 1834 et 1836.* Paris, 1838.

Ward, Christopher. *The War of Revolution.* New York, 1952.

Wied zu Neuwied, Maximilian, Prince von. *Reise nach Brasilien in den Jahren 1815–1817.* Neuwied and Frankfurt am Main, 1820.

_____. *Beiträge zur Naturgeschichte Brasiliens.* Neuwied and Frankfurt am Main, 1824–33.

_____. *Reise in das innere Nord-America.* Neuwied and Frankfurt am Main, 1838–41.

Wittke, Carl. *Refugees of Revolution. The German Forty-Eighters in America.* Philadelphia, 1952.

Wolf, Simon. *The American Jew as Patriot, Soldier and Citizen.* Philadelphia, 1895.

Wynkelmann, Hans Just. *Der/Americanischen/Neuen Welt/Beschreibung . . . Beneben einer wunderbaren Schiffahrt und Reise Beschreibung(!) nach Brasilien Hans von Staden/bürtig aus Homburg in Hessen. . . .* Oldenburg, 1664.

Wyfliet, Cornelius. *Descriptiones Ptolemaicae augmentum sive occidentis noticia brevis commentario.* Louvain, 1597. New edition, Amsterdam, 1964.

Zenger, John Peter. *A Brief Narrative of the Case and Trial of John Peter Zenger, printed in the New York Weekly Journal.* Lancaster, reprinted 1765. New York, 1765.

Zweig, Stefan. *Magellan.* Vienna, Leipzig, Zürich, 1938.

Illustration Sources

The author and the publisher thank the persons and institutions listed below who have provided illustrations for this book and have given permission for their use. Numbers following names are of the pages on which the illustrations appear.

Academic Printing and Publishing Institute, Graz: 59
American Heritage Publishing Co., New York: 90
Archives for Art and History, Berlin-Nikolassee: 22, 207
Art History Museum, Vienna (Collection Castle Ambras): 43
Bavarian State Library, Munich: 16, 46, 73, 123, 125, 195
British Museum, London: 49, 62, 63, 148; color plate, Köhler's map
John Carter Brown Library, Providence, R.I.: 17, 233
California State Library, Los Angeles: 303, 304
Collegium Carolinum, Munich: 211, 212
Forest Company of Riedesel Freiherr zu Eisenbach: 168, 169
Fort Ticonderoga Museum Collection, Ticonderoga, N.Y.: 166
Friedrich Wilhelm Prince zu Wied, Neuwied on the Rhine: 251, 253
German Museum, Munich: 32, 136, 137, 210, 299
German Press Agency, Munich: 380
Germanic National Museum, Nuremberg: 4, 15; color plate, Cortés
Gutenberg Museum, Mainz: 74
Keystone, Munich: 158, 209
Knoedler & Co., New York: 284
Lancaster County Historical Society, Lancaster, Pa.: 96, 97
Library of Congress, Washington, D.C.: 104
Linotype, Ltd., Frankfurt: 320
Martha Madler, Munich: 256
Hans von Martius, Munich: 254
The Metropolitan Museum of Art (bequest of Charles Allen Munn, 1924), New York: 149, 154, 163
Municipal Art Collections, Augsburg: 42
Museum for Folklore, Vienna (with the permission of the Zwettl Foundation, Lower Austria): 110, 118
Naval Museum, Madrid: 213
Natural History Magazine, New York: 128
Newberry Library, Chicago: 262, 263, 264, 265

New York Public Library, New York: 252, 286
Northern National Gas Co. and Joslyn Art Museum, Omaha, Neb: 287
Pennsylvania Council of Arts, Harrisburg, Pa.: 186
Picture Archives of the Austrian National Library, Vienna: 205, 223, 236, 243
Picture Archives Sepp Rostra, Augsburg: 12
Picture Archives Tasiemka, London: 348 (bottom), 355
Picture Archives of the Publishing House Bruckmann, Ltd., Munich: 40
Picture Service, South German Publishing House, Munich: 44, 82, 373 (right),
    151, 152, 221, 379
Felix Plattner, S. J., Zurich: 112, 114
State Graphic Collection, Munich: 257, 260; color plate, "Jungle Scene"
State Library "Prussian Cultural Property," Berlin: 5, 8, 51, 181, 218, 239,
    249, 272, 274, 277, 282, 312, 316, 318, 321, 323, 327, 331 (bottom), 335,
    337, 343, 345, 348 (top), 349, 352, 354, 358, 360, 362, 365, 367, 370,
    373 (left), 375 (left)
United States of America Information Service, Munich: 100, 146, 150, 183,
    290, 308, 331 (top), 332, 375 (right), 376, 377, 378
University of Texas Library, William H. Goetzmann, Austin, Texas: 311, 313
Wadsworth Atheneum, Hartford, Conn: 173
West Point Military Museum, West Point, N.Y.: 289
Yale University Gallery, New Haven, Conn.: 198

Author's Collection: 50, 132, 134, 142, 143, 160, 193, 222, 225, 232; color
    plates, *Rexia speciosa* and *Views . . . Guiana*
Collection of Droemer Knaur, Publishers, Munich: 10, 24

Index